The Autobiography of Dr Ben Horsfall

The Autobiography of
Dr Ben Horsfall

Memoirs of a Rare Bird

Badger Publishing

First published in 1992
Badger Publishing (Halifax)

The Autobiography of Dr Ben Horsfall
Memoirs of a Rare Bird

ISBN 0 9519024 0 7

Composed by Ryburn Publishing Services
Bound in Edinburgh by Hunter & Foulis
Printed by Ryburn Book Production, Halifax, England

Acknowledgements

It is with pleasure and gratitude that I acknowledge the help I have received from many sources which have, at last, enabled the publication of Dr. Horsfall's memoirs. Foremost amongst these are members of the Todmorden Orchestra, particularly Susi Shafar, Jean Hall and Jack Bednall for their commitment "to the cause". On Dr. Horsfall's behalf I would like to thank the late Mary Horsfall, Doris Duffy and Shirley Whitham for typing the manuscript. Particular thanks to Dr. Horsfall's lifelong friend Dr. N.J. de V. Mather for providing us with the foreword and a particularly fitting final chapter. Thanks also to the Royal Northern College of Music for allowing the reproduction of portraits in their possession and to Roger Birch for the cover photograph. In addition I am most grateful to Ryburn Book Production for their invaluable help and a 'crash course' in publishing.

It is regrettable that Dr. Horsfall could not witness publication of his memoirs but I am sure this book will be enjoyed by many and treasured by those of us who knew him.

C.W.

Foreword

The author of this candid and amusing work was indeed unique, in that in the realm of music the degree of Doctorate is rarely if ever associated with thirty years of professional orchestral playing with some of the greatest performers of the twentieth century. As Doctor Horsfall relates, even a desire to sit for the degree of Bachelor was queried by Sir Ernest Bullock, his examiner.

The ensuing pages contain the experience of a lifetime sadly interrupted by World War Two, but to people interested in music – especially those in Manchester and its environs – the revelations are a joy, and may be savoured and re-read with the revival of many delightful memories.

Although revealing erudition, acute powers of observation and a phenomenal photographic memory well-known at least to one lifelong friend, the author does not perhaps demonstrate the extreme sensitivity, the willing generosity especially to amateur musicians and the personal and professional integrity which were the foundations of the personality of Ben Horsfall. Whilst reading the following pages, however, one becomes imperceptibly acquainted with the thoughts of a very shrewd and interesting mind. It is more than regrettable that the work was not able to be completed.

In an endeavour to provide some form of ending, Doctor Horsfall's son and daughter asked a friend who knew him well and attended many of the Hallé concerts mentioned to compose a final chapter.

N. J de V. M.

Introduction

This book is mainly about people; players, composers and conductors with whom I have been closely associated all my life: I intrude from time to time in order to explain my presence in interesting and often amusing situations where great men have said and done memorable things.

The greatest musicians I have known, were, almost without exception, serene and self-effacing: the not-so-great were like Portia's 'quality of mercy' – 'twice blessed', with a touch of genius and more than a fair share of human frailty.

Men seldom become wise by talking, but it does not necessarily follow that wisdom will fill the heads of those who listen, particularly orchestral players who, throughout their professional lives, slowly and inexorably become anaesthetised by the incessant clap-trap of second-rate conductors.

Having introduced this state of orchestral players' anaesthesia, this is probably the most propitious time to pay some small tribute to the lesser known musicians in my life, and the efforts they made in devising the Three-stage System to alleviate its misery.

Stage I. The condition is not terminal, and initially recognisable! The Artistic Trance, as it ought to be designated, is vulgarly, and often quite mistakenly, called a sleep. The next give-away is, of course, closed eyes and in some instances even snoring. Constant vigilance is required. During the early 1930s detection inevitably resulted in the sack. Nowadays the T.U.C. protects its members from victimisation and wrongful dismissal.

Stage II takes a little more time. Unconsciousness gradually steals over the player, whose eyes *remain open*. Although this condition is more difficult to detect, very little real progress has been made.

Stage III is the ultimate of course, and can only be achieved after years of diligent study and self-denial. The player induces the coma quickly with his eyes open, *and at the same time looks intelligent*! An added refinement is to wear a smile, but this great gift has only been given to one person during my life – Stuart Knussen (senior) – and he was awarded a 'Black Belt'! (These highly prized badges have in more recent times become known as 'Cummerbunds', but let no one forget their glorious origins!)

Stuart used to sit directly opposite me in the orchestra, and if, after three minutes of the rehearsal, a smile took possession of his features, I knew that he was fishing in the South Sea Islands. He became such a master of this technique that he once complained during the statutory 15-minute break (when he invariably borrowed a cigarette from me*) that he found it very tiring making unnecessary trips backwards and forwards to Tahiti.

Another old gentleman in the Hallé First Violins who had reached Stage II of the System was Johnny Bridge. He was greatly respected by the youngsters in the orchestra, particularly by me. His experience of the orchestral repertoire and, indeed, of opera was phenomenal and whenever I sat near him in the orchestra he sounded to be playing *every* note, and bravely too! He was quite a wag, and like all good story-tellers began his anecdotes so very seriously that I believed every word, except the last. I am well aware that there is a season for Grouse and Salmon: there is also a season for the 'Messiah' which in 1930 was extensive and ran from late November to the middle of January. It is therefore not surprising that Johnny Bridge, who had not completely mastered the System should be an early casualty. He came to me, about the middle of December, very seriously, and whispered, "Last night I had a *terrible* nightmare – I dreamed I was playing the 'Messiah' – and when I woke up, I was!"†

An incident occurred one morning (I believe we were rehearsing Tchaikowsky No. 4) and the pizzicato movement had produced, as it usually does, a few disagreeable noises. Johnny Bridge came to me at the 'break' and said, "You are interested in Hans Richter, and that movement has taken me back a few years to an occasion when HE rehearsed it." He continued, "Richter was appalled at the same sort of ugly noise and was driven to shaking his fists and screaming, 'Mit dem Fleisch, nicht der BONE!' "

---

* Playing the 'cello seems to breed a race of cigarette borrowers! Haydn Rogerson, who left Manchester to join Beecham's Royal Philharmonic Orchestra in London, fooled me for years with a cunning cigarette trick. He, very shamefacedly, came to me every day to borrow a *light,* and he always fumbled in his pocket for a packet which always had ONE cigarette in it. This he always offered to me (with a sad and deprived look on his face), and I always said the same thing – "If that's all you've got, HAVE ONE OF MINE!!" That packet was a veritable gold-mine: it never wore out!

† This story has been told and retold in a variety of distortions – it is now in its proper context.

It is universally accepted that orchestral players cannot possibly know anything about music, other than acquiring some mechanical skill in manipulating a musical instrument, and are therefore fair game for the whims and caprices of any conductor in what must inevitably be a one-sided talking match. But shall we not laugh at them in our turn – provided that what we say is true?

Jesting Pilate said, "What is Truth?" and would not stay for an answer. Whether or not he already knew the answer has never been clarified, but he was certainly the first of a long line of perplexed human beings, including myself, who have been confounded by the adage that 'Truth never hurt anybody.'

There is an element of risk in telling true stories, however harmless they may appear: I have many times misjudged an audience and regretted the folly of hastily launching myself into a story when the situation was ripe and the story tailor-made. Always there is a dissenting voice, invariably bitter and loud, crying shame on me for tarnishing the image of his favourite conductor or deflating some ridiculous aspect of his national pride.

One such regrettably absurd situation arose in the Officers' Mess of a R.A.F. Maintenance Unit near Cairo in the summer of 1944. The sun temperature that day had reached a sizzling 126° and even in the late evening there was little comfort standing at the Mess Bar. Only the inexperienced officers were foolish enough to sit in the heavy leather chairs (which Air Ministry sees fit to provide in Messes all over the world regardless of the climate). The huge electric fan merely wafted the hot air about and cotton shirts were everywhere sticking to sweating bodies. Conversation was dull stuff and nobody had the energy to say anything or even listen, when quite suddenly, the C.O. gave voice to a singularly appropriate passing thought, "At this precise moment I would gladly give five shillings apiece for goose-pimples!"

In spite of the general willingness to laugh at anything which the C.O. might have said, I think the titter which greeted this remark was a spontaneous one – it may have been louder among the junior ranks than senior according to the deference considered to be his due, but in any event he was, in all minds, considered to be the only officer present who could possibly have afforded such extravagance.

My mind immediately conjured up from its archives an occasion when any member of the Hallé Orchestra would gladly have gratified his wishes at half the price!

I was soon (too soon) in full cry, and up to my ears!

I recalled a freezing foggy November morning in Manchester. The street lighting was not very effective and the traffic was noisy, bad-tempered and at a standstill. Inside the Free Trade Hall the fog and frost had seeped through, and any member of the orchestra who could wear an overcoat and still play his instrument, did so. Beecham was the unfortunate conductor and the piece with which he had begun the rehearsal was 'Don Juan' by Richard Strauss. Anyone familiar with this work or Tommy's repertoire will know that it was a great favourite with him: the three voluptuous females portrayed in the piece used to be vividly re-created under his direction – but not this morning!

He coaxed, cajoled, chivvied, prodded and tried every trick in his book, but he was powerless to infuse any warmth into the playing. The tone was thin and undernourished, but, above all else, the intonation was appalling!

It seemed an eternity before Beecham gave up the struggle. "Gentlemen," he cried, "it sounds like an EISTEDDFOD!"

He was a master of arch, drawling contemptuous inflections, but in this particular word 'EISTEDDFOD', he excelled himself – it came from the heart, and revived in some of us the memories of flapping great tents, wet grass, loose pages of music blowing about, insecure music stands and all the extraneous noises which characterise these rustic festivals.

I imitated Tommy as nearly as I could, giving the word the full treatment, and I was prepared to proceed to other anecdotes and monopolise the entire evening – but I had overlooked a fuming, funny little man with murder in his eyes for whom 'Eisteddfod' was a hallowed word. The very red face belonged to F/Lt. Roberts, a chapel choir-master from one of those unpronounceable Welsh mountain villages which had once been the Mecca for one of these gatherings.

The rest of the evening lapsed into a heated, but fruitless discussion on Home Rule for Wales and ended with a curse on Beecham which was not taken too seriously (on high) since he lived for a further 27 years.

This, and similar embarrassing experiences, have not in any way shaken my resolve to go on writing what I know to be the truth, incredible though it may seem.

Chapter 1

Sometime in the summer of 1926 I was auditioned by the Principal of the Royal Manchester College of Music, Dr. Adolf Brodsky, and accepted as a student.

Meeting Dr. Brodsky was a terrifying experience and I can remember quite vividly everything he said and did, as well as his dress and movements around the room. He carried with him on this, and indeed on all other occasions, two other items of wordly comfort – a glass of lemon tea (in a silver holder) and a cigar: they were part of his presence. He trotted into the room and, without any of the usual civilities, came to the music stand and picked up the three pieces which I had brought. "What are you going to play?" said he, grunting his approval of a study by Fiorillo and the Beethoven F major Romance, but the third – Oh dear! – it was a trifle called 'Dreaming' by Dr. Tertius Noble (one-time organist at York Minster). I had won a prize with this masterpiece at a local Co-op Musical Festival! Not having previously heard a Russian bear defending its cubs, I was not qualified to compare the sound with the growl emitted by Dr. Brodsky on this occasion. I suppose because of my youth, or the fact that this was our first encounter, he gave me a more gentle demonstration of his considerable dexterity in skimming music to remote corners of the room (or even out into the Hall) except this time he paid me the compliment of not first tearing it in half.

The Fiorillo study passed without comment and then on to such bits of the Beethoven Romance as the good Doctor permitted me to play. My cousin, who had made the journey in order to accompany me on the piano was cut short in every bar in which the fiddle was not involved. I didn't finish the piece, naturally. He got up from the huge leather chair which had completely enveloped him (it was still there 40 years later when I last went into the sanctum) and shuffled over to me, and very kindly said "There is no great talent, but if you work hard you will be a good player." then after a little pause, added, "You will be accepted."

In September 1926 I enrolled at the R.M.C.M. as a student and began the long road with a cheerful heart. I can never remember resisting the compulsive urge to 'fill in the gaps' between the facts of musical history which every student is expected to know, and the exciting game of projecting myself to other times and places, endeavouring to re-live great

Dr Adolf Brodsky, Principal of the Royal Manchester College of Music

moments in other men's lives or re-create the social conditions in which great musical events took place. I was a very curious and impressionable lad of 17 and Dr. Brodsky was the first important musician I had ever met: it was not surprising that he became the first object of my immature research.

The audition was the first time I had spoken to Dr. Brodsky, but I had previously seen him in public, or, more truthfully, someone had discreetly pointed him out in the audience of a Brand Lane Saturday concert in the Free Trade Hall. The occasion was a recital by Fritz Kreisler to which I had been taken by the kindness of a school teacher. I was a boy of 11 and wore my Sunday suit. Kreisler played the Grieg C minor Sonata with Charlton Keith, and then the Tchaikowsky violin concerto: after the interval he played two movements of the E major Partita by Bach and then on to countless of his own charming compositions which he played with such easy, charming grace that it worries me that these pieces are still in my 'too difficult' drawer! It was during the performance of the Tchaikowsky that my attention was drawn to Dr. Brodsky whose face was just visible to me: his eyes were filled with tears which occasionally overspilled, unchecked, down his cheeks.

I, along with every other student at the R.M.C.M. soon knew the thread-bare story of Dr. Brodsky's debut with the Tchaikowsky in Vienna on 4th December 1881. He had rescued the work from Kotek (who first tried unsuccessfully to play it) and later from Leopold Auer (who wouldn't admit that he couldn't).

Two characters who interested me for a very long time were present at the Vienna concert – Hans Richter the conductor, and Hanslick the critic.

Richter conducted performances with Brodsky in Vienna, London and Moscow, and it is significant that he came to Manchester as conductor of the Hallé Orchestra: he brought with him a great Wagner tradition and his name will appear many times in the course of this book.

Hanslick (immortalised by Wagner as Beckmesser in Die Meistersinger) wrote a scathing report of the Vienna concert in the 'Neue Freie Presse'. I was horrified when I read it, but all critics have this effect on me, and I share Dr. Johnson's opinion of the whole breed epitomised in the first paragraph of his essay 'Dick Minim the Critic' –

"Criticism is a study by which men grow important and formidable at a very small expense. The power of invention has been conferred by nature upon few, and the labour of learning those sciences which may by mere labour be obtained is too great to be willingly endured; but every man can exert such judgment as he has upon the works of others; and he whom nature has made weak, and idleness keeps ignorant, may yet support his vanity by the name of a critic."

I was 'allocated' to Arthur Catterall for lessons on the fiddle and I soon discovered that he was an excellent teacher – firm, patient and intensely serious. His teaching room was in the same annex – a back attic in a derelict house in Oxford Road, Manchester. The room itself

Arthur Catterall, Ben's tutor at the RMCM

overlooked the back of some very dingy houses trying to survive by taking in theatricals as lodgers. There was one tree, I remember, which appeared to grow out of smooth black undulating concrete: a few hens scratched for something to eat and I doubt if any of them could remember when grass last grew there. If any of the paying guests ever had an egg for breakfast, it must surely have been bought at the corner shop.

The furniture in Catterall's room was sparse to say the least, it consisted of a piano, which was never played, a music stand for the victim and a chair for the master.

Immediately underneath the echo-chamber was the waiting-room where each clutch of four pupils could leave their hats, coats and cases, and speculate on the likely state of the master's liver. Harry Blech and Charles Taylor were two in the same group as myself – the third, Eric Roberts, drove from the wilds of Wales each day in a Bentley sports car and constantly fidgeted with cigarettes which he lit but never smoked: he pressed the ends of them with his thumb until they looked like miniature trumpets. Eric and I have not met since those student days, but the others have become well-known since they gravitated to London.

Progress on the violin was never, with me, gradual and satisfying. Most musicians have at some time or other met the 'brick wall' – I knew it well, and experienced long periods of frustration and depression which I considered to be scant reward for the time I spent practising.

The lesson of which I have the most vivid recollection was an early one. Catterall allowed me to play about half of a study by Rode and then devoted the rest of the lesson to a patient explanation of the misuse of my available practice time. His advice, like the first Soprano recit in the 'Messiah' announcing 'glad tidings which shall be to all people', might also profitably be directed to the dwindling race of amateur orchestral players who invariably play every difficult passage 'pianissimo' regardless of the composer's dynamic marking or intention, and very much under tempo regardless of the conductor's direction. Those who do not evaporate altogether, hide behind their music stands until rescued by their more courageous but nevertheless foolhardy colleagues, who play wrong notes with great conviction, abandon, and evident self satisfaction.

Catterall explained with great tolerance precisely what studies are designed to do, and the cunning manner in which passages of technical difficulty are interpolated to disturb the rhythm, dynamics, poise and confidence. These must be diligently practised if progress is to be made and genuine technique acquired. He then stressed most of the pitfalls which await those who play single line instruments (and indeed the unwary pianist too) of playing every piece relentlessly from beginning to end – bravely at first when it is easy, a little slower here, a little softer there, accommodating awkward changes of position, a little gallop through the next easy passage and a sharp pull-up at the next dark patch which is glossed over very confidentially, and so on through another dreary day. Catterall played through the study (rather easily, I thought) then took out a pencil and enclosed three short passages in heavy brackets. "Now," he said, "at the beginning of every practice session play through this study once only AT THE PROPER SPEED AND WITH THE RIGHT DYNAMICS. You will come to grief at each of these passages which you will then isolate and practise exclusively for the remainder of each session. You will in a very short time be able to play them from memory. Walk about the room. Watch yourself in the mirror. Concentrate on the immediate technical problems and do not gape at the music or stare at the surrounding wallpaper. Never let peevish, shrivelled sounds escape you! Put mistakes right at once and be your own seviorist critic!"

I took this lesson very much to heart: the system of isolating difficult passages and practising from memory did not immediately produce spectacular results; just a feeling that I was making the best use of my time.

There was, for the remainder of the course, a very serious application to the new method of acquiring technique, it became intuitive, and continued during the pre-war period when survival in the profession of orchestral playing depended upon one's ability to play most, if not all, of the notes in the standard orchestral repertoire.

I have often drawn the attention of pupils to the danger of constantly adopting (in private) a constantly changing 'tempo of accommodation' in order to avoid coming to grips with the technical problems, and pointed out that ensemble-playing is impossible when all the combatants are oblivious of each other's problems. The response from students has never been encouraging – they all say "that's just common sense" and dismiss the advice with a contemptuous wave of the hand.

I was puzzled fifty years ago and am now completely mystified that Conservatoires and Colleges of Music (Royal and otherwise) provided then and still continue to provide excellent courses which will eventually launch instrumentalists on their first World Tour as concert artists, and disregard the inescapable fact that 99.7% of the disillusioned virtuosi will have to settle sooner or later in one or other of the National Symphony Orchestras – a career for which they are singularly ill-equipped.

Panels of solemn Conductors, Leaders and Principals sit annually to audition would-be orchestral violinists who regularly play the first movement of the Tchaikowsky, Brahms, Beethoven, Max Bruch or any of the concertos studied at College: no one else wants to hear them!

Most panels, I feel certain, would prefer to hear a candidate making a brave attempt to play the 'Corsair' overture of Berlioz, or the C sharp minor passage of flying semiquavers in the 'William Tell' overture, or indeed any of the 'naughty little bits' which abound in almost every piece in every orchestral programme. Every conscientious player will spend years getting to know the repertoire and will wonder, as I did, why Colleges of Music do not regard orchestral playing as an honourable career and provide adequate courses for it, instead of an orchestral class for the benefit of trainee conductors.

The remaining three years spent at the R.M.C.M. were uneventful: friendships were formed which survived the ten pre-war years in the Hallé and the twenty post-war years in the B.B.C. Northern Orchestra. Two contempories – Sydney Coulston and Clifford Knowles returned to the College as professors of the Horn and Violin.

I was, on two memorable occasions during my second year as a student, impressed by the modesty of Dr. Brodsky and R.J Forbes in displaying unique, impromptu examples of quite profound musicianship. The first and only time I ever played at an 'Open Practice' proved to be an exciting lesson in score-reading! College professors met regularly (too frequently for the students' peace of mind) to choose programmes and 'detail' their pupils to perform pieces being currently studied. The 'Open Practices' were concerts given fortnightly in the College Hall, Ducie Street, at which the public were admitted free of charge: there was no appeal against appearing on the list, and terrible was the retribution for not turning up or even remonstrating against the chore. The front row of chairs in the Hall was reserved by ancient custom for the 'Old Man' who sat with his Russian tea and puffed at his cigar in spite of the No Smoking notices which adorned the walls. He was unable to applaud, having both hands full, but he grunted from time to time.*

Catterall, in his wisdom, had put me on the list to perform the G minor Prelude and Fugue from the first Partita of Bach (it would, perhaps, be too much to say that I subsequently made a career out of the Partitas, but I did eventually get a College Diploma with the same Prelude and Fugue, and later a place in the Hallé Orchestra with the Chaconne!)

Bach, then as now, takes precedence in programme building, and in this particular concert I was quickly on and off the platform. The fright of my young life came in the 'green room' before I had had time to put my fiddle away. R.J. Forbes, another very formidable man who later became Principal, summoned me in a gruff, almost sour voice – "Horsfall, I want you!". I was a little bewildered to be back so soon on the platform with a fellow student, Ernest West, apparently without his instrument. I knew him to be an excellent trombone player and, half an hour later, I discovered that he was also an excellent pianist. He sat at one of the Steinway Grand pianos and played the Schumann A minor Piano Concerto from memory. At the other piano sat R.J. Forbes who launched him into this work with a thunderous chord of A minor which he played before I had time to open the tattered copy at the first page. Needless to say I was soon turning to page two, and then three, and so on: it was not the second piano reduction I had expected to find but a full orchestral score! R.J. obviously enjoyed my consternation and thus began my first lesson in score-reading! I was probably the only person in the Hall who knew, and could appreciate the fact that R.J. was not showing off, and really preferred to play from the full score – a truly amazing gift!

Dr. Brodsky was a celebrity, and almost everything he said and did was worth remembering. My regard for the 'Old Man', as he was affectionately called, seemed to oscillate between terror of his unpredictably violent temper and gratitude for just being privileged to listen to a few words of wisdom, and to hear him play – which, in spite of his great age, was sometimes unbelievably brilliant – although, I must confess, it was sometimes out of this world but not quite far enough out!

His Tuesday afternoon quartet class was always great entertainment for the spectators and sometimes a rather terrifying experience for the combatants. One of these sessions stands out in my recollection: it covered every aspect of his unique talent – and temper.

---

* Mr. Withers, The Registrar, who was aptly named and cast in the image of Wackford Squeers of Dotheboys Hall, like Cassius had 'a lean and hungry look': he would, without trial, have eagerly committed any student to the Tower of London for so much as having a packet of cigarettes in his pocket as he crept through the Main Hall.

The class was held in the Main Hall and there was always an aura of discipline and organisation whenever the Principal was involved. A ring of chairs surrounded the playing area of four music stands and chairs set out for the quartet: there was a special chair for the 'Old Man' which was strategically placed directly opposite his room-door. At 2.30 p.m. precisely he trotted out with tea and cigar and made a circuit of the ring of students sitting with their instruments on their knees (not the 'cello obviously). Having pointed his cigar at two violins, a viola and a 'cello, he sat on his little throne and the ordeal began.

We were all aware that this particular session would belong to Haydn, since the complete quartets (all 83 of them) bound like four Family Bibles were perched precariously on the stands in the centre circle. Who, on this particular day had decided which one to play, I shall never know, but they began playing Opus 76 No.4 in B flat. Whoever published that rather primitive volume of Haydn quartets had overlooked the elementary fact that, in order to practise or rehearse them, letters or figures are usually printed at intervals in the parts as landmarks to obviate the necessity of repeatedly going back to the beginning whenever the players 'get lost'.

This unfortunate group (in the first movement) gradually 'got lost' and one by one evaporated. To the surprise of everyone present the Doctor was extremely tolerant and, without any trace of anger in his voice, said, "Any fool can play za *notes* – when will you learn to play za *rests*?!"

He then, like R.J.Forbes, gave us a modest demonstration of how well he knew Haydn quartets and also how remiss the publishers had been in not identifying a few milestones for the straying sheep. He trotted over to the First Violin and pointed to the music, "Zis bar" and finally the 'Cello, "Zis bar". "So!" said he very approvingly, and trotted back to his chair.

Nothing happened to distinguish this session from any other until they arrived at the variations and lost themselves in the darkness of B flat minor (a remote key for Haydn). The good Doctor began trembling (erupting would be a better word) and leaving his tea safely behind shuffled at great speed towards the quartet stopping in front of the unfortunate First Violin. He shook his fists and his cigar ash at him and shouted "You feefty times a beeg *Donkey!* Eet is fife flats and you play za open strings!".*

Many years after I left the College I talked with Jimmy Shirley who had been a pupil of Dr. Brodsky immediately after the First World War. He was one of the privileged few who had lost his copy of the Bach Partitas during a lesson in Dr. Brodsky's slightly deaf period. Jimmy related how he managed only the first four bars of the Chaconne (from

* Since E, A, D, G are the open strings on the violin, the key signature of D flat major or B flat minor (B flat, E flat, A flat, D flat and G flat) rather hampers a violinist and deprives him of all his open strings.

the D minor sonata) when the Doctor grunted "More TONE!". After a third unsuccessful attempt to please the Doctor, Jimmy Shirley was horrified to see the 'Old Man' get up from his huge leather chair and charge towards him screaming "TO ME!". He grabbed Jimmy's fiddle and hacked his way venomously through the first four bars making the resin fly in all directions. "SO!!" he said, handing back his violin. Jimmy was astounded, and said to me very confidentially "If I had produced any sounds on the fiddle remotely resembling those excruciating noises I would have been unceremoniously expelled! – I nearly was for trying – two minutes later I was out in the Hall quickly followed by the two halves of my Bach Partitas."

Dr. Brodsky frequently conducted the Monday afternoon orchestra class and less frequently played concertos with it: on the latter occasions R.J. Forbes conducted. Sir Hamilton Harty sometimes came to the rehearsals ostensibly to look around. After all, the bust of Sir Charles Hallé looked down on the proceedings to remind us that the R.M.C.M. was founded as a training college for the Hallé Orchestra.

I was aware also that Dr. Brodsky had tried unsuccessfully to persuade Sir Edward Elgar to become Professor of Composition at the R.M.C.M. and that he played his B minor concerto at a Hallé concert. He certainly rehearsed it with the College orchestra: I can remember feeling very sad and not daring to say so. The technical passages were unbelievably brilliant and appeared to be thrown off with disarming unconcern, but the slow movement called for more than he was able to give.

A few months before I completed the course, Dr. Brodsky died, and was succeeded as Principal by R.J. Forbes.

The B.B.C. Symphony Orchestra was formed in 1929 and Arthur Catterall was appointed as its first leader; it was also the first major orchestra in Britain to offer employment (dare I say it?) to WOMEN. Several of Catterall's pupils left with him to join the B.B.C. Orchestra.

In this same year nearly half a million musicians in the United Kingdom were suddenly and permanently thrown out of work by the introduction of Talking Films and I began to feel as though all the doors were beginning to close in my face. The possibility of being absorbed into other careers in music was extremely unlikely. Teaching in schools was a dream someone had two decades later!

I did what was then expected of College students – I sat for the Associate Diplomas and applied for an audition to the Hallé: I also applied to the Birmingham City Orchestra because, unaccountably, they were advertising vacancies. Leslie Heward, who was appointed conductor, after the departure of Dr. Boult to the B.B.C. heard me play in Birmingham and I was offered a contract for the winter season of 1930.

I can remember very little of that audition except playing a few bars of the Berlioz overture 'The Corsair' and the first line of a study by

Mazas, in E minor, but every detail of the next audition, which followed a fortnight later in Manchester, I remember very well.

The Hallé Society had an office in Forsyth's music shop in Deansgate and I was invited to play for Sir Hamilton Harty in one corner of the huge piano showroom on the first floor.

He walked towards me very slowly, the whole length of the showroom: it was a very significant walk, which seemed to demonstrate Victor Sylvester's theory of 'contrary body movement' in ballroom dancing.*

I could see by the lack of expression on his face that there would be no vacancies in the Hallé Orchestra for at least ten years! He gave me a reluctant hand which felt like a cold codfish and he asked me sotto-voce what I was going to play. "The Bach Chaconne" said I. "Oh! very well." he said resignedly and walked to a chair about fifteen yards away.

Wednesday was half-day closing in Manchester and nobody came to the showroom: the only disturbance for the next quarter of an hour was the subdued noise of traffic along Deansgate. I was not playing from memory and was surprised to find that each time I turned a page he allowed me to go on and that it was his obvious intention to listen to every note! Seven pages of unaccompanied Bach! When I had finished, he came over to me, and this time relaxed his features into a little melancholy smile, and said "That is a wonderful piece!". As he walked away he said, quite softly, "You will hear from us." I expected to, in the normal course of events, but I was left guessing as to *what* I should hear. To my joy, however, I did later get a contract and instead of facing unemployment in the winter of 1930 I faced the dilemma of trying to satisfy commitments with two orchestras in two cities.

I often refer to the season 1930–31 as 'my L.M.S. period': it was rich in memories and experience which in my case were rather expensive. The rail fare from Manchester to Birmingham was 21/- in those days, and the fee for Birmingham concerts 25/-. The Hallé fee was 29/- and it was soon apparent that I could not indefinitely withstand the inroads made by the L.M.S.

Although I was eventually on nodding terms with a few station-masters en route I never got used to the slag heaps of Staffordshire, and at the end of the season it was not difficult to stop my migratory habits and to make a choice between the two orchestras. I settled for Manchester.

---

* The object of 'contrary body movement' in ballroom dancing produces the illusion that the gentleman 'leading' will not sway from side to side if his right shoulder moves forward with the left leg, and conversely the left shoulder and right leg. Professional dancers do it instinctively: amateurs look like John Wayne striding triumphantly across Arizona – overdoing it a little!

Chapter II

I felt like a travelling tinker during the winter of 1930–31, dividing my time between two orchestras and spending my limited income on rail fares and frugal living. The lodgings I had in Smethwick were homely and the landlady (a retired schoolteacher) was a forebearing soul, who besides being an excellent cook seemed to take kindly to my unpredictable comings and goings.

It was inevitable that I should make comparisons between the Hallé and Birmingham City Orchestras, and also between Leslie Heward (whose first season it was with the Birmingham City Orchestra) and Sir Hamilton Harty.

Paul Beard was the leader of the Birmingham City Orchestra and his younger brother and father sat at the first desk of violas. I sat with Herbert Downes at the third desk of first violins. (Herbert Downes later in his career turned his attention to the viola.) I was never happy in this orchestra: there was an atmosphere of resentment towards anyone taking the bread from an unemployed Birmingham mouth. At every rehearsal I was aware of a niggling intolerance, sometimes amounting to bitterness, but always with a deadly serious attention to trivialities such as 'getting the bowing right!' I was never referred to by name, but always as 'that Manchester fellow'! and Herbert Downes, whose accent, in those days, was a mixture of 'Brum' and Walsall, sniggered every time I ventured to speak, and said, with tedious regularity, "This guy don't 'arf talk funny!"

The Orchestra played as well as professionals are expected to play, and the rehearsals, which were always serious, were sometimes sour and cynical efforts to make dangerous corners safe: the concerts were, at best, free from accident and although some of them were good, none of them was memorable.

Leslie Heward, who was a fine musician, is easy to recall: he was frail and obviously a sick man: he tired very easily. He held his baton as an artist would hold a paint-brush, or most men a pen, between the thumb and index finger, which, like the other fingers were held out stiff and straight. His beat, like that of Sir Landon Ronald and R.J. Forbes, was always safe and reliable: his experience of conducting opera in the pit had probably taught him the useful lesson that an out-of-sight conductor has little chance of beguiling an audience with useless antics which

Scheherazade

would only mislead the players anyway. His ears were abnormally sensitive to pitch and quality, but at rehearsal he was often guilty of fixing some unfortunate member of the orchestra with a critical stare, and, when the inevitable mistake occurred, giving a resigned shrug of the shoulders which implied 'I was expecting you to do that!' Leslie Heward was extremely intolerant of 'hurrying', a common fault in most orchestras: he always vented his spleen on the third desk of first violins – Herbert Downes and myself – and 'Always on Sundays'.

On most Sunday evenings throughout the winter concerts of light classical music were given in the West End Cinema: the stage would not accommodate more than three desks of violins, which would normally be adequate for light classical programmes, *but* Rimsky Korsakoff's 'Scheherazade' crept into one of them and resulted in Leslie Heward indulging in one of those sadistical bits of mediaeval torture, which every orchestral player mistakenly believes was abolished with the Rack and Thumb-screw – the rehearsal technique of 'A desk at a time!' starting at the back.

Herbert Downes and myself never caught on to the cunning trick that sooner or later we would have to play every impossible passage absolutely solo in front of the entire, sniggering orchestra which seemed somehow to be aware that it would never be their turn! One of our most humiliating experiences was this passage from the last movement of 'Scheherazade' (a very brisk *one* in a bar).

I cannot vouch for Herbert Downes remembering the advice Leslie Heward gave us at the end of this ordeal, but I have carried it with me through life and have frequently passed it on gratis to those amateurs who crouch behind their music stands whenever they see demi-semi-quavers – 'IF YOU CAN'T PLAY IT – *LOOK* TO BE BUSY!".

A far more serious instance of 'hurrying' and having to play 'a desk at a time' was this passage from 'The Merry Wives of Windsor' by Nicolai.

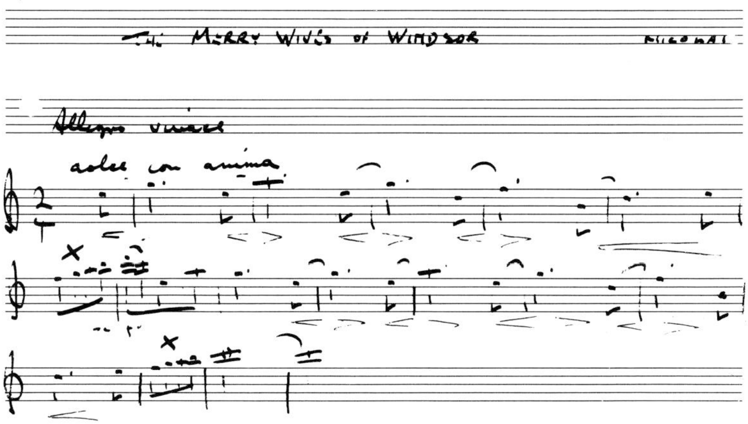

The Merry Wives of Windsor

The problem is rhythmical rather than technical and we were called upon to play these few bars over and over again for what seemed an interminable time. Every performance and every recording I have heard of this work since 1930 has been very near to grief in the bar marked 'X'.

In order to indicate the rhythmical telescoping I have contracted the offending bars in the printing. During the West End series of concerts there were two instances of Leslie Heward admitting to conducting works for the first time, and confessing to his inability even to start one of them – 'Beethoven's Fifth'. The other was Mendelssohn's overture to the 'Midsummer Night's Dream'. He brought to this performance a keen, fresh eye: his insistence on playing exactly what Mendelssohn had written proved a point which has escaped most conductors since, or, what is definitely worse, a point not considered worthwhile observing! In the exposition this passage appears – first violin part only —

Midsummer Night's Dream

It is abundantly clear from the precise placing (or absence) of the expression marks in both passages that Mendelssohn meant what he said.

The deadliest sin of all orchestral players is 'knowing' a piece too well. It requires only one or two in the ranks of a symphony orchestra to play by 'radar' or any other device to ruin the effect of 'sempre p' or a non-crescendo passage. Wallowing by instinct in Mendelssohn, particularly in all the wrong places, has done his delicate music no great service. Leslie Heward spent a great deal of time purging the 'Midsummer Night's Dream' of unwanted crescendos – he made his point.

Another deadly sin is uncertainty, which can spread through an orchestra like a bush-fire. In a concert where a new or unfamiliar work has pushed a 'well-known' classical symphony right out of the rehearsal schedule – watch, or better still, listen to the panic three or four bars before the end of the exposition. 'Are we making the first movement repeat?' is the question that no-one asked or answered at the rehearsal. The leader and the principals around him usually take the plunge and the danger passes, but not without leaving a few blemishes.

One of the Thursday concerts in the City Hall brought a brief re-union with Arthur Catterall, who came from his recent appointment as leader of the B.B.C. Symphony Orchestra, to play the Sibelius Violin Concerto. This concerto suited him well – I have never met anyone who could play the passages in octaves and thirds (which abound in this piece) quite as immaculately as Catterall. He always played from the music; in spite of his infallible memory he used to say "It is never worth the anxiety". I remember, on this occasion, sitting 'inside' the orchestra in order to turn the pages for him.

Having experienced a period of unemployment* I was determined to make the most of my heaven-sent opportunities as an orchestral player by studying for a University degree. I shall never, even to myself, ever be able to satisfactorily answer the question – 'Why?'.

I hadn't matriculated in order to enter the R.M.C.M., but it was necessary if it was my intention to go on to a University course. On 1st January 1931 I enrolled at Durham for the Mus.B. degree and also paid a fee of £4 to Wolsey Hall Correspondence College, Oxford, for courses in English, French and all the ramifications of Mathematics – Algebra, Euclid and Arithmetic. Wolsey Hall guaranteed to get me through the Entrance Examination in Music in September, 1931, or continue to coach me until I did, at no extra fee! There were stringent rules to be observed: all weekly work was to be despatched to the far-flung tutors, postmarked '6 p.m.' on Fridays (in those primitive days mail was delivered first post on Saturday mornings anywhere in the British Isles for 2d.). Solutions and new work were despatched to students from Oxford, at the same time, ensuring that no student had the solutions to hand before he sent off his work. I was never tempted to disobey the rules except in the case of the Rev. W. Williams residing in the Isle of Man, who fairly let himelf go, in red ink, on my French! There was only *one* essay in the whole nine months' course which ever drew from him a word of praise or thanksgivings: it was 'A Visit to the Circus' – I promptly memorised it!

The matriculation was not a matter of life and death, but I applied myself diligently to the task and, in September, set off to Durham with a light heart.

In the English examination I remember being very confident about the set work which was Shakespeare's 'Julius Caesar'. In the essay I also remember that I could not spell the word 'umbrella' (I lost a lot of time debating whether or not it should be 'ar' or 'er'!). In one of the mathematics papers I didn't know the formula for calculating the speed of a train in relation to the radius of a curve and the elevation of the outer banking rail (and I have gone through life not knowing it!). I did, however, win the first prize for initiative in the French paper: I struggled through the grammar with great difficulty, and my heart sank when I saw the choice of subjects for the essay – 'Talking Films' headed

---

* Music was not an insurable occupation until 1948. In the pre-war years there was no unemployment benefit or Social Security.

the list because, in 1931, it was a topical subject. Having decided that 'A Day at the Seaside' would offer most scope for my limited vocabulary, I, like a true north-countryman, set out for Blackpool, where I spent six tortuous lines of my very worst French exhausting its pleasures. However, it *'pleuved chats et chiens'* – roughly, *very* roughly translated – it 'rained cats and dogs' and with great relief I darted into the Tower Circus where I spent the next two pages blinding the examiners with my very best homework! Needless to say I passed, but justice has since been done: the only time I ordered a boiled egg in France I got a glass of water! I had better luck in Austria and Switzerland: at least my limited knowledge of German has been honestly acquired.

In pre-war years all British symphony orchestras, with the single exception of the B.B.C. offered only seasonal contracts to orchestral players. To be IN the Hallé Orchestra in 1930 meant a series of weekly concerts in Manchester, on Thursdays, from mid-October to March. The concerts were sometimes repeated, using fewer strings, in Bradford, Sheffield or Nottingham on Fridays, and promoted in those cities by private enterprise.

During the summer months, seasonal employment of a very different nature was never difficult to find. Llandudno Pier, Scarborough Spa and Bridlington Parade supported orchestras of considerable strength (between thirty-five and forty players) which were usually drawn from the Hallé and Liverpool Philharmonic Orchestras.

It is inevitable that youngsters like myself, occupying back desks, should be regarded as reserves for the out-of-town concerts and our most pressing problem during the winter months was keeping body and soul united: the answer lay in the deputising system.

The break periods of most orchestral rehearsals were like the Stock Exchange: the older players were always first in line for engagements with local amateur choral societies (which in 1930 were prolific and repetitive in their productions of Parry's 'Pied Piper', Stanford's 'Revenge', Stainer's 'Crucifixion' and a host of forgotten masterpieces) but what is more to the point, they never refused a date however many clashes occurred. Having sorted out the best paid engagement, or the one involving the least travelling time, they were then willing to allow the crumbs to fall from the table. "Are you free next Tuesday? Good then go to Bolton Victoria Hall – it's 'The Creation', 2.30 p.m. rehearsal, d.j. (dinner jackets)".

There are several unwritten rules in this insidious game: never try to do the job better than the person for whom you are deputising! nor accept the engagement directly from the Society for the following year.

It was a very bewildered young man who turned up for his first Hallé concert in the old Free Trade Hall: it was an extra date – a Municipal Concert in the fortnightly Monday series, and it preceded the grand opening of the Hallé Thursday series a few days later. The rehearsal at 10.30 in the morning was for everyone else a cheery re-union of suntanned men licking salt from their lips and shaking sand from their hair. Charlie Collier was even replacing some of the harp-strings which had broken in the open-air bandstand at Scarborough Spa during his summer season.

Sir Hamilton was unusually bright and made a few quiet comments about 'how well you all look' and 'this programme need not concern us for very long' and 'let us try a few bars of Rienzi' which we did. The trumpet player, Alec Harris, played his solo A natural (with which note the overture unfortunately begins) and the orchestra immediately responded with the oldest and stalest joke in the business – everybody began to tune as noisily as it was unnecessary The rehearsal ended at 10.40 a.m. with the quiet assurance from Sir Hamilton that "We shall play this programme as usual."

I was sitting on the back desk with a charming and very experienced old gentleman from Liverpool - Johnny Whitehead – who realised my predicament. "Well, young man" he said kindly "I think you would be well advised to look at one or two of these pieces!" I did, for the rest of the morning and most of the afternoon, and I have been looking at them steadily ever since. It was the usual Wagner programme and they were ALL there! the Tristan 'Prelude and Liebestod', Klingsor's 'Magic Garden' and 'Good Friday Music' from Parsifal, 'Forest Murmurs', the 'Ride of the Walküre, Siegfried's 'Journey to the Rhine' and the Funeral Music from 'Götterdämmerung', the overtures to 'Rienzi' and the 'Flying Dutchman', and the Venusberg music from Tannhäuser'. In fact not much was left out!

I was the only newcomer in the ranks of the Orchestra and the brevity of the rehearsal made me painfully aware of the insignificance of my contribution to a programme of unfamiliar Wagner played 'as usual'. Tradition dies very slowly in orchestras where vacancies rarely occur, or are not artificially created, and after pondering all day on the words 'as usual' I realised that every note of that memorable concert had been authentic Wagner, and a rich heritage from Hans Richter. Many of the older members of the Orchestra remembered him as the conductor of the Hallé before the First World War, and two of them – Sam Holt and Johnny Bridge – played opera seasons with him at Covent Garden. Sam Holt, the first trombone in the Orchestra, was also Professor of the instrument at the R.M.C.M. He possessed the legendary perfect 'embouchure' and was able to produce gradations of tone from *pp* to *ff* without apparent expenditure of breath. Above all he was the Grand Old Man of the Brass Department and not in the least forbidding to an eager and inquisitive young man like myself. I had experienced some thrilling sounds in my first concert and Sam answered my questions with great patience: the sound which intrigued me most was the brass entry in the Introduction to Act III of 'Die Meistersinger'. The chord of G major took away my breath and I can only liken its impact to the launching of a huge ship – 'sideways with an enormous slow squelch' Sam Holt explained that 'soft-tonguing' was difficult to achieve unanimously throughout the entire section because instruments of different lengths and bore do not respond or speak at the same time. The method of non-incisive tonguing had been introduced by Richter. He also pointed out many other places where this effect can be quite shattering, for instance, the entry of the brass choir in bar 54 of the Prelude to 'Lohengrin', also the overwhelming entry of the sleep motif in 'Wotan's Abschied und Feuerzauber'.*

Another of the soft-tongued chords with a special significance for me is the E major chord at the beginning of Act I of 'Götterdämmerung' which seems to illuminate the stage and awaken Siegfried: it sparks off the miraculous interlude known to everyone as the 'Rhine Journey' and thereafter the whole tragedy of 'Götterdämmerung' is written into Brünnhilde's thoughts as she watches Siegfried disappear from sight towards the Rhine. Wagner said that 'the art of composition is transition' and, when asked how the 'Ring' could ever end, said enigmatically "The music will reveal all!" I may be alone in my belief that in the epilogue of 'Götterdämmerung' (when Wagner has despatched the character and dispensed with the spoken word) the music is sublimely liberated, and ends with a moving reference to the pathetic figure of Sieglinde, mother of Siegfried, whose love and sacrifice transcends the mythological world of demi-gods, cunning and treachery.

I have digressed a little since I recalled my first rehearsal with the Hallé and reflected on the Wagner tradition inherited from Richter. Nothing could be further from my thoughts than to suggest that Sir Hamilton came to the rostrum that evening and snapped his fingers to let the Orchestra loose on a programme which Richter had rehearsed thirty years before.

'It is incumbent on those who never change their opinion to be secure in judging properly at first.' Since 1935 I have been unshakable in my

* The next reference Wagner made to this sleep motif was in bar 37 of the 'Siegfried Idyll'

Sir Hamilton Harty

belief that the Hallé was, until 1933, the finest orchestra in Europe and Sir Hamilton Harty the greatest conductor I have ever known. He was supremely self-assured, undemonstrative, niggardly in the size of his beat and his gestures, but always in complete control. Cassado was the only soloist who ever momentarily disturbed his composure. At all other times there was about him an aura of quiet self-confidence. He had a prodigious memory for the occasional blemish which had perhaps marred a previous performance, and although he never referred to it at rehearsal, his keen glance betrayed the fact that he and the player concerned had a little secret. A wry smile or the slightest of nods was usually all that passed between him and the culprit, and the incident was never resurrected. On the rostrum he was a serene whispering giant: his features betrayed nothing of his innermost thoughts or anxiety (if he ever had any) and there existed between him and 'his' orchestra a relationship which transcended mutual respect – he was venerated. I never heard him raise his voice at rehearsal: perhaps the whispering was a clever ruse, but everything he had to say was felt to be directed so personally and confidentially that not a word was missed and the discipline was so good that he never had the occasion (nor the time) to repeat himself.

For a little while I was mystified by the enormous range of expression and the spontaneity of the sounds he created by minimal gestures. He had the most eloquent left hand which never made superfluous movement and obviously enjoyed an entirely independent existence from the right.* With it he could restrain and control the natural exuberance of the strings, or encourage them to unleash rich, virile, sonorous sounds which defied the limits imposed by the printed symbols of piano, crescendo, forte and other artificial methods of producing 'expression' in music.

Sir Hamilton is easy to recreate in the imagination – he had one foible, which I never understood, several characteristic gestures (including one which remained a confidence between him and the first violins), and an entire absence of antics, although I sometimes felt that he allowed his affinity with 'Till Eulenspiegel' to show a little too much, particularly in out-or-town performances, when he used to strut, swagger and whistle with obvious relish But after all, 'Till' was one of the Orchestra's virtuoso pieces, and audiences in 1930 were less inhibited in their enjoyment of music. The Hallé audience stood a little aloof from this generalisation: it had to support a reputation for discernment – based on what, I do not know – and in the early thirties this reputation had already begun to show unmistakable signs of fraying at the edges. It would be an exaggeration to say that Hallé subscribers scattered in all directions after every concert rather than commit themselves to expressing a black and white opinion of what they had just heard, but whenever I trapped and spoke to anyone I had just seen enoying the music, they invariably put me off until they had read Neville Cardus in the following morning's edition of the 'Manchester Guardian'!

The foible which puzzled me for years was no whim or caprice. Sir Hamilton began every concert by drawing himself to his full height (which was considerable) and holding his right hand with baton at the alert position as if he was about to start, he spent an interminable time fumbling with his left hand under his dress coat on his right bosom – he looked like Napoleon in reverse, and almost as serious! In spite of being Irish, he was not a Catholic, and certainly was not counting his beads; but the ritual was regularly performed.

Reginald Stead and I are now two survivors of the First violins of Harty's last years with the Hallé. We sat together for ten pre-war years and later resumed our close association in the postwar years with the B.B.C. Northern Orchestra. Whenever we meet, the conversation, will sooner or later get around to the incredibly beautiful sounds the Hallé strings used to make, and inevitably to Sir Hamilton's little secret with 'those on his left'. Memorable moments in music do not occur every few

---

* Most conductors fall into the 'Grecian Urn' category where both arms produce elegant curves in contrary motion. Only one (J.B.) ever went through life doing the breast-stroke.

bars, and Harty knew very well where they were! He would, on these occasions, hold out his left hand to us, and with his head slightly on one side, give us one of his rather rare melancholy smiles (as if to indicate that at last our moment of glory was at hand) "Now, boys" was all he whispered, but the response was always electrifying.*

As an accompanist Sir Hamilton was immaculate: in my orchestral experience since his departure from the Hallé scene, many conductors of international reputation and breath-taking stature have failed to re-unite soloists with orchestras at all the infamously dangerous joins and corners, by varying widths from a whisker to a tramcar. They are constant reminders of Sir Hamilton's infallibility in this important facet of a conductor's technique.†

As a composer Harty wrote for the Hallé Orchestra: there was in his music (even the transcriptions of Handel's 'Water Music' and Music for

---

* One instance which springs immediately to mind is the long awaited entry of the first violins in the Epilogue of Tchaikowsky's 'Fantasy' Overture, 'Romeo and Juliet'.
The top B natural is a wonderful sound if it is willed into existence by vibrato and a fast moving bow which scarcely touches the string.

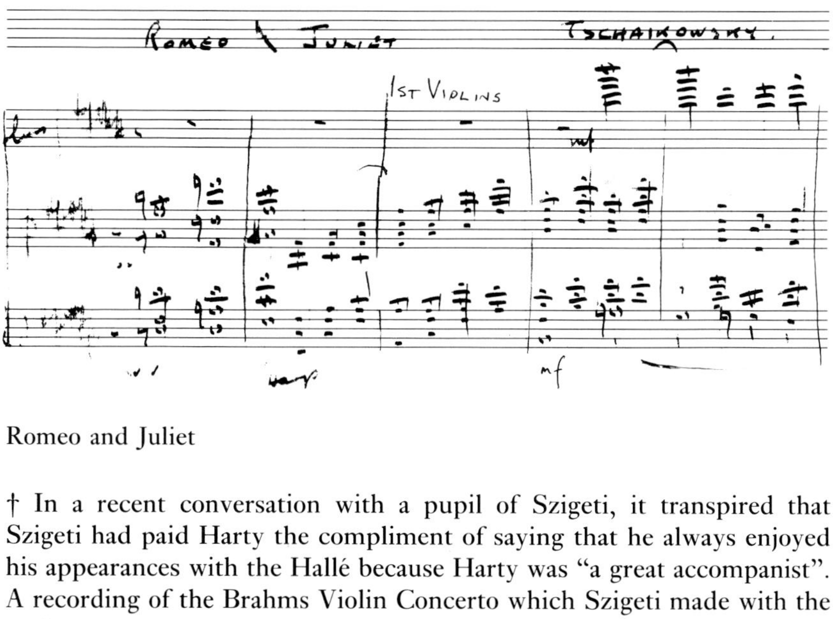

Romeo and Juliet

† In a recent conversation with a pupil of Szigeti, it transpired that Szigeti had paid Harty the compliment of saying that he always enjoyed his appearances with the Hallé because Harty was "a great accompanist". A recording of the Brahms Violin Concerto which Szigeti made with the Hallé in 1931 has recently been re-issued: this recording went 'in the can' first time! Only the cadenza (as far as I can remember) was repeated six times, until Szigeti was satisfied.

the Royal Fireworks') perhaps an overabundance of his own inimitable personality, but it also exploited the technical brilliance of individual members of the Orchestra. The 'Comedy Overture' abounds with passages unmistakably written for Archie Camden, Joe Lingard, Sam Holt and the Whittaker family of wood-wind players. Performances of this piece were always witty, sparkling improvisations and however worthy his music may be of a revival, I am very much afraid that the 'Comedy Overture' played by just any orchestra with just any conductor would sound like an Eskimo playing the 'Blue Danube'.

The more serious compositions such as the tone-poem 'With the Wild Geese' and the Violin Concerto were never considered by the critics generally, and consequently by the Manchester audiences in particular, to be music from the top drawer, but the woeful neglect of his music in this country has been offset by its increasing popularity abroad.

Chapter III

The foregoing chapter may indicate that the appraisal of Sir Hamilton Harty as a conductor was the hasty opinion of my first few impressionable days as an orchestral player. Between 1930 and 1933 I was spoiled – for life! Every concert enriched my musical experience and was in some way or other memorable and exciting.

Harty had already become internationally famous through a wide circulation of brilliant recordings which the orchestra made at this time, and it was no secret that the two series of concerts which he presented in the old Queen's Hall in 1929-30 and 1930-31 attracted representatives from orchestras in America, and that the 'rave' notices of the London concerts were reproduced in the American press.

It was no surprise to anyone when he accepted invitations to conduct in the States (except perhaps the Hallé Society who regarded Sir Hamilton as a provincial conductor) and little harm was done when the tours were undertaken during the long summer vacations.

The highlights of my first season with the Hallé (1930-31) were the six concerts presented in London: they proved to be tremendously successful. The first one on November 14th, which also included 'Le Carnaval Romain' and 'The Royal Hunt and Storm' was devoted mainly to a spectacular performance of the Berlioz 'Messe des Morts' which required Brass Bands in each of the four corners of the Hall. The second, a fortnight later, was a mammoth programme of the Brahms E minor Symphony and the Schubert 'Great' C major, cunningly separated by Suggia playing a very relaxed Elgar 'cello concerto. Never has the Elgar been in better company! The third in the series, on Friday, 12th December, was in many ways unique, and requires a little explanation. In pre-war days the Hallé Society could ill afford the expense of extra rehearsals, and the statutory three hours for a two-hour concert was all that a conductor was allowed. It is not surprising therefore that conductors had to be either very good (since they could not afford the luxury of overmuch talking) or cunning enough to devise programmes which could be repeated in geographically isolated places on consecutive days. The Queen's Hall concerts fell into this latter category except – for some inexplicable reason – this one. The concert in the Free Trade Hall, Manchester the previous night had gone predictably well, but Reginald

Stead and myself were confronted with, and confounded by a completely changed programme when we arrived in London for the 2.30 p.m. rehearsal. 'Ein Heldenleben' (all thirty-five breathtaking pages of the damned thing!) had replaced the Mahler symphony 'Das Lied von der Erde' the major work in the previous night's concert. Harty, predictably, began the Queen's Hall rehearsal with the unfamiliar piece but it ended in an uproar ten minutes later! At this point it becomes necessary to introduce the main character in the fracas – Alfred Barker – who had succeeded Arthur Catterall as leader of the orchestra only a season before. Alfred was what a professional musician would describe as 'a natural'. He looked as if he had been born with a fiddle under his chin: everything about his playing looked easy and mechanically perfect. He made glorious relaxed sounds without any trace of apprehension or nervous vibrato, but there was a little of the Gypsy somewhere in his make-up which sometimes betrayed a coquettish charm, and at others, a casual air of temporary disinterest in the proceedings. Why Alfred should have decided at 2.40 p.m. to sprawl out his legs and slump into a casual mood, I shall never know. Harty was obviously set upon making history with his 'London' concerts and, as everyone familiar with 'Ein Heldenleben' is very well aware, the Hero's love-life is portrayed with great eloquence by the solo-violin. It is a long and difficult section covering a wide range of nineteenth century teutonic emotions leaving precious little to the imagination! Alfred to the horror of us all, began his solo, somewhere in the no-man's land between 'casual' and 'sloppy', and a very sick and deflated Harty stopped him in his tracks and said "Alfred, it won't do!" "Oh," said Alfred rather breezily, "it will be all right tonight." (how often have I heard that fatuous remark?). Harty put down his baton, then with great dignity, and in complete silence, walked off the platform. The Orchestral Manager was Harry Mortimer, who played first clarinet*: he left the platform in a state of embarrassment and said rather sheepishly "I'll see what I can do." He returned some minutes later, looking very serious – "He won't come back. The rehearsal is cancelled."

So, for the second time that season, I faced a public concert on a ten minute rehearsal (and in *London*, too!). It seemed an interminable wait until 8.15 p.m. and it was with some trepidation that I looked around the distinguished audience, thinking of the disgrace to follow.

The Princess Royal graced the concert with her presence, as she had most of them, and also attending this one were G. B. Shaw, J. R. Clines and Albert Sammons, who sat under Alfred Barker's nose about six rows from the front of the stalls.

---

* not to be confused with Harry Mortimer the trumpet player

The first half of the concert consited of Beethoven's Seventh Symphony and Moiseiwitsch playing the Rachmaninoff C minor Concerto – all very nice; but it was 'Ein Heldenleben' which filled every heart and mind in the audience with eager anticipation and those on the platform with varying degrees of terror and despair. Whether or not Alfred Barker prayed or practised, or both, or from whence came the message or the inspiration, will forever remain a mystery, but that performance of the 'Hero's Life' was not only the highlight of a memorable season, but the greatest playing I have ever heard from an orchestral leader in my lifetime of music making.

The fourth concert in the London series took place on 9th January, 1931 and consisted of 'great bleeding chunks' of Wagner, but with a difference. This time the chunks were bigger and fewer: the first half of the concert was Act I of 'Die Walküre', and the second, which began with a new version of the 'Tannhäuser Venusberg Music' (in which the sirens singing 'Come to these Bowers' were represented by the two back desks of the first violins!) ended with an impressive performance of Siegfried's 'Death March' and the Finale of 'Götterdämmerung'. The evening proved to be a triumph for the soprano Oda Slobodskaya who sang the part of Sieglinde in 'Die Walküre', and of Brünnhilde in the Finale of 'Götterdämmerung': she was living proof that a 62 inch bust is not the first requirement (or physical qualification) of any soprano aspiring to sing Wagner! In fact she was so frail in appearance as to be perfectly cast as any of the consumptive heroines in Opera who regularly and inevitably die on sofas singing healthy fortissimo top Cs. I cannot remember, precisely, whether I stopped playing, or gasped, or laughed, or just looked up a few times, but the sounds which this incredible woman emitted were unbelievably beautiful. She appeared with the Hallé on two more occasions during that season and passed, unaccountably, into limbo.

The concert on 23rd January was the fifth in the London series and my first experience of Sir Hamilton Harty conducting a Sibelius symphony, this time the fifth in E flat.

Sibelius, as a composer, was little understood in 1930, in consequence of which, musicologists and writers of programme notes were extremely active in producing volumes of high-sounding, pseudo-knowledgeable, airy-fairy bits of journalistic jargon about his 'distinctive, original style' following 'no accepted rule or law', movements 'in a sort of free variation form, (a priceless definition!), 'organic growth', 'metamorphosis', 'terse, pithy phrases' (this one was getting warmer!) and a host of other clever-sounding snippets from musical terminology which were of no real help to anyone.

Harty was a composer with the rare gift of recreating music as if he were at the heart of it: his affinity with, and understanding of the qualities which distinguish one composer from another made his performances, in my opinion, stylistically perfect.

This performance of Sibelius was a lucid demonstration of the inimitable way in which pithy, pregnant motifs can, at each re-statement gradually shed the strong characteristics which have identified them and appear to re-group into *new* shapes which are curiously *familiar.* This may, in some elementary way, explain metamorphosis to a non-musician, but it would have been more difficult to explain the musical logic of this breakaway, skittish fragment in the first movement:

gradually gaining momentum and generating relentless, uncontrollable energy, with the violins in wave after wave of soaring ostinato crotchets until they reach the top E flat when the movement crashes. The silence was terrifying!

The last concert of the series on 6th February consisted of *two* great works, and a very interesting small one. The two major ones were 'Symphonie Fantastique' by Berlioz and the D minor Concerto for Piano and Orchestra by Brahms.

Harty's reputation, as a conductor, had been considerably enhanced by his performances of Berlioz, but it did not wholly depend on it. Any conductor whose reputation does, is a fraud! Berlioz has already done all the work and what he has to say is brilliantly said, but he has never been a favourite with me. Success is assured for any Berlioz item in a programme and applause is usually spontaneous but never prolonged: satisfaction is short-lived, like a straw fire. In any case, I feel to have been whipped into a patriotic frenzy and cheated by an orator with nothing but trivialities to say.

Backhaus played the Brahms D minor Piano Concerto immaculately, and this performance has always held a special place in the storehouse of my memorable musical experiences. Some two years before at one of my violin lessons, Catterall, in one of his gentle, fatherly moods, had stopped me in my tracks as I wallowed about in the slow movement of the Mendelssohn Violin Concerto! I was, in fact, laying on great thick helpings of that accursed stuff 'interpretation'. "Horsfall," said he, "be content to make beautiful sounds on the fiddle and to phrase intelligently. If the music is any good – and this is – let it do the talking. You may, one day, play the Brahms in public: if that ever happens and members of the audience turn to each other and say 'Isn't the Brahms a wonderful work?' then, my boy, you will be a great player!" I cannot remember what Backhaus looked like that night, and I was probably too involved in playing the notes to have any opinion about the performance, but I would eagerly have agreed with anyone there who said "Isn't the Brahms a great work?".

Handel's 'Watermusic', the interesting 'Suite' with which the concert began, is a much more contentious item. Harty has, in recent years, been mercilessly set upon by pundits for his arrangement of this 'Suite' and also of 'Music for the Royal Fireworks' – not because they are priceless gems of stylish orchestration but because post war Britain is now firmly in the throes of reactionary 'cults' which could be classified under a common title of 'back to nature'. Handel has been the principal target for this reformation, with some justification perhaps, because the 'Messiah' got a little out of hand during the second half of the nineteenth and the first half of the twentieth century. Grandiose performances of four hundred voices with matching orchestras were aided and abetted by mammoth organs lending a hand (and two feet)! The reaction to hefty Handel has produced a wide variety of 'realisations' of Handel's masterpiece. 'Authentic' manuscripts are coming to light with alarming frequency as evidence that the grotesque ornaments and coloratura cadenzas which are now bringing tears to the eyes of honest Yorkshire choral folks, have the authority of 'someone who was there' – in 1742! Goebbels once said "If you tell lies big enough, loud enough and often enough, somebody will believe them!"

The original performance of 'The Water Music', out of doors and on a choppy tidal river, must have been something to forget. It is inconceivable that Handel could have ingratiated himself with King George I (unless the King was tone-deaf) with a bargeful of horn players blowing more wrong notes than right ones on valveless instruments, accompanied by a clutch of coarse, indescribably out of tune, farting Fagotti! There is no record of George I throwing up his royal arms, praying for a tidal-wave, or summoning his Royal Scuttler to pull the plug out of the offending vessel – just a brief note in the programme that 'a reconciliation was achieved' – or did they reach agreement that Handel would 'never do it again'? Handel was always in a hurry, and the scoring of some of his greatest works was left bare and perfunctory.

Mozart had no compunction in adding flesh to the bones of the Handel Oratorios which he prepared for performance in the house of Baron van Swieten in Vienna in the early 1780's. The 'Messiah' lost nothing by Mozart's additional accompaniments, and I believe that the vitality which Harty infused into the Water Music will contribute more to its immortalisation than some of the Quakerish versions which I have recently played.

As I have already pointed out, six of the Hallé Manchester concerts were, with the single exception of 11th December, duplicated at the Queen's Hall in London the following nights. The major work in Manchester on 11th December was the Mahler symphony 'Das Lied von der Erde' which was its first performance at a Hallé concert. This work was replaced at the London concert on 12th December by 'Ein Heldenleben'.

Every concert was for me a first performance of something, and for the next two years I was much too busy absorbing new experiences to notice that the Hallé Society was extremely tardy in giving first performances to well-established masterpieces, although a great many works of Arnold Bax and William Walton were performed soon after they were completed.*

There was nothing unusual about the first performance of Ravel's 'Bolero' but the repeat 'by popular demand' a week later was a sensation. At the rehearsal, Harty gave no indication of the reason why he required us to be ready, on the platform, at 7.15 p.m.: he walked on, very solemnly as usual, and began the 'Bolero' whilst the bewildered dribs and drabs of an sudience were looking for their seats or standing in the aisles just gaping at the Orchestra. In spite of the loud bang which finished the piece, nobody either appreciated the performance or even realised what this incredible exhibition was all about – it was like a bad dream. Harty re-appeared at 7.30 p.m. to conduct the concert having purged it of what, in his opinion, was an obnoxious work.

On one other occasion during that winter season did Harty puzzle me by making a sly, profane remark, which took some of the gilt off his wings. In pre-war days, the Hallé gave fortnightly concerts in Bradford and Sheffield: the Bradford concerts unfortunately could not be given in St. George's Hall (because in those days it was a cinema). The Eastbrook Hall was the only available building, and to say that it was never intended to be, or be suitable for a concert hall, is the understatement of this century. It was a Chapel, and a very stark one to boot, probably built by a band of nineteenth century temperance workers with large families

---

* I can dimly remember rehearsing a symphony in G minor by E.J. Moeran, who was sitting in the auditorium. When and where is a mystery: I cannot find a reference to a performance in a Hallé programme, neither can I remember ever playing the work in public. The music was not in manuscript – the printed part was published by Novello.

who fervently believed that the only passport to happiness in the next world was to be completely wretched and miserable in this! The conductor was obliged to make an entrance from behind the organ gallery and make his gestures in the pulpit. Round about him was room only for twelve or fourteen players: the rest of them were dispersed on each side of the organ and were consequently out of sight and sound of each other. It was an octagonal building, and the audience in the balcony could see only part of the orchestra, and those on the floor could, at best, only see the conductor – the remainder were better off at home. All the seats were made of shapeless, bare wood, and they squeaked abominably: they were only dusted when people sat on them, and the place had a most peculiar smell. There was never room on the platform for a soloist, so that the concerts were always orchestral and usually repeats of the previous evening's Manchester concert. The rehearsal was normally a 'seating' one at 6.30 p.m. (or just before the doors opened).

On the evening in question Harty came down to the pulpit, looked around in disgust, shivered and said (very disdainfully) "This place *reeks* of *stale* Methodist prayers!".

A few years later, on February 7th, 1936, I remember Beecham conducting a Hallé concert in this Hall which ended with the Sibelius Sixth Symphony. As I have already explained, only a few players could be accommodated anywhere near the conductor. On this occasion Alfred Barker (the leader) and Harold Jones sat on Beecham's left, and immediately under his nose sat Johnny Whitehead and myself – so close, in fact, that in his more energetic moments our music folders were in danger of being scattered by his baton. Anyone familiar with the Sibelius Sixth Symphony will recollect that it is a dreary, meandering piece, and it has never been regarded as good box-office music; on this particular evening it matched its surroundings. Tommy, who probably was regretting its presence in the programme, was in artificial full cry throughout the work. It never really got off the ground and he began grunting and singing: his baton quivered in front of my face in all the most unlikely places, in fact, in all the places where there was nothing to quiver it for. Finally, he gave it up, and shrieked in a voice which could be heard in Laisterdyke, "Haven't they gone home – yet?!".

Sometime after 1934, when Delius died, the Delius Society issued several albums of recordings which Beecham had, with great dedication, produced. One Friday evening we arrived at the Eastbrook Hall for a seating rehearsal to find that all the seats in the body of the hall had on them a leaflet waiting for the attention of whoever came to the concert. We, in the orchestra, had no idea what the leaflets were about, and we were obliged to wait until Tommy came to conduct the second half of the concert before our curiosity could be satisfied. He addressed the audience in his best, slow, patronising drawl, with his eyebrows arched so high as to be somewhere on the top of his head "Ladies and gentlemen (pause) if you will remove the pamphlets upon which you are at present seated (pause) you will observe the picture of a man whose misfortune it was to be born in this *town*!" The rest I have forgotten, but it was not calculated to impress the local inhabitants of the city with the recordings. They took it well, as audiences usually did, because even when he was in deadly earnest, nobody took him seriously.

A short time ago I was passing the Eastbrook Hall on foot; its shabby, derelict appearance sparked off a game which I all too frequently play, of projecting my mind to other times and places, people, conversations, and incidents, in lightning flash-back until I begin to talk to myself and become oblivious of my immediate surroundings. (This insidious game can be very dangerous when car-driving. How many times have motorists looked out of the driver's window when held up at traffic lights and discovered that they have been on automatic pilot for twenty miles without the faintest idea how they negotiated the intervening distance and the route taken?) The Eastbrook Hall was a grim reminder of the poverty and wretchedness of the working classes in the woollen industry in the late nineteenth century and the particular brand of Socialism which my father used to ram down my young throat. There were so many Pakistani immigrants with whom I was rubbing shoulders in the street that I was quickly, by association of ideas and the help of a magic carpet, transported to Cairo and Aden where I served during the war. I was soon reviving conversations with a Moslem batman whom I inherited from my predecessor with the Aden Protectorate Levies, and listening with great interest to those priceless words of Mohammedan philosophy which were motivating his useless life. The one edict most frequently on his lips has probably been responsible for the astronomical crime rate among Moslems for centuries – 'Allah will provide – but he does not throw it into the nest!' Mohammed's words of wisdom did eventually seep through to the Western World via Karl Marx, whose encyclopaedic 'Distribution of Wealth' has been condensed into one simple axiom which has brought happiness to countless millions – 'It is all right, on religious grounds, to put your greedy hands into anybody else's pocket.' Unfortunately, this cosy advice has produced a very popular pastime which is getting a little out of hand, with too many hands finding fewer pockets. Soon we shall be faced with the dilemma of either wearing immunity badges for identification or sewing up our pockets for protection.

From January to March 1931, besides playing for the first time such monumental pieces as the Elgar Symphony No. 2 in E flat, Delius's 'Appalachia', Liszt's 'Faust Symphony', Mozart's Double Concerto in E flat (with Harty and R. J. Forbes) and the Beethoven Choral Symphony, I met, for the first time, three great soloists – Schnabel, Szigeti and Cassado.

My first impressions of Schnabel were confirmed on each subsequent appearance he made as soloist with the Hallé. He could, and often did, play more wrong notes on one page of his music than most soloists of comparable standard make in a lifetime; the great moments in every performance were usually sublime and I found myself oscillating so violently between praise and blame that I labelled him (quite privately, of course) as a 'profit and loss' pianist. I often felt like the referee who has the difficult job at a World Heavyweight Title Fight (which has gone its full distance) of awarding the fight to one or other of the contestants – on points! Schnabel always gave me the impression that he was about to do battle with the pieces he played, and was prepared, if necessary, to lose a little blood in so doing. The first piece I heard him play was the Brahms B flat concerto (15th January 1931). It was so huge in conception, staggering in tone, technique and contrasts that I readily forgave him for the blemishes. He was even more successful, at a later concert, with the Brahms D minor, which I remember being in every way gigantic, but in the 'Emperor' he overplayed Beethoven's rebellious spirit, and enjoyed only moderate success in coping with the notes.

On 29th January, 1931, Szigeti appeared as soloist in the Beethoven violin concerto. About this time he also recorded the Brahms which I have mentioned earlier in reference to Harty's genius as an accompanist. In trying to recall Szigeti I find it much easier to remember *what* he played and *how* he played it than to recollect his personal appearance or his temperament and character.

His technique was flawless and his intonation impeccable: the quality of the sound he made was intensely satisfying, and expression, if any, was on such a high plane as to be almost not there. Like Catterall, whatever he played, he enhanced the stature of the composer.

Cassado, who played the Dvorák 'cello concerto on 26th February, 1931 was always my favourite 'cellist, playing, on this occasion, the greatest piece ever written for the instrument. He never seemed to enjoy the reputation his playing deserved: perhaps he was born at the wrong time or perhaps his name was easily confused with Casals: but whatever the reason, he was never, in my experience, eclipsed by Casals. I must confess, in all fairness, that when I did eventually hear Casals, or play with him, he was over the hill and rapidly disappearing from sight down the other side.

It has never been my good fortune to avoid nostalgic and sometimes embarrassingly painful farewells to great soloists and singers. Besides Dr. Brodsky and Casals, Artur de Gref playing the Grieg was an experience I can never forget – his left hand was before his right by such a margin that I found it hard to believe. Frank Mullings singing in the 'Messiah' in the Albert Hall, Manchester could not produce a musical sound on the first top E in 'Comfort ye'. He burst into tears and left the platform.

In lighter vein – Tetrazzini made so many farewell appearances at Brand Lane Concerts in Manchester that the last three had to be changed to '*Definitely* the Last Appearance'. The bouquets were becoming symbolic of wreaths for a dead talent!

Cassado was a natural player without problems; his tone was lush and there was always an aura of improvisation about his performance. He seemed to be slightly unpredictable and he was so extrovert that he talked incessantly throughout the rehearsal. He was spontaneous but I sometimes felt that Harty was uneasy with him: he was always expecting the worst to happen – and it never did. In fact Cassado was a devilishly exciting player.

On Friday the 13th March, at the rehearsal in Sheffield, I made my first 'domino' with the Hallé. Counting the opening bars of the Scherzo of Beethoven's 'Choral' Symphony has always been a trap for me, but over the years I have managed to get it right.

The last concert of the season, a week later, was a Pension Fund Concert and devoted entirely to Wagner.

Chapter IV

In the 1931–32 Hallé season there were first performances of a great many works which unaccountably have remained for me the first and only performances – Arnold Bax's Symphony No. 3 and his overture to 'A Picaresque Comedy', two pieces by R. Strauss – 'Festival Prelude' for organ and orchestra and 'Burleske' for piano and orchestra. There were also first performances of the 'Mussorgsky Pictures' in a new orchestration by Ravel, Gershwin's 'American in Paris', Sibelius's Seventh Symphony and the Walton 'Viola Concerto' which Tertis played (in addition to the solo viola part in 'Harold in Italy'). January 21st, 1932 was a great first night for the Tallis 'Fantasy' and the 'Nursery Suite' (Elgar) and also the English premier for the Tenth Symphony of Shostakovich.

A very young Jelly d'Aranyi played the Brahms Violin Concerto on March 26th and on the 12th November I had my first experience of one of the seven wonders of the world - Bach's B minor Mass, in which the Bass was Arthur Cranmer.

Most appetites for music, however rapacious, are normally satisfied by a performance of the Brahms D minor Piano Concerto, and only a glutton with a mean, mercenary streak expects anything else in a programme. The work demands, besides the elementary details of technique and musicianship, the physical strength of a lumberjack and the endurance of a marathon-runner, yet, on January 28th, before Schnabel did battle with this mammoth piece, he loosened up by playing the Beethoven Concerto No. 1 in C major.

Just before the war Horowitz went a stage nearer winning a gold medal – by playing the Brahms D minor in the first half of the concert and the Tchaikowsky B flat minor in the second.

Many standard works in the orchestral repertoire such as 'Don Juan' and 'Don Quixote' by Strauss, and Elgar's A flat Symphony were adding to my experiences, and the Beethoven and Brahms Symphonies, which formed the basis for most of the 'out-of-town' concerts, were still unfamiliar and exciting.

The concert on February 11th was planned with the obvious intention of utilising the two soloists in every item in the programme (with the single exception of the overture). Szigeti and Cassado played the Brahms

Double Concerto in A minor in the first half, and each had a solo spot in the second. Szigeti played unaccompanied Bach, and Cassado the Rococo Theme and Variations by Tchaikowsky – brilliantly.

Violinists do not normally include the Brahms' Double, or any other double concerto, in their brochures, neither do 'cellists (in spite of the limited repertoire for the instrument) and bringing two soloists together, in one place, at one time, and in one mind to play this work is usually a triumph of diplomacy and administrative skill. The Hallé Society was amply rewarded on this occasion.

Szigeti's unaccompanied Bach, which was the G minor Prelude and Fugue from the First Partita, was of great personal interest for me: I had played the piece for the associate Diploma at the R.M.C.M about two years before. Whether from courtesy or relief or a quick trip to Cox's bar, I don't know, but every member of the orchestra except me fled from the platform. I stood my ground (or sat my seat) and I was left to enjoy a private lesson from Szigeti, in public. At the end of the short recital I realised that I too had an audience, and a very distinguished one: Sir Hamilton, with a very broad grin on his face was standing at the foot of the stairs which led to the platform talking to a group of first violins. He was saying, as I learned later, "I just *had* to come round to this side to watch Horsfall enjoying himself".

One of the greatest obstacles to the appreciation of music is a stubborn resistance to the persuasion that 'music' is sound, and not printed paper. The inadequacy of the printed symbols of music to represent a composer's thoughts has been an insuperable problem for centuries, and a composer's intentions become increasingly obscure when the printed page is transmitted from place to place, or what is more important, from one generation to another until his thoughts, together with his reputation, recede into history. Under Patronage, where composers directed private performances of music never intended for posterity or publication, manuscripts which have survived convey little more than a speculative idea of the actual performances. Haydn, for example, enjoyed many privileges at Esterhazy, but was nevertheless restricted in publishing his music until after the death of his royal patron in 1790. By far the greater proportion of his 134 symphonies written at Esterhazy were directed by Haydn from the harpsichord: 'expression' and nuance of the simplest kind were decided on the spot, and the improvised continuo part which Haydn supplied to fill out the harmony and provide rhythm and texture were never set down, thus creating acute problems of authenticity when these early symphonies are performed.

In spite of the sophisticated expression marks and the subtlety of dynamics and nuance which have adorned music since the beginning of the 19th century, composers remain entirely at the mercy of performers (or middlemen) to recreate the symbols, and breathe the breath of life into the inanimate crotchets and quavers according to their understanding. God preserve me from the man who says "I can only play what I see" – it isn't good enough!

The extremities of seeing and understanding were never more clearly illustrated than in the exemplary Beecham who was the greatest architect of living sound I have ever known. He was inimitable in shaping music as it happened and he always, at rehearsal, appeared to be disinterested or even disdainful of the printed paper. As he turned the pages of a score little grunts used to escape him which would clearly have said "So that is what that delightful passage *looks* like." He conducted from memory because it was expected of him, but his memory was often suspect and he frequently stirred the pudding: he used to sing until he arrived at a landmark, proving beyond doubt that he knew the outlines even if he had forgotten the notes.

One other supreme example of the perfect 'middleman' between composer and public was Fou Ts'ong. Professor Proctor-Gregg persuaded him early in his career (6th May 1960) to give a mainly Chopin recital in the Whitworth Hall of Manchester University. The audience proved to be sparse and exclusive: sparse because Manchester audiences then, as now, have to be repeatedly told how good an artist is before they stir off their doorsteps to listen, and exclusive because those who attended were prepared to enjoy themelves, and they did, immensely. The recital was unbelievably uninhibited. He saved the miracle until the very end, as an encore he played the Chopin 'Berceuse' – after which I would have run from the building if he had played another note! It was godlike in its simplicity: obviously he had never heard Pachman or Paderewsky play it, or listened to anyone telling him how it ought to go: he held the fragile piece so gently in his hands that Chopin seemed to have passed the manuscript to him with the ink still wet, and then sat down and played it. I shall never again recapture that moment.

It is probably an exaggeration to say that I have, in the last 45 years played the Sibelius Symphony No. 2 with every conductor who ever drew breath: but so it seems to me, because no other work ever takes me back with such speed and certainty to November 19th, 1931 when I first played it with Harty – he was the only conductor who ever got it right! I never regarded Sir Hamilton as an authority on Sibelius, or anyone else, but there existed between himself and Sibelius an affinity which made the music flow, and the musical ideas grow, develop and fragment so lucidly that the common tree appeared to shed, from the same branches, an abundance of different fruits.

For the connoisseur only, here is a piano reduction of two passages from the Scherzo and Trio of the Second Symphony. In order to illustrate that the joins are more difficult visually than aurally, I have simplified the note values (not the notes) and added approximate metronome markings as an indication of how Harty showed greater concern for sounds than symbols (which in the case of Sibelius are bewildering, e.g., what does '*poco a poco meno ff*' mean? – would not 'diminuendo' do just as well?).

GP
Timp
GP
GP
GP
GP
GP

Allargando
Allegro moderato

SECOND VERSION to illustrate the pulse relationship between Scherzo and Trio, also the transition to the Finale.
Note values changed and approximate metronome markings inserted in order to demonstrate the 'aural' simplicity of the transitions.

There were two small points in the Siegfried Idyll which Harty insisted on having right, although he never seemed to labour them –

The crotchet rest in bar 28 if meticulously observed will expose the first violins for the crotchet B natural which forms the anacrusis octave leap, as it was at the beginning of the piece.

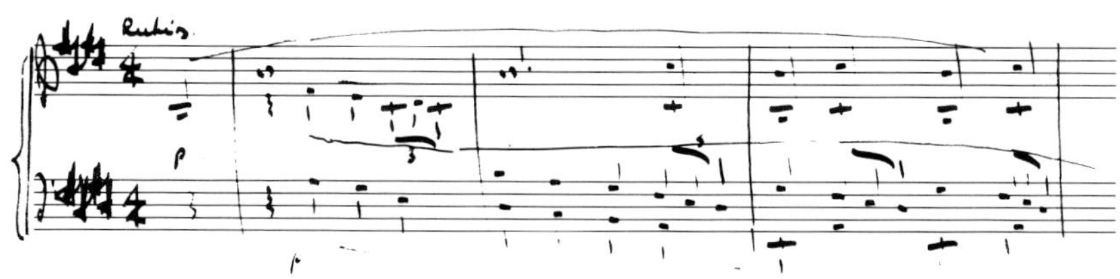

2nd Symphony by Jean Sibelius © Breitkopf & Härtel, Wiesbaden

In bar 105 the first violins hand over the F sharp to the second violins. The smooth change can only be achieved if the first violins hold the note over the bar line or by the second violins fractionally anticipating their entry.

Chapter V

The season 1932–33 began like any other, harmlessly enough, with a Wagner concert, and a succession of world famous artists playing well established pieces. Suggia played the Schumann, Rosenthal - Liszt and Chopin. Mischa Elman played the Bach E major (walking about the platform trying to stick his fiddle down our throats) and the Tchaikowsy (which kept him far too busy to be giving us lessons).

Some of the works enoying a first performance in Manchester, were Mozart's Symphony No. 29 in A, Sibelius' Symphony No. 1 and the Tone Poem 'Tapiola'.

Muriel Liddle made her debut with the Hallé playing the piano in Saint Saëns' Symphony No. 3 in C minor. When I met her in Birmingham recently she was playing the harp, and understandably failed to recognise me, I was far too gallant to remind her that I knew her 45 years ago.

November 17th was a memorable first performance of 'Belshazzar's Feast' in which Denis Noble sang: there were other performances with the Huddersfield Choral Society but I cannot remember the dates.

On the 8th December Myra Hess played the Brahms D minor Piano Concerto thus discrediting my previous observations that this concerto is exclusively a masculine enterprise.

On December 15th I played for the only time in my life a Strauss Ballet Suite – 'Schlagobers'. I cannot remember anything of this work.

After the performance of the 'Messiah' Harty left us for a tour of America which turned out to be momentous. He came back to us on February 9th for the remaining concerts of a season which proved to be his last with the Hallé.

There were three concerts during Harty's temporary absence in America which made a lasting impression on me. On January 19th I met for the first time an astonishing French conductor, Pierre Monteux, and on February 2nd an equally sensational Englishman – Sir Thomas Beecham. Both these extraordinary men were dominant figures in my orchestral life for the next 30 years. Some of my observations of Sir Thomas Beecham have already been published, I make no apology for repeating some of them here, and they will be recalled in context, authenticating some of the stories which have, through distorted repetitions, lost their original 'point'.

The concert on January 26th was, sadly, the last time I met Sir Edward Elgar who conducted a performance of 'The Dream of Gerontius'. The whole day was heavily charged with emotion: he received a standing ovation from the orchestra at the rehearsal, and, in the evening, from everyone in the Free Trade Hall. The entire proceedings seemed to be an excuse to pay tribute to him. Throughout both rehearsal and concert he sat in a commodious arm-chair, and he did very little more than paw gently at the air with his baton to direct the playing and singing. The response from everyone on the platform belied the tragically tired conducting – the performance was what it deserved to be – tremendous.

There was one personal incident at the rehearsal which ought to be recorded – Sir Edward had given us all the impression that he would rather stop occasionally and have a chat than play relentlessly on through a piece which seemed to be giving him little satisfaction. A few bars before the end of Part I (which takes only 40 minutes in performance time) he began to smile, and before long his 'tummy' started heaving up and down with what might vulgarly be called a belly-laugh. He turned in his armchair with some difficulty and pointed with his baton to one of the two V.I.P. boxes at the back of the (old) Free Trade Hall. "The first performance of this work in Manchester" he said, "was a great civic occasion, and the Lord Mayor with his official party occupied that box. Richard Strauss was with me and we were introduced to the Lord Mayor just before the performance began. It was obviously the first concert he had ever attended in his life and he didn't recognise me, neither was he particularly interested in my name or that of Dr. Strauss. "Oh, sit down anywhere" was all the Lord Mayor had to say, and we all endured the first 40 minutes in silence. Just before the end of Part I Richard Strauss and I got up and excused ourselves because I was most anxious to be backstage and have a talk with Hans Richter, who was conducting. I said, very apologetically, 'I'm afraid we shall have to go now, my Lord Mayor' to which he replied, rather painfully, 'And I wish to God I COULD!'" Sir Edward went on chuckling to himself for some time and we took that to be the cue for a long coffee-break. The rest of the rehearsal I remember as being friendly, cosy and a little sad.

The only information which preceded Pierre Monteux to Manchester came through the orchestral bush telegraph:* he had a reputation for

* This system is older than Reuter, and just as reliable, although there is probably not a grain of truth in the old story that the pigeons now roosting in great numbers on the roof of the Free Trade Hall are descendants of the noble breed which carried messages to and from our brothers in the London Philharmonic.

having 'the smallest beat and the biggest fee in the business', and since none of the older members could enlighten me further, I was full of apprehension on the morning of January 19th, 1933.

The platform of the old Free Trade Hall could be approached on either side by a flight of eight or nine steps which curved away under the balcony (in a quarter circle) and disappeared into the hinterland, back-stage. Sitting in the first violins I had a perfect view through the avenue between second violins and violas of anyone coming up the stairs on the other side. Nuttall, the porter, who usually came on to the platform to place the conductor's scores and baton neatly on the music stand, appeared at 10.30 – empty-handed, which was surprising. He carried off the conductor's desk, and this single-handed duty got the inevitable ironic cheer from the orchestra; but Nuttall was quick to learn, and the music desk never appeared again at any subsequent concert conducted by Pierre Monteux.

I was ill-prepared for the maestro when he at last appeared, and I am sorry to admit that I burst out laughing. Monteux had a rather big head and he wore a huge drooping moustache: his cheeks were ruddy and his whole countenance radiated impish joy. His round body bounced up the stairs, and he trotted to the rostrum beaming at everybody like a naughty little boy whose mother had just chased him up the steps for stealing a plateful of jam tarts which he had obviously eaten judging by the size of his belly. All he had with him was a baton, and all he said was "Debussy".

I have been trying very hard all my life to introduce legislation probibiting some conductors from mauling certain pieces, but with no conspicuous success: on the morning of January 19th my head was filled with a very different kind of legislation. I would gladly have precluded any other conductor from conducting 'L'après-midi d'un faune' as long as Monteux remained alive. He was a phenomenon, if that means an unusual person so strange as to excite great wonder. He had a photographic mind which was infallible. Twice within the first five minutes of the rehearsal his memory was put to the test: firstly, I regret to say, by the First Horn 'trying it on' and secondly by the Harpist who ought to have known better. The horn player, quite unnecessarily, asked him about a note in his part 'which he wasn't sure about' (this is called 'taking the micky'). Monteux was full of genuine concern and told him all the notes in the bar which was queried, and the bar before, and the bar after, and also where the crescendo and diminuendo marks started and finished, in fact, he would have written out a new part for him. Raymond Meert thanked him, rather shamefacedly, and muttered to those near him "This one knows what he's doing". The first entry of the harp was an unexpected shock to Monteux – Charlie Collier gave one of his spectacular flourishes which (like the Turkish Delight) was full of Eastern promise to be 'all right tonight'! but Monteux raised his cautionary finger, gave one or two 'tut-tuts' and then calmly told him of all the wrong notes which had escaped from his instrument, and reminded him of the notes Debussy had written. No-one else that day, nor for the next thirty years ever tried again to deceive Pierre Monteux.

The rest of the programme covered a wide variety of styles from Mozart's Piano Concerto in D minor with François Lang as soloist, to Beethoven's Symphony No. 7 in A, 'Till Eulenspiegel' and 'Les Préludes'.

'Discipline' is a very inadequate word to describe the nerve-end communication which existed between Monteux and members of the orchestra, however widely dispersed on the platform. He directed every nuance and inflection and took breath for the players in the wood wind section before every solo or important entry. In spite of the 'small beat' he was always in control, especially of the little notes which were always miraculously 'placed' by a sub-divided beat.

Monteux rarely spoke at rehearsal except perhaps to correct mistakes or omissions in the parts: he never showed displeasure or any sign of anxiety. His modesty was disarming and he seemed always to be serenely aware that he was a conductor for the connoisseur: I believe that the esteem in which he was held by orchestral players all over the world was a source of wonder and amazement to him. He was the most self-effacing of all 'middlemen' between composers and discerning posterity, and he always seemed conscious of the fact that the primary function of a conductor is to help. In the longest speech I ever heard him make, he said "Composers write their music with loving care, even the little notes: it is our duty to play them all!". He included himself in that observation, and any gestures which contributed to the rhythmical control of 'busy' passages was anticipated and executed with unerring instinct and minimal fuss.

At a Hallé concert some years later he was conducting the 'Firebird' Suite of Stravinsky. The first allegro 6/8 is the passage which suggests the great 'flapping of wings'. Monteux, to everyone's surprise, conducted six quavers in a bar. He said, almost apologetically, "The music sounds so much quicker when we play all the notes!" He was also the only conductor who ever began Strauss's 'Don Juan' beating four crotchets in a bar. On these rare occasions I can remember having the satisfaction of playing every note!

Sir Thomas Beecham was also a phenomenon, but of a different kind, he was more amusing than amazing. The first concert I ever played under his direction, on February 2nd, 1933, was preceded, the day before, by an extra rehearsal in the Memorial Hall, Albert Square, Manchester.

Those members of the Hallé Orchestra who remembered Richter could also remember attending young Mr. Thomas Beecham's 21st birthday celebrations in St. Helens in order to indulge his conducting whims. He continued to indulge them throughout his long life (with inestimable benefits for the rest of mankind), and the extra rehearsal was just an example of the adage that 'he who pays the piper calls the tune' – the tune on this occasion being 'Ein Heldenleben'!

This rehearsal, like many more in later years, was to be one of Sir Thomas's working sessions, and not enlivened by wit or lively incident. He sat throughout the entire afternoon with his spectacles perched perilously on the end of his nose, turning the pages of his score and nodding recognition of a landmark here and there as he refreshed his memory. He made no attempt to conduct or to make a performance of any of this difficult work, and he appeared to pay little attention to what we were playing. It was soon evident that he wished to evade questions from individual members of the orchestra about the manner in which solo passages would eventually be played, or even the usual questions concerning doubtful notes. Wally Jones, the tuba player, asked him whether the 'F' in a particular bar should be sharp or natural: "What would you like to play?" asked Beecham, not taking the trouble to check. "I think it should be F sharp" said Jones, very pleased with himself. "Then you must play F sharp" was the unsatisfactory reply. Tommy later admonished Wally Jones for 'making the most' of a solo passage – "Damn it, man! he has only just met the young lady." It was obvious to us all that the Hero was not going to have any 'leben' until the following day.

Sir Thomas, at the rehearsal in the Free Trade Hall the following morning, was back to normal, or so I was informed by the older generation. Also in the programme was 'Brigg Fair' by Delius with which he began the rehearsal. Many extra wood-wind players were required for this piece and there was a great commotion, naturally, as all the extras scurried on to the platform to find their places, trying not to be late for what was probably the only engagement they had had for months. Tommy was a devil in situations like this, and was enjoying every second of the skirmish when his eye fell on the fourth oboe player – Donald Hargreaves – who was the least successful of the awkward swarm of new-comers, in fact, if there was anything awkward a man could have – Donald had it! His hair, which was never combed, was always over his eyes like an Old English Sheepdog, and he wore tiny gold-rimmed spectacles on the end of his nose which were useless to him because he always looked over the top of them. He chattered incessantly but never finished a sentence because he stammered so badly, and the black boots which he wore summer and winter, rain or shine, were at least three sizes too big for his feet. His crowning glory at 10.30 a.m. was the full evening dress suit he was wearing for the evening concert. The dress-coat would have been considered obsolete in 1889 and the *black* bow-tie looked as if it would drop off before 7.30 p.m. He wore some kind of limp, home-knitted cardigan, and as he wriggled to his place he kicked over a music stand or two, and tried to rescue some of the parts he was scattering about the platform. He finally collapsed in his seat, breathless and quite unable to blow his instrument.

Beecham was in convulsions, watching every perilous step.

Eventually, when he was able to find his tongue, he turned to Alfred Barker with one eye shut and the other one very wide open, and said "Who is that curious individual? he looks as if he'd slit your bloody throat for sixpence!"

A few years later he was up to his tricks again in a programme which included the 'William Tell' Overture. Stuart Knussen, the first 'cello was late for the rehearsal, and Beecham, who had walked past Knussen's empty chair on his way to the rostrum, shouted "William Tell!" to the orchestra and began thrashing fresh air with his baton in the direction of the empty chair (the piece begins with one solo 'cello). The manager called to Tommy from his place in the wood-wind section "He's on his way, Sir Thomas." "Yes, I know" said Beecham drily, "but *where*, in God's name, *to*?"

For the remainder of that day he was in a very serious, music-making frame of mind. Besides the Delius 'Brigg Fair' in the first half of the concert was the Symphony No. 34 (K338) in C by Mozart. Delius he championed all his life and Mozart he worshipped: having set his heart on a superlative performance of 'Heldenleben' I cannot recollect another concert with Beecham which surpassed this one, or one in which I was more aware of his involvement, concentration, control and attention to the minutest magical detail. He never relaxed his grip on the concert and he was more than his usual eloquent self on the rostrum: he radiated rhythm and vitality, and I had my first experience of the manner in which he could inspire orchestral players to give more than normally could be expected of them in the line of duty. To be physically exhausted at the end of Beecham concerts became routine experience.

The following week, Harty was back from what had been a highly successful tour of America to complete what was to be his last season as the conductor of the Hallé Orchestra. The first concert on his return was a Monday 'Municipal' on February 6th and the programme, which I cannot remember, was a run of the mill affair. The rehearsal was enlivened soon after it began by a cry of "Damn!" from the rostrum – Sir Hamilton had broken his baton and thrown into the auditorium the piece which remained in his hand. The little speech of explanation was of great interest to me. "That baton was the only one I used during the whole of the American tour, and, within five minutes of my return to Manchester, I break it!" In the quiet of the afternoon I had some difficulty finding the broken tip among the clutter of furniture on the platform, but the main piece was easier to find on the floor of the hall. I carefully re-united them at home with the aid of a little glue and the baton is still in my possession.*

The concert on February 9th was distinguished only by the reappearance of Schnabel playing the Beethoven C major Concerto and yet another example of the current practice of re-writing Schumann symphonies. Mahler, the supreme egoist had almost convinced the world that Schumann could not write for the orchestra, and the orchestral parts in general circulation in 1933 contained very liberal red ink amendments to prove that he (Mahler) could make his symphonies tolerably playable.

The version of the Fourth which we played on February 9th was the work of another 'arranger' this time no less a person than Harty. The public obviously liked it, and the B.B.C. used the arrangement for a few years, but I was probably a little prejudiced in my appraisal of yet another example of 'dabbling' with Schumann and I was greatly relieved, after the war, when it was generally felt that Schumann wasn't a bad composer after all and that his symphonies sounded rather well when left alone.

The following week, Solomon appeared for the first time playing the Tchaikowsy B flat Concerto and there was a first performance of Weinberger's Polka and Fugue from 'Schwanda the Bagpiper'. The critics in Vienna had been rather severe with Weinberger who (so they said) had come on to the stage after its first performance 'to take a bow for all the composers represented' in this too popular piece.

February 23rd was the first performance of the Ravel 'Tombeau de Couperin' and Cassado played the Elgar. On March 2nd I played in what must have been the only performance of the Delius 'Mass of Life' which had *not* been conducted by, or received the blessing of Sir Thomas Beecham. The last two concerts in that season had violinists as soloists. Jelly d'Aranyi played the Mendelssohn, and Henry Holst the Brahms. The Pension Concert on March 23rd was the last concert which Sir Hamilton Harty conducted in Manchester, and with it came to an abrupt end an episode, which, like the immensely satisfying aesthetic experience of reading 'Pride and Prejudice' for the first time, can never subsequently be recaptured.

Although Harty had had leave of absence for the American tour in 1933, it was the first time that such a visit had encroached upon a sacrosanct Hallé season, and it was abundantly clear (in view of the success of that tour) that Harty could no longer be held on an exclusive contract or regarded as a provincial conductor: his resignation was inevitable.

In the light of subsequent events it is a chastening thought that a decade later rich were to be the rewards for any British conductor who went 'on missionary work abroad' – with or without an invitation.

---

* Now at The Lisburn Museum, Lisburn, Co. Down

The guest conductors who were engaged in profuse numbers from 1933 onwards to provide all subscribers with new faces to look at, were also to infuse new ideas and interpretations into the Orchestra. The ideas were so confusing and conflicting, and the results so negative and temporary that its greatest attributes – character and tradition – were gradually dissipated until, long before 1939, it had become a very ordinary provincial orchestra.

Chapter VI

Symphony Orchestras in Britain were, in the decade before the Second World War, largely self-supporting, and for the short winter series of concerts orchestral players were engaged on the basis of a single fee for a statutory 3-hour rehearsal and 2-hour concert.

The repertoire of the Hallé Orchestra in 1933 was enormous and in spite of the limitations imposed by 3-hour rehearsals, new works were introduced and the repertoire extended by the common-sense expedient of cutting a few familiar corners in 'grand old pieces' and utilising precious rehearsal time absorbing the new music.

The new works which Sir Hamilton Harty introduced to Manchester audiences were more than adequately rehearsed, and the standard works which were sometimes played 'as usual' produced exciting and predictably excellent concerts.

The inescapable fact remained, however, that the Hallé Society, unsubsidised to the point of near extinction, could not, on economic grounds, afford the crippling expense of extra rehearsals or offer the guest conductors engaged in the season 1933–34 the luxury of them. 'As usual' became a meaningless phrase, and has remained so ever since.

There was one guest conductor during the season 1933-34 for whom the limitations of a 3-hour rehearsal had no terrors: it would be true to say that he was always capable of conducting 3-hour concerts with 2-hour rehearsal!

On November 23rd, Henry J. Wood conducted the Verdi Requiem and Brahms' 'Song of Destiny'.

Henry J. was a lovable, boisterous old bear, who bellowed his way through every rehearsal and charged his way relentlessly through every concert without a vestige of subtlety or finesse. He was greatly beloved by the 'extras' in the orchestral world, who depended on engagements playing rare, exotic and expensive instruments such as the F Trumpet, E*b* Clarinet, 2nd Harp, Oboe d'Amore, Bass Clarinet, Contra Bassoon, etc. Henry J. would not conduct an orchestra, amateur or professional, unless players were engaged to play every note in the score according to the composer's directions. He is now remembered and revered (by those who never knew him) as the inventor of the Last Night of the Proms.!

It was from the series of Brand Lane popular Saturday Orchestral Concerts that the Hallé Orchestra (or its free-lance players) derived a major part of their income and it was not surprising that Henry J. was engaged to conduct most of them. Every rehearsal, and there were many, followed the same hilarious pattern: the younger players were trapped in the band-room or ante-room by Henry J. and his tuning fork (a contrivance which looked like an empty cigar-box with a tuning fork sticking out of it). The older generation knew the trick, and were on the platform early, but there was no escape. Every player with an instrument in his hand was relentlessly pursued by Henry J. banging on his infernal contraption. He followed them all over the place until satisfied that everybody had heard the damned thing. Instruments vary in pitch when carried from one room to another, but he persisted in this ridiculous ritual all his life.

The first desks of second violins and violas instinctively retreated from the rostrum whenever Henry J. appeared. He had the most unusual baton which bore all the characteristics of a lethal weapon: the handle was a five-inch piece of rolling-pin out of which protruded at least thirty inches of pointed stick – and how he waved it about! The 'lebensraum' near the rostrum was a necessary precaution against grievous bodily harm; the rehearsals resolved themselves into running commentaries which he read out from the scores. (His music was liberally marked in thick blue pencil, with illuminating bits of wisdom such as 'speak to 'cellos', 'intonation', 'watch the beat, double basses', 'don't hurry', etc.) But it was the voice which irritated me most!

If there is a hate relationship which exceeds in violence that which belongs exclusively to a Lancashire/Yorkshire Roses cricket match it exists between a Yorkshireman and a Cockney. Henry J. was unbelievable at rehearsal – he never stopped bellowing and he always repeated the tail-end of every tedious comment. I cannot record the accent, but the remarks are easy to remember: "Leave nothing to charnce, gentlemen, nothing to charnce, gambling all right on the Stock Exchange, the Stock Exchange, but there's now plice for it in music, now plice for it in music" – "Second position, 'cellos, second position – it ain't in chune, it ain't in chune" – "Watch it, basses, watch it." But the one which evoked the biggest titter around the orchestra was "Pianissimo, gentlemen, pianissimo" with a beat which indicated *fff* in any conductor's language. He never repeated any music or put anything right which was blatantly in need of correction, and at the end of every rehearsal he breathlessly used to tell us at what time the concert would end – "The concert will finish at 9.28 precisely – 9.28 precisely! Good-day, gentlemen, good-day!"

There was nothing unusual about the performance of the Verdi Requiem except the presence of an invention of Henry J. to announce the end of the world – it was a huge one-skinned bass-drum, at least six feet in diameter, which looked like an inverted children's paddling pool;

there was also a Gong to match, and I cannot stifle a chuckle every time I see the sub-titles of a J. Arthur Rank stupendous film production, wondering if the gong which Tommy Farr is whacking in slow motion was borrowed from the Henry J. Wood collection.

Members of the public cannot any longer be mystified at the duties of 'inside' players at each desk of a string section in any modern orchestra. They stop playing at the foot of every right-hand page of the music and turn the page slowly if the music is dificult, and, God willing, in time for their colleagues to proceed without interrupting the music too noticeably. Henry J. would have none of this ancient custom in the overture to 'Tannhäuser'; his inventive mind contrived a special set of string parts in which the last four pages of the piece were arranged and pasted in pairs, one above the other, on one huge double sheet of cardboard, in such a way that they were all visible at the same time, thus obviating the necessity of 'turning' during the conflict between the Pilgrims' Chorus and the surging, passionate, Venusberg music. There were advantages for all in this absurd arrangement – Henry J. was happy in not halving the string sound for three or four seconds, and the players were deliriously happy and contented during the whole twelve minutes of the piece, hiding behind the sight screens not caring one jot or tittle who the bowler was or which were the googlies he was sending down.

The bogey of limited rehearsal time must have tormented the guest conductors from overseas, and the programmes presented by Robert Heger and Nicolai Malko were tentative and exploratory: enterprise and caution are curious bed-fellows and for the first time in my life I experienced the drudgery of working at music which was not worth the effort, and producing concerts which never 'got off the ground'.

The main work in Heger's first programme in Manchester was 'Variations on a theme by Mozart', an incredible piece of sophistication by Reger who was so carried away writing thousands of superfluous semi-quavers that he missed the point of Mozart's disarmingly simple and delicious caricature of a theme. Robert Heger was preoccupied for most of the rehearsal rummaging about in the maze of superabundant notes hoping that the niggardly attention given to the Kodály 'Marosszék Dances' would not betray the fact that its first performance in Manchester was little better than a run-through.

The second concert Heger conducted was devoted to two works – the 7th Symphony of Bruckner and the Dvorák Violin Concerto in which Arthur Catterall was the soloist. In spite of my high regard for Catterall as a teacher and soloist and the fact that I seldom saw him, the concert was a turgid, un-memorable affair.

Nicolai Malko, who conducted only one concert during this season was an enigmatical, unemotional man. He was small in stature and wore half-moon rimless spectacles: his features were full of character although he registered neither pleasure nor pain: he rarely spoke, possibly because his English was bad, but he gave the impression of being detached and uninvolved in the proceedings. His conducting was undemonstrative but infallible: he was always clear in his directions and he never reacted with impatience to mistakes nor indeed registered any satifaction whenever the orchestra was playing well. His presence on the rostum created the impression of firm, inflexible control: he never smiled, neither did his music, and the concerts he conducted in Manchester over the next few years were always very serious, consistently good, and entirely without incident worth recalling.

The concerts in February 1934 were, in a variety of ways, momentous. John Barbirolli – 'J.B.' as he later became affectionately called – was a very ambitious young man who conducted a very straightforward concert on February 8th when Schnabel, quite out of character, played Mozart in B*b* K.595, and the orchestra gave its usual rousing performance of the 'Eroica'. He was less successful with his concert a week later, however: it was devoted entirely to Elgar. In the first half, the 'Enigma' was sandwiched between the overtures 'Froissart' and 'Cockaigne', and in the second, Albert Sammons played the B minor Violin Concerto. It was obvious soon after the rehearsal began that he could have spent three hours on every piece in the programme, and like every other disastrous rehearsal, the fuss, and attention to microscopic detail in the early stages highlighted the elementary fact that great areas of the programme would inevitably be neglected. Tempers began to fray at the edges, and Albert Sammons was far from delighted with the time allotted to his concerto.

In situations when inexperienced conductors waste precious rehearsal time finicking with unimportant details, orchestral players are extremely reluctant to extend the tedium beyond the statutory limit. The Hallé Orchestra was no exception and at 1.30 p.m. precisely, there was a great groan of relief and the Orchestra scattered in all directions – not only from the platform, but from the building.

There were three exceptions to this general exodus – J.B., myself and Ted Stansfield, the bass fiddle player, who appeared on the platform sometime after 2 p.m.

J.B. remained on the platform, shaking with nerves and frustration: he was chain-smoking and fidgeting with a pencil as he turned the pages of his scores back and forth. I was sitting towards the back of the balcony, nibbling at some sandwiches and feeling a twinge of sympathy for J.B. although his present predicament was of his own making.

If the sandwiches were not very tasty my mind used to stray from the Free Trade Hall to the Chop House in Brazennose Street where I should meet Sam Holt and enjoy his company and a steak at 6 p.m. on this, and every other Thursday. I invariably carried with me the miniature scores of the music we played, and used the lunch hour to make notes of little gems of wit and wisdom which had been dropped by either soloist or conductor during the rehearsal. There was nothing to record on this day except the visual plight of J.B. who was unwilling to leave the platform and too preoccupied to notice that the third person (Ted Stansfield) was edging his way between the music desks on his way to the rostrum clutching a portfolio, which was tentatively offered to J.B. J.B. was in no frame of mind to give audience to Ted Stansfield or spare a glance at the contents of the portfolio: he waved him disdainfully away before he could utter a syllable, and a very crestfallen Stansfield made his way off the platform. Neither of the characters in this silent performance on the stage was aware that I was sitting in the balcony munching sandwiches to the accompaniment of a rather noisily ticking Free Trade Hall clock, and the scratch of J.B.'s pencil. I knew what the portfolio contained and was impressed by Ted's persistence on this, and many other similar occasions, to show its contents to the most unlikely and uninterested people. The incident would have passed from my mind had I not been sharply reminded at 6.45 p.m., as I walked into the bandroom to change for the concert, that Ted Stansfield was an incredibly good teller of stories relating to himself: in fact he was a fascinating, bombasting buffoon. Every Thursday evening he changed in very good time and sprawled his 18-stone figure in a huge wooden chair in front of the bandroom fire (which in those days resembled the fires in any porters' room on any railway station – at least half a hundredweight of coal burning in the grate and halfway up the chimney, with two bucketsful at the ready to top it up: there would be more burning away on the stone floor than ever appeared in the passengers' waiting room, and always a kettle simmering as it stood 2 feet away from the fire). Ted invariably took up his position in order to hold forth to the younger members on some topical points of interest in which he had been personally involved. On this particular evening he had an audience of three who seemed eager to listen to his latest tit-bit: just as I walked into the room Ted had reached the climax of his story and was just beginning to say – "After the rehearsal this morning, HE SENT FOR ME to show him the Photographs!!"

Although 'the Photographs' were certainly not worth the time it takes to explain their existence, Ted Stansfield's five-string double-bass was his whole life. Nature had endowed him with the frame of a gorilla and huge, hairy hands to match: the inescapable fact that the double-bass was the only musical instrument he could possibly have played was not enough for Ted Stansfield's ego – he had to build an instrument unique among double-basses which only he (or Fafner) could manipulate. It became his pride and joy: on every occasion when a note on the lower string became imminent he used to fidget and then grin all around the Free Trade Hall before he pounded hell out of some harmless low C in order to prove conclusively that he alone in the world could do it! He bequeathed the monster in a handsomely inscribed mummy-case to the Royal Liverpool Philharmonic Society and it now stands, gathering dust, waiting for the Death-watch Beetle in the bowels of the Philharmonic Hall. No-one knew where the key was kept the last time I was curious enough to have a peep at it.

To watch Ted crouching over his contraption was a spectacle which everyone deserved to see perhaps once in a life-time, but Ted considered it to be of national importance to have his photograph taken (by a professional photographer) in the 'pounding position' on every concert platform in England and Wales. Consequently, it became a familiar sight during the seasons 1931–32–33 to find Ted patiently compiling the dossier on himself and his precious instrument which he henceforth carried with him and showed to every member of the musical profession who was not agile enough to escape his attentions or recognise the portfolio. J.B. had obviously heard all about it!

There was one story which he featured about twice a year at his Thursday evening fireside sessions, and every guileless newcomer to the orchestra was obliged, sooner or later, to listen to it. The saga of one of his First World War exploits lost nothing on each repetition, and I confess to encouraging a few additional performances of a practice which became known in the Second Great War as 'shooting a line'!

Ted had a turn of phrase peculiar to his native Rochdale, which was on his lips every few seconds – 'I thought nowt about it'. This nauseating piece of false modesty implies that feats of extraordinary skill were frequently and nonchalantly performed with consummate ease and tossed aside as not worth mentioning. Mr. Stansfield survived the First War in the Pay Corps, well behind the lines, and it is not surprising that bravery and acts of gallantry and sacrifice were never features of his war-time exploits – let us leave him to tell his best story in his own words:-

"I was walking down the street in (some obscure little French town) when I heard some music coming from a theatre. The doors were open so I strolled in and stood at the back: there was an orchestra in the pit rehearsing 'Oberon' (overture by Weber) so I just ambled down to the front and had a look over the 'railings'. There was a double-bass lying on its side just asking to be played so 'I thought nowt about it' – I jumped over the top and picked it up and joined in." At this stage in the story Ted always became more deliberate and laid emphasis on every meaningful word – "Well, as you know, there is a passage of semi-quavers in the Allegro section" – pause – "so when we came to it 'I thought nowt about it' I just trickled 'em in – but the conductor gasped and fell off the rostrum." (Another pause for effect.) "When we'd finished the overture, he came over to me and said, 'Who are you?'. When I said 'Stansfield' he stepped back, flabbergasted like, and when he recovered he whispered 'Not *THE* Stansfield?!'"

Sir Hamilton Harty with Ted Stansfield and his Double Bass

Chapter VII

The concert on 22nd February promised to be the event of the 1933–4 season, and I had for some time looked forward with the keenest anticipation to the visit of Igor Stravinsky to conduct a programme of his own music. At 9.45 p.m. I didn't leave the Free Trade Hall – I escaped from it!!

The printed programme which the audience had unwittingly bought on its way in was, like the road to hell, 'paved with good intentions', but it bore no resemblance to what they eventually heard. They did, however, know when to go home because the concert ended with the 'Firebird Suite' (which the orchestra knew very well) and which the programme announced as the last item. I wish that I could forget the rest of that disastrous day.

After only a few minutes of the rehearsal it was apparent that Stravinsky was a very poor conductor, and was expecting the orchestra (by some miracle) to grasp his unfamiliar idiom, and play his music impeccably AT SIGHT, without any help from him. The rehearsal was a shambles and Dushkin, with many stops and starts, bravely finished the Concerto in D: that work survived until the concert, as did the 'Firebird Suite', but three works – 'Fantasia', 'Feuerwerk' and 'Pastorale for Violin, Wood-wind and Piano' – just died. I can remember Maurice Whittaker (who was a member of the celebrated family of wood-wind players) voicing the opinion of all his colleagues concerned in the performance by refusing to play the Stravinsky pieces which they were meeting for the first time that day!

The rehearsal ended in a confused silence. No one had the authority to suggest that there should be an extra rehearsal in the afternoon, nor even believed that such a rehearsal, if authorised, would have salvaged anything from the wreck. The printed programme now in front of me is meaningless: all I can remember of the very sick concert was the appearance in the evening of a grand piano, with Dushkin and Stravinsky playing an interminable number of make-weight pieces for violin and piano (the titles of which were not announced) to a mystified audience which seemed resigned to listening to whatever came next in these very strange goings-on. They went home after they recognised the 'Firebird', which was the last item anyway!

The concert on 1st March was the last in the trio of concerts devoted entirely to one composer. The Elgar concert on 15th February had been an anxious one, and the Stravinsky a near disaster! but the concert on 1st March was, in my recollection, the last Delius programme Sir Thomas Beecham ever conducted in Manchester. The main works were 'Eventyr' (which I have never played since) and the 'Appalachia Variations'. Beecham was President of the Hallé Society, and in this, the first season of guest conductors, it soon became clear that he had taken as many of the concerts as he could squeeze into his busy life, and it was equally obvious that he was 'Cock o' the Midden' in Manchester and enjoying every scintillating minute of it. This rehearsal and concert revealed more than any other the extremities of his brilliant wit and satire, and his genius as an architect of musical sounds. His casual appearance on the platform at 10.40 a.m. (late, as usual) was an indication that music was the remotest thought in his head: he was jaunty, relaxed, and even more than usually ready to gossip. As he sprawled on the rostrum looking towards Alfred Barker to start something, he muttered, almost to himself, "The other day I met 'Flash Harry' – the 'Monte Carlo Croupier'!" and continued in this vein, disdainfully, until Alfred Barker asked him, in a whisper loaded with slander, if he had heard that Henry J. had run off with his secretary. "Highly creditable," was the lofty reply, "but hardly credible." The rehearsal eventually began, but with a difference; Tommy knew this programme very well, and, as he had never in his life previously done, or was ever likely to do in the future, did not intend to waste his unique talent by giving a superlative performance (at the rehearsal) of any piece to empty rows of seats. He was 'Tommy' to us in the mornings, but a very aloof Sir Thomas Beecham at public performances. Although the rehearsal was, in some respects, a routine refresher course, he was less in need of it than the orchestra, and indulged himself by frequently leaping to his feet and actually conducting a bar or two before relapsing again into his chair and going through the motions. The weakest chink in Beecham's armour also highlighted his strength – he could never *tell* a player how a phrase should go or intimate the subtlety of phrasing by whistling or singing: his toneless vocal efforts were hilarious, and the noises he made went up and down like a nobleman endeavouring to be sick with dignity. He had no sense of pitch and if the passage was identifiable at all he was rarely within a fourth or fifth of the actual notes. Whenever he broke out into song – which is the stock-in-trade of most conductors – he invariably addressed himself to 'Mr. Flute' or 'Mr. Oboe' (never by name) and his little outbursts were often quite meaningless to the bewildered players – but whenever the offending passages were repeated at rehearsal he would leap to his feet and direct all his eloquent gestures to the persons concerned. "That's the way" he would say approvingly, and sit down again.

The rehearsal of 'Appalachia' (when he finally got around to it) was enlivened by one of his most brilliant examples of rhetoric. Although there is a chorus used in this work, we, in the orchestra, were not in the least surprised to find that not a single member of the Hallé Choir was present at the rehearsal: Tommy had rehearsed them (presumably with piano) on the previous evening, and like all choral concerts in those primitive pre-war days chorus and orchestra came together for the first time at the performance – like fruit and pastry in restaurant apple-pie! It became apparent as the rehearsal proceeded that we might expect voices later, because he 'sang' in the oddest places with great violence and very little conviction. At one point he became more than usually agitated, and sprang to his feet making the wildest of gestures to a very silent and mystified orchestra. When he gained some semblance of composure he sat down and delivered the following persuasive address.

"Gentlemen, at letter 'J' the choir will sing a generous portion of the work unaccompanied. At letter 'K', however, they will have contrived, by some mysterious means, to arrive at a key far removed from that in which they began. I would, therefore, exhort your collaboration by performing some cues you will observe if you cast a long and penetrating glance at your music. In this manner we hope to *lure* the choir back, if not to the original key, at least to some nearly related one, and that is all I would like you to remember – beyond the elementary detail of creeping in at the right moment!!" This was the first of Beecham's stylistically perfect examples of rhetoric which impressed me: the tempo of his delivery, always in a grossly exaggerated and patronising drawl, seemed to say, "Have patience my friends, and I will transform this trivial incident into a cosy little gem of wit and saucy humour!". He had, like Sir Winston Churchill and Samuel Johnson, the instinct for choosing and manipulating the *only* word in the English language which could, by innuendo and inflection, render a harmless situation ridiculous and hilarious. It is a great pity that so many of his finest stories were, like Gray's flower, 'born to blush unseen and waste its sweetness on the desert air!' and also a dubious compliment that he invariably excelled himself in ribaldry whenever he addressed the Hallé Orchestra!

The whims, caprices, foibles and eccentricities of this remarkable man have become legendary: the stories, wonderful as the best ones remain, were too fragile to withstand the misquotation and distortion to which they have been subjected since his death by over-eager biographers. In later life I entertained little doubt that some of the situations which sparked off his wit were artificial and manufactured, and that some of his spontaneous out-bursts were not the brilliant improvisations they appeared to be. Nevertheless, it is extremely difficult to denude him of the notoriety which he obviously enjoyed, or to escape the fact that he dominated English musical life for half a century and brought to an end (for me) an era of great conductors.

There was one small piece in the programme of which Beecham was very proud. He had persuaded Delius to compose the entr'acte 'The walk to the Paradise Garden' as a trifle of scene-shifting music in 'A Village Romeo and Juliet'. It was new to us at this concert, but quickly established itself as one of Tommy's most famous 'lollipops' (his word for encores). At the rehearsal he gave the piece no more than the usual cursory run-through, checking that the publishers had printed the right notes and that all the extra exotic instruments were present with someone to play them. He gave neither hint nor indication of how he intended to perform the piece at the concert, and with a few more pleasantries we were dismissed.

Most orchestras in this country carry, like mediaeval armies, a small entourage of hardy followers endowed with the compelling urge to 'get to know' the combatants and to talk to someone back-stage at the interval of every concert. The Hallé was no exception and in pre-war days the auditorium in the old Free Trade Hall was separated from the steps leading to the stage by only a flimsy curtain, and members of the audience who were so inclined had easy access to backstage during the intervals of concerts. The 'following' at all Beecham concerts were not only more numerous, but were invariably more concerned with watching his antics than listening to the music. One of them gave voice to a stock phrase on every occasion – "If conductors *must* caper about on the rostrum – give me Sir Thomas!". But the question universally asked was "How do you follow him?" and my less than honest reply was always "We don't follow him – we are *with* him!". Sitting at the back I ought to have admitted that we were sometimes lost and that some of his astonishing pianissimo effects were the direct consequence of floundering helplessly about and listening for some tangible snippet of recognisable tune, or waiting for the front desks to give us a hint of their whereabouts in the music.

Sir Thomas was not the greatest conductor I ever played for, but he was, without the slightest doubt, the cleverest. He invariably frittered away his rehearsals, whatever the programme, in a curious mixture of buffoonery and aimless meandering through pages of boring crotchets and quavers; but his attitude at every concert was a sharp reminder of the enormity of his ego – he couldn't bear to be ordinary at doing anything! However impatient the audience became, he was never punctual in his life, nor did he ever acknowledge their applause with much more than a disdainful half-nod of his head, or a twitch of his imperialistic beard. He had, at a very early age, dispensed with all the conventional gestures which might be considered as the stock-in-trade of conducting 'technique'. He was unique, not only in his distinguished appearance, but also in his 'presence' on the rostrum.

In the first few moments between turning from the audience and assuming control of the orchestra he went through a familiar routine of reaching for a baton (wedged between music stand and folder on the first desk of the 'Cellos – to his right) which he clutched in both hands in front of his body, like a Praying Mantis. Then, throwing out both arms in a movement akin to smoothing out a table cloth he turned his head from side to side, fixing every member of the orchestra with a pair of unusually bright eyes, dispelling all illusions that he was the same man we had met earlier, or that the rehearsal had given us any indication of what was to happen. Before a sound was heard there was always an aura of instant discipline* and expectancy.

Rhythm and vitality oozed out of him, and whenever a situation demanded precision, he used to 'freeze', and his perky knees and elbows became the most eloquent parts of his anatomy. Everything about him radiated the clearest indication of encouragement or restraint – except the baton, which he rarely used at climactic points in the music. The most spectacular antic in his repertoire was the uppercut with his clenched left fist which would have felled an ox: a superfluous gesture for the percussion players (who do not normally bang their noisy instruments in wrong places) but introduced to the benefit of the audience, who loved to see at least one example of this manoeuvre at every concert. The baton which he often held limply at his side, or even slightly behind him, (like a dentist concealing his forceps) was sparingly used, except for pointing the most delicate and subtle moments in Haydn, Mozart and Schubert. It was a characteristic gesture akin to dipping a pen into an imaginary ink-well, and he quite predictably used it at 'recapitulations' (such as in the G minor Symphony of Mozart) or 'returns' to the opening motive in the Rondos of Haydn symphonies (which the composer in his inexhaustible wit and fertility had endeavoured to conceal). Beecham used to 'point' these moments of magic as if to say "*That* is why Haydn is a great composer – the 'surprises' remain 'surprises' although we know they are there!".

---

* The discipline had little to do with fear and less to do with respect, since he went to great lengths at all other times to convince *us* that he was just playing at being a musician, and the public that he was a fascinating charlatan. However unpredictable he was in his behaviour on and off the rostrum, his intentions were abundantly clear at the commencement of every concert – 'I am going to enjoy every note you play just the way you've always wanted to play them!': he then, with the greatest guile, set about the task of shaping the phrases and sentences and building the climaxes just the way *he* wanted them to go.

Beecham had many cunning tricks: one of them was the knack of leaving 'diminuendos' at the ends of phrases perilously near to being missed altogether, and many times at many concerts when I have seen his own blue-pencil sign looming up, has the thought momentarily crossed my mind – "He's going to forget this one!" when the music has taken a sudden dive into near obscurity – with electrifying effect. He also knew the secret of creating vibrant, living sounds which bloomed and blossomed with spontaneous joy.

A phrase frequently on his lips at rehearsals, "How should I know what will happen tonight?" epitomised his approach to music making: every concert was an exciting improvisation which invariably came off. I was convinced that every piece I played would never sound 'quite like that again', and in common with many other orchestral players I was exhausted at the end of his concerts.

After one particularly beautiful performance of Schubert's C Major Symphony, Alfred Livesley, (the first Oboe) who had excelled himself in the slow movement, said, quite philosophically, as we were sauntering away from the Free Trade Hall, "I wish I could play as well as that every day!!".

Having described Beecham's presence on the rostrum as he was about to begin the Delius Concert on March 1st, I must apologise for digressing and recording my impressions of this extraordinary man during 30 years of my life as an orchestral player.

The strange affinity which existed between Delius and Beecham gradually became manifest in the little pieces – 'Summer Garden', 'On Hearing the First Cuckoo in Spring' and the entr'acte 'The Walk to the Paradise Garden'. Beecham had a truly amazing gift for creating 'atmosphere' and a 'stillness' of warm, vibrant sound which was like a halo – without a beginning and an end. No other conductor in my experience has ever achieved this new dimension in musical magic: the effect of the 'near to nothing' awareness of sounds was like rolling morning mist, through which a shaft of sunlight, or a breath of air, made momentarily visible a hazy, scarcely discernible figure. The sounds, which were constantly dissolving and re-forming, defied aural analysis and, since Beecham never rehearsed his conjuring tricks, I shall remain mystified how Delius conceived and wrote down such indescribably beautiful sounds, and how Beecham became infallible in re-creating them.*

The concert on the following Thursday, March 8th, was, by comparison, extremely dull. Egon Petri was the soloist (for whom I felt

---

* The creation of other pieces has similarly bewildered me – "L'après-midi d'un Faune' and the orchestral epilogue to 'Götterdämmerung' are but two of my seven wonders of the world.

a twinge of pity, he having spent months of his life learning the piece) and R.J. Forbes (his colleague at the R.M.C.M.) was the conductor. The work to be performed for the 'First time at these concerts'* was the Busoni Piano Concerto – with Male Voice Choir!

Beethoven was probably unaware that his Choral Symphony would spark off such grandiose pieces as Berlioz' 'Messe des Morts' and Mahler's extravaganzas in the shape of Cantatas-cum-Symphonies, Two-Act Operas-cum-Three Movement Symphonies, and the Symphony of a Thousand Extras. (Cecil B. de Mille would have been proud of that one!).

It was inevitable that we should deserve a 'Piano Concerto – with Male Voice Choir' if only to put an end to further speculation on 'What will they think of next?'.

Someone *did* think of something! – Havergal Brian wrote a Gothic Symphony for Full Orchestra (plus thunder-machines and rattles), Two Choirs and Two Brass Bands. There were so many combatants at a recent revival of the work in the Victoria Hall, Hanley, that an audience could not be accommodated. The performance, however, could be heard for miles around by just leaving the doors open!

Beecham conducted the Pension Fund Concert on the 22nd March for the first time. There was nothing remarkable about Pension Concerts except that members of the orchestra gave their services, as indeed did the conductor and soloists (if any could be found). The music played was never profound and there was usually an aura of relaxation and enjoyment. It was always the last concert of the season and an occasion for saying 'goodbyes' among players, and sometimes audience too. Beecham was the ideal choice of conductor for these none-too-serious 'jamborees', but this particular concert was unique even for Tommy. He had chosen a programme of music which later became known as a 'lollipop', and which would have raised a few eyebrows at the end of Llandudno Pier! At this rehearsal there was no restraint for the howling, wordless chorus which occurs in the operatic version of the 'Polovtsian Dances' – I can't remember whether or not he raised a cautionary hand at the concert, but there was pandemonium at the rehearsal! The overture to 'The Meistersinger' was always in the folder for Beecham's popular concerts: if the item was included in the printed programme we, of course, played it, but if not he invariably played it as an encore. In later years this work was superseded by the 'Adagietto' from Bizet's 'L'Arlésienne', which he conducted unbelievably slowly, but with exquisite care.

---

* The second performance of the Busoni followed very quickly on the heels of the first – on November 8th, 1934, to be precise, and so to bed!

Chapter VIII

In the halcyon days of the 'thirties seaside holiday resorts and some inland spas provided orchestral concerts as a major attraction for summer visitors: Scarborough, Bridlington, Llandudno and Harrogate being the main centres in the north of England and North Wales. The personnel of these orchestras was drawn mainly from the Hallé and Liverpool Philharmonic Orchestras, and relaxing for twenty weeks in the summer sunshine became a way of life for professional musicians, playing golf, tennis, and also, in my case, watching Yorkshire County cricket at Scarborough: there was, in addition, a bonus of a nine-day Cricket Festival.

Sargent conducted for two seasons at Llandudno (a fact he tried hard to erase from his, and everyone else's, memory), Basil Cameron conducted at Harrogate, and at Bridlington A. Barker directed a smaller but excellent orchestra of soloists. At Scarborough, where I returned year after year, there was an autocratic old gentleman who was a much better musician than he was a conductor: Alec Maclean directed an orchestra of 36 which included the luxury of a harp! Alec Maclean was brave enough to assess his audience as he walked to the platform and make substitutions willy-nilly to the printed programme. 'Glamorous Night', 'The Arcadians' and 'The Geisha Girl' selections gave way to the 'Eroica' and 'New World' symphonies, and by flattering them into believing that they deserved what they got, he created a regular following of genuine music-lovers. S. Kneale Kelly, who followed him as conductor, readily gave in to every request for rubbish (in an effort to please a 'wider public') and succeeded only in driving the Spa Company into near bankruptcy.

The only season I played in Margate was the summer of 1934. Herbert Lodge was the conductor, and the players he recruited from Manchester were Leonard Hirsch, Stuart Knussen (senior) and Keith Cummings (who shared lodgings with me). Although Keith was a viola player, he drove me up the wall and along the ceiling by practising the 24th Paganini Caprice on his violin in the next bedroom for 4 hours every day for 20 weeks! Because of my involvement in last-minute preparations for the Mus.B. Finals in the September examinations at Durham University I was obliged to turn a deaf ear to his losing battle with the excruciatingly out-of-tune octaves in A minor (a key to which I became acutely sensitive). The dead of night became the only time I could escape from the Paganini Caprice (but not his snoring) and profitably spend studying: I had, however, overlooked a very observant landlady who objected to me 'wasting' electricity, so I literally had to burn candles'.

The orchestra at Margate was extremely versatile – and brittle. It dissipated daily into Salon Groups, Dance bands and Light Orchestras, uniting only once a week on Sunday evenings in the Winter Gardens for the celebrity Concerts. These concerts were unique since the 'celebrity' occupied the stage for the whole of the second half; an arrangement which created problems for Herbert Lodge and his Orchestra, but not for the audience. The Margate Patrons of the Arts were very different from their medieval counterparts: they patronised the orchestra by drifting nonchalantly to their reserved seats in varying degrees of lateness – from 15 to 50 minutes – according to their 'breeding' and holding conversations with their recognisable brethren (also down from London for the weekend). The night Sophie Tucker appeared as the 'celebrity' only the usherettes were present to applaud the first item on the programme!

One of the celebrities in the 1934 season presented me with the exciting opportunity of meeting 'the voice'. Paul Robeson was thrice blessed with the brains and supreme artistry to match the most thrilling sounds I ever heard emerging from a human throat. He was a huge, genial man of great modesty who sang first of all a few arias with the orchestra and then a great many songs with piano; he brought with him an accompanist, and so successful were they that they eventually exhausted the music they had brought. The audience clamoured for more, and Paul Robeson (who was talking to some of us in the wings) said, quite resignedly, "Ah well, all I have left now is Shakespeare!" and he walked back on to the platform and held a spellbound audience in the palm of his hand by reciting generous portions of 'Othello'.

My trip to Durham for the September examinations was without incident. Candidates were quite predictably expected to know something of three British composers who died within a few weeks of each other in that year – Elgar, Holst and Delius – and I remember being asked a question by Sir Ernest Bullock (at a long viva voce examination) to which he did not expect an answer, and to which I could not, 44 years later, give a satisfactory reply. The set-work on which the 'viva' was based was Berlioz' 'Damnation of Faust' – a work which Harty had meticulously rehearsed with the Hallé, and publicly performed more times than I could remember. I was not expecting to be tripped up on such familiar ground, and, having been asked all the right questions, was a little surprised at the end of the private session to hear Dr. Bullock say "What do you do for a living?" and in the next breath – "Only church

ORGANISTS come to Durham for degrees in music – why on earth do YOU need one?". Later, at the convocation ceremony in the cloisters of Durham Cathedral, another great British composer – Sir Arnold Bax – was awarded the honorary degree of Mus.D.

The Hallé winter season 1934 began on October 18th with a quite exciting concert conducted by the Hungarian-born Georg Szell. He was, in those days, a tall, thin young man with a lean and hungry look: he wore rimless spectacles and there was about him an intensity I have always associated with Czechoslovakian conductors. Raphael Kubelik, who came on the scene years later was, in many respects, a carbon copy of Szell.

The major works in the programme were 'Tod und Verklärung' Op. 24 of Strauss, and Brahms' C minor Symphony: the performance I remember as being first-rate, but the rehearsal had a most unusual start. We pounded out only the first 2 bars of the Brahms when the conductor stopped to deliver a well-prepared speech which began with the words "I can hear Hans Richter in this orchestra," and he then rushed into a long, flattering tarradiddle about the Orchestra's reputation abroad, and what performances he intended to give with us in Manchester. The introduction to the Brahms is very impressive, as everyone knows, but never before have two bars created such a disturbance.

There was nothing in this concert, or the following one a fortnight later, to suggest that he was a strong candidate for the post, but on his second visit to Manchester in February 1935 he set his heart on making history with a performance of Schumann's 4th Symphony, to the exclusion of everything else in the programme. 'Neglect' would perhaps have better described his treatment of the other two works – the 'Fairy Tale Suite' by Suk (the son-in-law of Dvorák) and the *First Performance* of Dohnányi's 'Variations on a Nursery Song' for piano and orchestra, with the inimitable fire-brand Eileen Joyce as soloist!

The Suk was, technically and stylistically, fairly straightforward to play and presented few problems to the orchestra in spite of Szell's cursory treatment, but the Dohnányi was a major disaster.

The Hallé Society had allocated an extra rehearsal, presumably to grapple with the difficulties of this new piece, but Szell threw the precious time away quite nonchalantly on his beloved Schumann. Eileen Joyce, having been kept waiting at the second rehearsal for what seemed an interminable time, stamped onto the platform and banged through the work with such determination that nowhere were soloist and orchestra within hailing distance of each other. At the end of this sulky run-through she almost ran to the rostrum to ask Szell what he intended to do about such treatment, but Szell almost shovelled her off the platform with the age-old musician's blasphemy – "It will be all right tonight!". She stalked off the platform with angry, hurried strides and before she reached the top of the stairs leading to the dressing rooms, Szell impatiently shouted "Back to the Schumann". At the performance there was no rapport between soloist and conductor, and at its conclusion Eileen Joyce completely ignored Szell: after taking her bow she walked off the platform and did not reappear. Neither did Szell at any subsequent Hallé concert, and I have never met him since.

The only newcomer to the Hallé scene in the 1934–35 season was Carl Schuricht who conducted 'Daphnis and Chloë' and 'Till Eulenspiegel' in an otherwise uninteresting concert, and there was a lack of enterprise in many of the concerts given by guest conductors on 'return visits'. Sargent conducted the B minor Mass and 'The Planets', and Beecham, in all but one concert, was content with the 'Eroica' (which he described as 'a grand old piece') and several performances (on tour) of 'Scheherazade', and Tchaikowsky symphonies. Even the annual performance of the 'Messiah' did little for me: Bairstow conducted, and although I ought to have respected him – after all he was professor of Music at Durham – I could never feel anything but contempt for his sour, sarcastic voice and complete lack of humour.

The concert on November 29th was in many ways unique. Cardus (in his book on Beecham) states quite categorically that he persuaded the Hallé to give a performance of Dame Ethel Smyth's 'The Prison' which Beecham 'did not conduct'. Around 10.30 a.m. on this Thursday, November 29th, someone bearing a striking resemblance to Beecham strutted on to the Free Trade Hall platform and sprawled into the armchair on the rostrum. Having assured himself that music was provided for the players he addressed himself to the orchestra at large, and then to Mr. Barker in particular – "Gentlemen, I will now demonstrate how remarkably simple conducting really is – Mr. Barker, how does this piece begin?" "Moderato, four in a bar," replied Alfred Barker. "let us begin," said Tommy, aimlessly waving his arms about, until the novelty wore off. It was apparent to us all that until a full score arrived, from some source unknown to him, he had no intention of proceeding with the rehearsal, or taking any interest in a piece which he, like us, was meeting for the first time!

Dame Ethel eventually arrived looking like Queen Victoria at Ascot, wearing a very wide-brimmed hat which was drooling artificial fruit and vegetables, and carrying a huge copper ear-trumpet in one hand and a huge family album (which presumably was 'The Prison') under one arm. The score was passed on to the platform and deposited on Tommy's desk, where it remained for the rest of the day. This was the only occasion I can ever remember Tommy conducting from music, for the obvious reason that he was sight-reading, and whatever virtues the work may have had, or Cardus imagined it to have, they did not emerge that day.

There was one other non-successful concert with Beecham near the end of the winter season – March 14th, 1935. The work he introduced for the first time in Manchester was 'Rossiniana' by Respighi, a very difficult piece which seemed then not to be worth the effort of preparing, and has quickly passed into obscurity.

The most important concert in the season was on March 7th, 1935 when Rachmaninoff introduced his Rhapsody on a theme of Paganini, opus 43, to the British public. If it could be said that Rachmaninoff had a country, then a fellow-countryman, Malko, conducted the concert. Very few words were exchanged at the rehearsal, and those, presumably, were in Russian, since I had no idea what they were talking about: whatever was said could not have been meant for our ears because Malko passed nothing on to the orchestra.

My first impressions of Rachmaninoff were vivid and lasting. His presence was, in many ways, startling as he walked on to the platform: he was very tall, with short cropped hair, his complexion was the colour of stone and nothing in his features betrayed the fact that he was alive. He didn't speak, and as he walked slowly to the piano he held both hands, drooping quite limply, in front of him, about chest height; he was wearing loose cotton gloves which looked ready to drop off. As he sat at the piano he carefully removed the gloves and placed them on the woodwork at the left-hand end of the keyboard and then stretched out his hands to touch the keys, which was the silent signal to begin. At this rehearsal, as indeed on at least half-a-dozen other occasions, I sat immediately behind Rachmaninoff, and was completely mystified how this great man produced such an enormous range of tone, dynamics and expression of the noblest kind from his FINGERS. His arms, which were abnormally long, commanded the entire keyboard without the slightest movement of his body or inclination of his head: his countenance, though immobile, betrayed (at least in my imagination) a trace of melancholy, and there was, in his impenetrable stare and reluctance to communicate, a cold presence at the piano which belied the unbelievably warm sounds which came from it.

The predominant wish in the heart of every aspiring pianist is to acquire sufficient technique to be able to wallow unashamedly in Rachmaninoff's music. Emulating the great man is not easy of achievement, and the qualities in him which completely disarmed me on this memorable day were his immaculate playing, his modesty, and the restraint which he imposed on any suggestion of a 'big tune'.

The two taciturn gentlemen in charge of the proceedings seemed reluctant to begin, which was in marked contrast to our anxiety to 'get at it'. We were eventually rewarded by a run-through of the work: nothing was repeated at the rehearsal and only once did Rachmaninoff speak. In the Eulenburg edition of the miniature score Var. XV is judiciously marked in brackets '(Orchestra Tacet)' which means that, in the likely event of the conductor not knowing the precise whereabouts of the soloist, if he doesn't bring in the orchestra at the half-way stage no serious damage will be done!

Rachmaninoff began the variation pp like a gust of wind blowing frost from the trees; the iced diamonds sparkled and cascaded without accents or bar lines. Malko joined him with uncanny skill and without fuss, and all finished the Variation in perfect accord. This performance was the only one in my recollection which was better with the orchestra than without it! Var. XVIII which followed close on its heels has since become one of Rachmaninoff's famous 'big tunes'; he played the first statement of the tune (which is 'solo') with great dignity, and then accompanied the violins with his rubato triplet figure almost urging us to enjoy ourselves. He actually spoke to the orchestra only twice during six visits to Manchester in the 'thirties, and this was one of them: turning to the First Violins before continuing with Var. XIX he said, with a very wry smile, "You play that NEARLY as well as I do!!". I don't know whether or not it was intended to be a compliment: perhaps it was a warning to future generations not to over-do it!

Chapter IX

The early concerts of the Hallé season 1935–1936 were conducted by a very excitable Italian conductor, Vincenzo Balleza, introducing to British audiences a long string of not very exciting works by 'modern' Italian composers – Pick-Mangiagalli, Castaldi, Martucci and Respighi. Neither the conductor nor the music made any lasting impression on me.

Beecham dominated the pre-Christmas series with four quite exceptional concerts: the first, on November 21st, introduced Emanuel Feuermann to Manchester in two works – the Haydn 'Cello Concerto in D major and the solo 'cello part of 'Don Quixote' by Strauss. The rehearsal for this concert saw the birth of one of Beecham's most famous stories - since mauled, mutilated and misquoted until it has become a bizarre music-hall joke. The best of Beecham's witticisms usually evolved from ONE word cunningly placed at the climax of a sentence of well-chosen adjectives, delivered in a patronising drawl which convinced anyone within earshot that gems of the English language were being frittered away on trivialities. The rehearsal began late, as usual, with 'Don Quixote'. Beecham had brought his own orchestral parts with him, and the Hallé librarian – Harold Ball – had already held a long conversation with Tommy in the green-room, prior to distributing the parts among the players. Besides his duties as librarian, Harold Ball was a well-known percussion player and had played opera seasons with Beecham over a long period of time – in fact they were on intimate terms, which is the point of the story which follows. Having distributed the orchestral parts of 'Don Quixote', Harold Ball took his place in the 'Kitchen Department' as the third of seven players required for this interesting but noisy piece. Tommy was in a 'thinking' mood and there was never enough of the 'wind-machine', 'thunder-sheets', 'lightning cracks', 'sheep bleating' and all the rest of the noises off, which, of course, the extra players were delighted to demonstrate. Every member of the orchestra was dumbfounded when Tommy stopped the over-exuberant team of noise-makers to demand, "MORE," from them, and (with a naughty twinkle in his eye) he addressed himself to Harold Ball – who was standing with a huge pair of cymbals in his hands – "My dear fellow – what is your name?" Harold Ball's face was a study – he looked around the orchestra as if to ask for confirmation that "this man is *barmy*

– he knows damn well who I am!" and then he replied to Tommy, with contempt in his voice, "Ball, Sir Thomas!" "How very SINGULAR'" was Tommy's reply – almost too readily for it to have been a spontaneous joke. I hope that this anecdote can now be laid to rest.

Maurice Ward (Principal Viola in the London Philharmonic Orchestra) who attended the rehearsal and probably heard and enjoyed the 'ball' incident, lost no time (at the interval) in relating another instance of Beecham's extravagant use of a single word, and the lengths of self-indulgence to which he would go in order to produce embarrassment to others and a belly-laugh for himself. A few days before, the London Philharmonic Orchestra had given a concert in the Victoria Hall, Hanley, and after the rehearsal in the late afternoon Beecham was strolling away from the Hall in company with Maurice Ward and David McCallum (the leader of the orchestra). The stroll was, in effect, the progress of an entourage with Tommy the central figure, draped nonchalantly in a lightweight, grey Raglan coat thrown about his shoulders, hobbling along with as dignified a step as his gout would allow. The trio of wandering minstrels came quite suddenly, and obviously by accident, upon a 'Pot Fair': Tommy, without a word to the others, turned majestically into it. 'Pot Fairs' are peculiar to the north of England, and more numerous, naturally, in the Potteries than anywhere else in the world. They are long, ramshackle, open-ended grottos, brilliantly lit and filled to bursting point with sub-standard miscellaneous items of crockery: everything has to be sold by auction, and it is usually the non-stop chatter of the auctioneer at the remote end of the tunnel which attracts the curious public into the den. The trained eye of the auctioneer, having spotted Beecham and his distinguished friends standing in the entrance, quickly signalled to his clerk to ask which items interested them. Tommy, with a serious face, pointed with his walking- cane to a tottering stack of chamberpots which were standing quite near (like the leaning tower of Pisa). The clerk showed no outward signs of anything he may have felt, and staggered with his precarious load up to the auctioneer's bench. The auctioneer banged the table a few times with his hammer and cried out "Am I bid five shillings for these useful items?" "Six!" shouted Tommy, quite unnecessarily, and the hammer came down on what had been the swiftest sale of the century. The clerk dutifully brought the bargain pile of pots and put them down at Tommy's feet, and Tommy, with great deliberation, dropped three florins into the palm of the man's hand. "We have to keep books y'know, sir – a sort of register of sales, sir. What name shall I put, sir?" "PHILPOTTS!!" said Tommy, very seriously, turning on his heel and stalking out into the street, leaving a bewildered clerk with a pile of pots and six shillings.

The Beecham concert which followed on November 28th was a Wagner evening at which Joan Cross and Walter Widdop sang. Beecham was in a pernickety mood at the rehearsal with two works – 'A Faust Overture' and 'The Siegfried Idyll', both of which were superbly played at the concert. At a later concert he also gave a spectacular performance of Berlioz' 'Symphonie Fantastique'. The second half of the season began on January 9th, 1936 with a shabby concert conducted by Ernst Ansermet. The programme included three straightforward pieces Schumann No. 4, the Sibelius Violin Concerto and 'Introduction and Allegro' for strings by Elgar. The two works which 'frayed at the edges' and caused irritation, frustration and bad temper at the rehearsal were 'Portsmouth Point' by William Walton (first performance) and 'Iberia' by Debussy. Both pieces presented the same intrinsic, insoluble problems: the basic quaver unit of time (which moves too quickly to beat) alternates 2/8, 3/8, 2/4, 5/8 and 7/8 in a bewildering sequence, and, although Ansermet may have been the most sensitive conductor in the world and possess a finely-tuned pair of ears, he succeeded in losing the Hallé Orchestra by beating down-beats in all the wrong places. He lost his temper at the rehearsal and committed the unforgivable sin of accusing the first violins of 'not being right' and 'not being in tune' and all the general, unspecific griping associated with a conductor's privileged position. Tommy Matthews (who was sitting almost under his nose) also got tired of Ansermet's niggling, and played one of the difficult passages in 'Iberia' absolutely solo and very loudly. "Now, what's the matter with that?" he said, at the risk of being sacked for daring to speak. "Oh – Oh, nothing," said Ansermet, taken aback. He then went silently on through a seething rehearsal which mercifully did not erupt again. At the concert Ansermet created a record which lasted for years – he stopped the orchestra after a few bars of 'Iberia' and began the piece again!! The Hallé Orchestra was spared a second visit, in fact I have not seen Ansermet since 1936.

The concert which followed on January 16th was conducted by Sir Landon Ronald and consisted of three works which might be regarded as belonging to the 'heavy brigade': the overture 'Leonora' No. 3 by Beethoven, the Brahms violin concerto and the Symphony No. 1 in A*b* by Elgar. I can remember Sir Landon rehearsing the Beethoven first and then making a curious, tentative announcement in a stage whisper – "Now for it – I have never met this gentleman before, and I understand he can be rather trying!" He was referring to Huberman, who was the soloist in the Brahms, and for whom we were eagerly waiting. I also had never met Huberman before, and was unprepared for his unprepossessing appearance: he had many unfortunate deformities which did not in any way hamper his playing, but his manner was brusque (particularly to conductors, who probably have their own 'bush telegraph' where soloists are concerned). Sir Landon coped with his eccentricities with commendable patience, and the rehearsal and concert passed without incident.

One of the most disconcerting of Huberman's oddities was a steel-haired bow which he put across his knee during every tutti passage and rubbed violently with soft (and very squeaky) resin. The next stage after a steel-haired bow would, of course, have been a 'file', and to say that his performance of the Brahms was 'manly' was the understatement of the year – he fairly whacked the hide off it! Another of Huberman's afflictions which added considerably to the feeling of revulsion was a horrible squint: this one was quite unusual because the eyes, which were turned outwards, were unequal in size. He also addressed members of the orchestra without leave of the conductor, and was rude to everyone.

I have already said that the most successful concerts I ever played with Beecham were the purely orchestral ones: he was by no means an inflexible conductor, but he did not yield too readily to other ideas, or take kindly to the role of accompanist to strong personalities. Huberman and Beecham met on one occasion at a Hallé concert. I cannot recall the date, although the rehearsal was a very lively affair. Huberman began his tantrums and his tricks very early: he was not in the position of being able to refer to the full score on the conductor's desk because Tommy conducted from memory, so he addressed himself to everyone all around the orchestra willy-nilly. Beecham's eyebrows arched more and more with every interruption, and his face assumed a familiar look of astonishment – "Mr. Huberman," he said, very deliberately, "if you will kindly address your observations to me, there is a distinct possibility that I *may* be able to *re-direct* them to the right quarter!"

Sir Landon Ronald conducted another concert on January 23rd which included Elgar's Second Symphony, and an interesting first performance took place on February 6th when Beecham introduced Sibelius' Sixth Symphony in D minor to the Hallé audience in Manchester, and on the following day to the Bradford public in the Eastbrook Hall – I have already quoted Beecham's remarks concerning this work, which he made in an extremely audible stage-whisper at the Bradford performance (p.41).

The concert on February 27th was the only time I met Horowitz. It was a gigantic programme in which he played the Brahms D minor Concerto in the first part and the Tchaikowsky B*b* minor Concerto in the second. There were several passages of such brilliance in the Tchaikowsky that the gasps of astonishment in the audience were actually audible on the platform, as if there was an irresistible urge to applaud. The most incredible moment in the piece was at bar 348 in the development section of the first movement, when he unleashed the cascade of double octaves at such a speed and with such clarity that everyone present felt that they were experiencing the performance of a lifetime. The technique, which was obvious and amazing in the Tchaikowsky, was his servant in the Brahms: it was a physically and musically huge performance without distortion or roughness, and it was the performance I would have expected from the composer himself, who treated technical passages with a kind of negligence. The concert must have taxed his strength: he had with him a handkerchief into which he coughed incessantly during every tutti passage at the rehearsal, as well as the concert, but like Rachmaninoff, his appearance belied his superb playing.

In spite of Sir Thomas Beecham's enormous repertoire, and the number of his concerts in which I took part, it has been a source of disappointment to me that I never played in a performance of the 'Messiah' with him. According to his many friends and admirers there was nothing sanctimonious about his concept of Handel's most successful opera. Whatever were Beecham's views about Verdi's non-liturgical 'Requiem' he certainly gave a performance of this work on March 5th 1936 which could only be described as rip-roaring Italian opera. He enjoyed every spectacular minute of it without twitching an eyelid – and so did I. The concert on March 12th was another appearance of Rachmaninoff playing, this time, his 3rd Concerto in D minor. This performance was only the second at a Hallé concert, and the conductor was R.J. Forbes who, besides conducting the concerto splendidly and unobtrusively, gave a fine performance of Dvorák's D minor Symphony (numbered in those days No. 2, but since the re-classification of Dvorák's symphonies, No. 7). The programme stated the fact that this work was 'last performed in January 1903' and I have never understood why this symphony remained for so long neglected, and, even now, has never enjoyed the popularity of the 'New World' or No. 8 in G.

Beecham conducted the last concert of the 1936 season which included the 'Symphonie Fantastique' of Berlioz, and also the extra concert for the Pension Fund which included 'Scheherazade' and my bête noire the Divertimento No. 2 in D for Horns and Strings K.334. This essentially soloistic piece of Mozartian chamber music used to sound tentatively poisonous when played by tutti strings, and it appeared far too frequently in programmes by Harty, and now by Beecham, as a 'virtuoso' piece to show off the First Violins. This work always meant a great deal of private practice – and prayer. I was not sorry when it dropped out of the orchestral repertoire.

Chapter X

The Hallé season 1936–37 was not an exceptional one: the soloists were the established favourites playing or repeating the established masterpieces. Schnabel played the Brahms D minor, Moiseiwitsch the second performance within a year of Rachmaninoff's Paganini Variations. Feuermann played the Dvorák with Beecham and Gieseking (whom I remembered as a superb Mozart player) this season played the 2nd Rachmaninoff, not exceptionally well.

Pierre Monteux (after a year's absence in the United States of America) conducted the first two concerts. The soloist at the first was Arthur Rubinstein who played the Brahms Concerto in B*b* No. 2. Monteux was the first conductor in my experience to place himself inside the orchestra, with his back to the piano soloist, thus modestly effacing himself from the audience. Rubinstein has, in his long career, made several pronouncements that he doesn't practise before public appearances, in order to leave something for the heat of the battle; he probably, at the rehearsal on October 15th, 1936, was 'leaving something for the performance', which did not please Monteux, who rebuked him in FRENCH! Rubinstein turned to the 1st Violins, and quite shamefacedly said, "That was the finest music lesson I have ever had!".

The second half of the concert was devoted to a rare performance of Dukas' 'La Péri' and yet another magical performance of 'L'après-midi d'un Faune'. The 'Firebird' ballet suite by Stravinsky which concluded a fine concert again demonstrated Monteux's propensity for sub-dividing beats, even in quick tempo, in order to accommodate difficult technical passages: under Monteux's direction there always appeared to be time to play all the notes.

On one occasion, early in my experience, Monteux had expressed the profound opinion that composers write every note with loving care – it is our duty to play them all.

Beecham, too, often created the illusion that his tempi in allegro movements were too slow – his great secret lay in the fact that 'rhythm and vitality in music are unrelated to speed!'.

Monteux conducted a purely orchestral programme the following week: it was the last time he appeared in Manchester until the late 'fifties. The major work was the César Franck Symphony which musicologists were, in 1936, already endeavouring to despatch into oblivion by describing the work as an Organ Sonata composed in the organ loft at St. Clotilde in Paris, with pauses here and there for adjustments in the registration. César Franck's self-critical conscientiousness as a composer had an equally conscientious advocate in Monteux, who insisted on the right instrumentation (two F trumpets and two Cornets) and with great patience produced internal balances and beautiful orchestral sounds which made this performance unique in my experience.

Monteux's incredible photographic memory was always a source of wonder to me, and at the rehearsals of the Ballet Suite 'The Three-Cornered Hat' by Manuel de Falla he gave another example of an unprepared recitation of what the composer had actually written, what was likely to happen, and what the orchestra (surprisingly for him) had misinterpreted.

The offending passage was the ending of the Miller's Dance (the string parts of which are quoted from figure 9).

There is a natural, though unforgivable tendency in most orchestras, amateur and professional, for dynamic markings to be attracted to each other, e.g. crescendo will invariably be accompanied by accelerando and conversely diminuendo by ritardando. The last twenty-four bars of the Miller's Dance are conveniently divided into three eight-bar passages, galvanised together by an all-embracing crescendo. The Hallé Orchestra's natural urge to accelerate scarcely required de Falla's indications of 'Pochissimo più mosso', 'Più animato' and 'Ancora più vivo' to fling themselves into a rumbustious ending to the Miller's Dance, but the otherwise imperturbable Monteux showed considerable annoyance and shook his fist at us, shouting "Non, non, non!". He then spent a great deal of rehearsal time purging the orchestra of an irresponsible reading of de Falla's intentions: pointed out (from his memory) that the first eight bars of the passage are clearly marked 'Pochissimo più mosso MA RITMICO' and the second have a new basic tempo which is 'more animated': at figure 10 the indication 'Ancora più vivo' contains a final cautionary reminder from de Falla 'MA IN TEMPO'. Monteux insisted on three distinct levels of increased tempo without the slightest trace of accelerando to spoil the effect of the crescendo from 'p' at figure 9 to the fortissimo secco 'A' minor chord which ends the Dance.

The 1936–37 Hallé season was the fourth after the departure of Sir Hamilton Harty as its permanent conductor, and although the Hallé Committee were steadfast in their belief that guest conductors would infuse new life and ideas into the orchestra, and perhaps give the subscribers an opportunity to see the President (Sir Thomas Beecham) in action, it was apparent even to the programme-sellers that 'things were not the same'.

9 Pochissimo più mosso, ma ritmico
stacc.
sul G
cresc. gradualmente
stacc.
cresc. gradualmente
stacc.
cresc gradualmente
pizz.
cresc. gradualmente
mf marc.
cresc. gradualmente
cresc. gradualmente
mf marc.
J. W. C. 43

Più animato
arco ad lib.
f
cresc. sempre
arco ad lib.
f
cresc. sempre
arco ad lib.
f
cresc. sempre
f marc.
cresc. sempre
arco
f
arco
cresc sempre
sempre pizz.
J. W. C. 43

10 Ancora più vivo, ma in tempo
ff
fff secco
ff
fff
ff
fff secco
ff
fff secco
ff
arco
fff secco
J. W. C. 43

In spite of very few changes in personnel since 1933 the orchestra was gradually losing its character; its uninhibited playing which had made it world-famous and the brilliant individual characteristics of some of the wood-wind principals were beginning to fade, almost imperceptibly, in the teeth of the younger breed of ambitious, and sometimes ruthless, guest conductors, who considered it to be a sacred mission in life to teach orchestral players how to bow and blow their instruments. The cumulative effect of finicking and niggling over insignificant details at rehearsals produced lack-lustre performances which rarely reached a standard Harty would have considered to be adequate.

Of the guest conductors for the remainder of the 1936–37 season, the three elder statesmen Sir Landon Ronald, Sir Henry J. Wood and Sir Thomas Beecham were guiltless of teaching the orchestra the rudiments of music, and also aware that their established reputations in London were unlikely (in the slightest degree) to be tarnished by an enjoyable day of missionary work in the Provinces.

Sir Landon Ronald was a gentleman who (like Monteux) radiated good humour and earned the respect of the orchestra: he presented three programmes of conventional masterpieces (in which it was apparent that he had not discovered any hidden secrets) and was relaxed enough to guide the orchestra through works which would, in any event, be traditionally well-played. There was a feeling of mutual trust whenever Sir Landon Ronald raised his baton: although his conducting technique was of the 'Grecian Urn' contrary motion variety, and more safe than spectacular. He quite often smiled benignly during the performances, which may perhaps have been an indication that he knew and appreciated the fact that the playing was better than the conducting.

The three concerts conducted by Sir Henry J. Wood were in every way normal and predictably anxious. He slapped once through everything at the rehearsal, talking (if that is the right word) incessantly: he invariably finished the rehearsal with time to spare, and the new works, old pieces, difficult ones, easy ones, all received the same cursory treatment, with the inevitable result that his concerts were just sight-reading sessions without the running commentary. He enjoyed a reputation (in my younger days) of tackling anything and giving an 'airing' to more new works than any other conductor: but there is a fine distinction between courage and foolhardiness.

Two works which appeared in the programme received short and shabby shrift – the rarely-heard 6th Symphony in C minor by Glazunov, and the first performance of Symphonische Minuten (Op. 86) by Dohnányi. The Dohnányi, which is a miniature symphony in five movements, lasts only twelve minutes, and is scored for a large orchestra with celeste, harp and glockenspiel. The Scherzo (Allegro vivace) alternates between 3/8 and 2/8 with the added complication at one point of naming four straightforward bars of 3/8 followed by four of 2/8. It would be fruitless to apportion the blame between conductor and orchestra for never at any time being in contact with each other, either at the run-through or the concert, but whoever wrote the programme notes was 'psychic' – he said that "the movement comes to a breathless, spirited conclusion".

The Glazunov Symphony was unfamiliar to most orchestral players then, as it is now, and deserved far more attention than it received at the rehearsal: a bash at the notes was not enough. It would be an exaggeration to say that the performance was in tatters, but it was far too anxious and tentative for any enjoyment to be derived from it, either on the platform or in the audience.

Sir Thomas Beecham, who was President of the Hallé Society, had undertaken in 1933 to conduct as many concerts in Manchester as his commitments elsewhere would allow. In the season 1936–37 not only had the number of his concerts in Manchester shrunk to five, but the programmes were, by his standards, singularly unenterprising: the main works presented were symphonies Nos. 1 and 3 by Brahms and the 'Eroica' and No. 7 in A by Beethoven. His own orchestra, the London Philharmonic, was attracting the best players available and rapidly becoming the finest orchestra in Britain: quite predictably Beecham's attitude towards the Hallé changed from a serious application to maintain high standards to one of patronising a commodity which he knew was gradually becoming second best.

The programmes were such that he was quite capable of conducting them at any hour of the day or night, without notice. It was apparent to the members of the orchestra that he was in no mood for work on his intermittent visits to the Free Trade Hall. He was reliably unpunctual at the rehearsals and, if it were possible, wittier, funnier, and more relaxed than in previous seasons. The performance of the Beethoven symphonies impressed me least of all: for many years I held an entirely personal view that Beecham was secretly afraid of the giant who appeared to be standing at his elbow, constantly reminding him that his music was full of traps. Beecham's memory was not infallible and we had experienced, in the previous season, one of his inexplicable lapses in the Emperor Concerto: he had whacked a thunderous E*b* major chord on the *silent* third beat of the ante-penultimate bar in the first movement. Unfortunately, some of the unwary players near the rostrum responded with a feeble, half-stifled squeak. Tommy pouted and looked around quite disdainfully, as if to say "Beethoven is entirely to blame – he ought to have written a chord just there!".

The performance of the 'Eroica', which he described as a 'grand old piece', was disappointing: the restarts after the pauses (which regularly occur in the variations) were irritatingly and consistently not quite together. On March 4th I was a little more than disappointed by his performance of the 7th Symphony. I was embarrassed by a rather naughty public demonstration against this well-established masterpiece. The first three movements were uneventful, but Tommy had other ideas about the last! He braced himself for it, and his roguish eyes seemed to say "You all believe this to be a great work. I will now illustrate that the last movement is unutterable rubbish, which belongs to the Old Kent Road". He then let it rip, and proved his point!

He similarly took leave of his senses on another very different occasion many years later, conducting the B.B.C. Northern Orchestra in a broadcast from Rossall School. Beecham had spent the entire nostalgic day revisiting every nook and cranny of his old school; looking at the destruction his boyish pen-knife had done to the desk he once occupied. He eventually arrived on the platform for the broadcast obviously very happy and a little tipsy. I shall never forget the performance (or crucifixion) of the overture to 'William Tell': it went airily along until we arrived at the 2/4 vivace. Beecham didn't let it rip – he whipped it into such a froth that neither we, nor the countless millions at the other end of the 'contraption' could identify the damned thing. (He always referred to the B.B.C. and microphones as 'The Contraption'.)

In the years immediately following the death of Sir Edward Elgar, his two symphonies were frequently played at Hallé concerts. John Barbirolli, who conducted only one concert in the 1936–37 season, included Elgar's 2nd Symphony. Sir Landon Ronald, the other champion of Elgar, had already given a performance of the 1st Symphony, and the B minor Violin Concerto, with Henry Holst as soloist.

The most significant concert in an otherwise dull and unenterprising season was a performance of 'L'Enfance du Christ' by Berlioz, which Sargent conducted on February 25th. Isabel Baillie sang the part of Mary, and the other soloists were Roy Henderson, Stewart Wilson and Robert Easton. The programme notes announced the interesting fact that the work had received its first performance in England at a Hallé concert in 1880, but was last performed in 1888. There was nothing in the 1937 revival to suggest that 'L'Enfance du Christ' was a neglected masterpiece and that Berlioz was a grossly underrated composer.

Sargent conducted seven of twenty concerts in the 1936–37 Hallé season; an indication perhaps in some minds, particularly his, that he was the favourite for the part of permanent conductor. At one of the rehearsals he turned abruptly to Alfred Barker (the leader) without addressing him by name and said, "Are these OUR parts?". Before the astonished Mr. Barker could reply he went on to use his baton as a fiddle bow, making some motions of up bows and down bows on an imaginary fiddle: "Then bow that passage THIS WAY FOR ALL TIME!".

Orchestras can sulk in perfect accord and with great subtlety: attitudes towards certain conductors can be mutually adopted in a few minutes and maintained – in varying degrees of smouldering hostility – for life. After the departure of Sir Hamilton Harty in 1933 the standard of orchestral playing in Manchester declined. At the end of this, the fourth season of guest conductors, the concerts had become, to the more discerning members of the audience, disappointing experiences, and in many cases, to the members of the orchestra, anxious and disagreeable ones. It was apparent to Neville Cardus (whose articles on cricket and music adorned the Manchester Guardian) that the policy which the Hallé Society had, perhaps too eagerly, adopted four years before, was at last bearing fruit – of a particularly wizened variety. Precisely to where Neville Cardus was directing the responsibility for the sub-standard concerts I shall never know, since I never avidly read anything he wrote, but it became obvious towards the end of the season, in two witty speeches from the rostrum (which the audience loved) that Sir Thomas Beecham's corns were being trampled on. Entertaining as these skirmishes between Beecham and Cardus turned out to be, they were of little concern to the public: the old adage that 'where there's smoke there must be fire' greatly heartened the players and gave rise to a strong and persistent rumour – that Harty was coming back! How this diplomatic miracle was to be achieved no-one knew, but the entire orchestra (and, I believe, Neville Cardus) were aware that such an attempt would have been the salvation of the Hallé Orchestra.

The Spring of 1937 was the second of four extremely happy seasons I spent on the Pier at Llandudno, playing mornings only (Sundays excepted) from 11.00 a.m. until 12.45 p.m. between Easter and Whitsuntide. Perhaps I can be forgiven for regarding the whole period from Easter to Whit as a relaxed Spring holiday: the weather was invariably good and the engagement scarcely interfered with golf, tennis and all the other pleasures which a single young man has a licence to pursue.

The combination of piano, violin, viola and 'cello was small, but the reason for its existence was dictated by the tenants of numerous Souvenir Kiosks, Tobacco Shops (and a café at the end of the Pier) insisting on some attraction being provided to tempt off-season promenaders to walk along the Pier. The pianist George Atkinson was an exceptional player, and a most unusual character. To say that he was a harmless man would not adequately describe him: he was a retired Solicitor and a major shareholder in the Llandudno Pier Company. There were two expressions which never crossed his lips during the four seasons I made music with him – "I think ...." and "It is my opinion that ....". Needless to say, it became a challénge to me during our daily 'coffee intervals' to bait him with questions which demanded direct answers or opinions. His legal training never deserted him, and although he monopolised the chatter at our daily friendly intercourses, he was never off his guard. He frequently cast cautious glances around the never-too-busy café, and even under the table, to be reassured that the hosts of people he might mention were not eavesdropping or that any snippet of conversation could possibly be recorded. To any question his reply was always prefaced by, "Well, as it were, some people might sometimes be inclined to think ....". It is small wonder that this charming man was affectionately known in the profession as 'George AS IT WERE Atkinson'!

George, who was the musical director, (without ever exerting any authority) brought with him every morning a very carefully chosen programme of easy pieces: we were never really extended and there was an aura of pleasant relaxation in playing for a handful of people who were obviously resting from their walk along the Pier, or, as often was the case, Parsons writing their sermons whilst their wives knitted socks. Applause was rare, partly because so many hands were preoccupied doing more useful things and partly because the audience always appeared to be in and out of the café. If we were required to play solos in any programme, the meticulous George would ask almost apologetically at least two days in advance: "if we minded".

One morning George came well-prepared to take the 'solo-spot' himself by playing the 'Andante' and 'Rondo Capriccioso' in E minor by Mendelssohn, which he accomplished without disturbing anyone in the audience. The performance did, however, spark off an incident in his long memory which occupied the whole of the fifteen-minute coffee break to relate, and must be the prince of all 'shaggy-dog' stories! The only hesitation there was in his narrative was in fixing the exact date between August Bank Holiday Sunday or Monday evening in 1904 when he played *this very piece* before a packed audience in the GRAND PAVILION! One thing emerged as a certainty – it was a very hot, sultry evening, and he perspired abundantly. He then went on to describe the performance bar by bar until he introduced the subject of his story – he suddenly felt something crawling on his neck, "And, as you are very well aware, (as it were) Mendelssohn keeps both hands of the pianist very busy during this work. There are no rests in the Rondo, and it would have been unthinkable to stop playing before 2,500 people in order to flick off this mysterious 'thing'!"

Having nibbled away three finger nails and neglected my coffee until it was cold I waited eagerly until George eventually arrived at the climax of his saga – "Well, gentlemen, as well you know, there is a pause 𝄐 just a few bars from the end of this wonderful piece, and I was almost frantic leading up to it (possibly marring the performance) but when I arrived at the pause – DO YOU KNOW – IT LEFT ME – FROM THAT DAY TO THIS, I HAVE NEVER KNOWN WHAT I HAD ON MY NECK!!"

George monopolised the conversation during many coffee intervals, always in a confidential whisper and liberally interrupted by furtive glances around the room whenever he mentioned a person by name, however harmless were his references even to the dead and forgotten. In the first half of one of our morning sessions we were about to play a Waldteufel Waltz from a very old and tattered set of parts which George had brought along from the Pier's main library. The 'cellist, Leonard Baker, handed his part around (not a long process, since there were only four of us) for a general confirmation that it was quite impossible to read the notes. The reason was not the obvious one that the notes were badly printed, but the more obscure one that the notes had been obliterated by corrections to the value of the rests, each of which had been initialled 'E.S.' in ink. George allowed a stifled titter to escape him, which was a certain indication that the origin of the initials 'E.S.' would be the subject for discussion at the coffee break.

The initials belonged to Ted Stansfield, (the inventor of the five-string double-bass) who tried so hard to be famous, and whose exploits in the Hallé band-room have already been mentioned in an earlier chapter: we learned from George in the course of his narrative that he had been regularly employed by the Pier Company for about thirty years. It was, therefore, not surprising that Edward Stansfield had, during his long engagement, played from every bass part in the library, and furthermore, in his ridiculous conscientiousness, had corrected every printer's error, initialled it, and made quite certain that, if the Pier Library lasted for a thousand years, posterity would remember with amazement (if not pride) that Edward Stansfield had been around!

The story which George had to tell us concerned another comic character in the big orchestra by the name of Gus Wood (a bassoon player) who, like all his suffering brethren in the orchestra, had to listen day after day to Ted Stansfield 'just mentioning' that he had corrected yet another mistake in a bass part. George set the scene for his story in the Grand Pavilion on a very hot August evening (there was always a trace of red-carpet and decorum in George's voice whenever he mentioned the Grand Pavilion!) The orchestra was playing an interminable selection from 'Patience' by Sullivan, which contains practically everything in the Opera. George thought that some people might be inclined to think that it was perhaps a little on the long side, and that some of the players, in the sultry conditions, were perhaps finding it a little difficult to give the work their undivided attention (what a delightful way of preparing us for the simple fact that Ted Stansfield had dozed off at his post). "Well, as you know, in the final section marked 'molto vivace' there is a sudden silent pause bar – what do you think happened?" (as if he still hadn't recovered from the shock) 'Mr. Stansfield went 'Zoomck' in the silent bar! – but that wasn't all –

Mr. Gus Wood, who was inclined to buffoonery, let loose a shriek of laughter – in the Grand Pavilion' – and shouted to Mr. Stansfield, "TED, MARK THAT SOLO!!!" (presumably with the initials E.S.).

George frequently brought to our daily coffee-breaks the welcome tidings of lucrative 'jobs up the line' such as a week of 'The Chocolate Soldier' or 'Our Miss Gibbs' with the Colwyn Bay Amateur Operatic Society, or perhaps a few ditties at a local middle-class wedding reception. One of these surprise engagements nearly cost a life – mine! – which was miraculously spared by God's gift of acute sense of pitch. George told us very briefly that we should receive a guinea for playing the National Anthem at the conclusion of a meeting in the Grand Pavilion that evening: the dress was Dinner Jackets but we would be obliged to sit through the meeting and wait for a signal from the platform before leaping to our feet to earn the fee. (Needless to say, George did not bring either music stands or music to this performance – we knew it.)

It was with a light heart that I joined the others that evening in a specially prepared pit in the Grand Pavilion: I listened in amazement (and ignorance) to the chairman, Lloyd (Mark Anthony) Griffiths foaming at the mouth, in Welsh, whipping 2000 Welshmen into nothing short of a Unilateral Declaration of Independence and the immediate recall of the Welsh Embassy to London. I ought to have connected this demonstration of patriotic fervour with the bonfires which I had seen burning on every mountain top for miles around: flags had been fluttering on every public building and almost everybody I had met in the streets was wearing an emblem, but in all honesty I was in another world when the signal came from the platform to play our solitary and expensive contribution, the National Anthem. Listening to the Welsh language for two hours is akin to an anaesthetic, but I leapt to my feet and played a very loud G natural – the key-note and note which launches 'God save the King'. George responded with a loud chord of E*b* major which blended very well with my G natural (the 3rd of the chord of E*b*) but it brought to an abrupt end my loyalty to the Crown. My G natural was followed by an F natural and then E*b*: the rest of the concerted efforts of the quartet were drowned by 2,000 lusty Welsh throats singing 'Land of my Fathers' (in Welsh, of course!).

Having fortuitously escaped a lynching, I chuckled all the way back to my lodgings in Colwyn Bay, alternately awarding myself a medal for bravery (or foolhardiness) and considering the punishment for conspicuous cowardice in the face of an overwhelming enemy. I finally awarded myself the C.D.M.*

---

* Cadbury's Dairy Milk

The boarding house in which I was comfortably lodged in Wymntay Road, Colwyn Bay, was very efficiently run by a Cornish couple, Mr. and Mrs. Isaacs whose only daughter had married a professional musician. Mrs. Isaacs was, by this connection, a little more understanding than most of the insecurity of a semi-itinerant profession. She was an excellent cook, and since I was the only guest in the house during the slack pre-season period I enjoyed personal attention. Mrs. Isaacs let it be known (indirectly, through neighbours and acquaintances) that "that nice Mr. Horsfall was such a homely young man – he doesn't want his meals in the dining room – he likes to eat with us in the kitchen".

The truth of the matter was the fact that Mr. Isaacs fascinated me, and that Satan himself couldn't have kept me out of his company. He owned a solitary taxicab, which was not only his pride and joy, but his only means of contributing to the family business. During the slack pre-Whit period his daily chores consisted of lighting the kitchen fire, bringing in the coal and polishing his taxi in readiness for the high season. When these duties were conscientiously performed, he established himself in a large wooden arm-chair in front of the huge iron fireplace and digested every word of his daily newspaper. It was in this position that I found him every lunch-time: to say that I hurried back from Llandudno would perhaps be an exaggeration, but I looked forward to lunch with keen anticipation. I knew that the lunch would be a good one and that Mr. Isaacs would be all eagerness to solve the world's problems, which in 1937 were of some magnitude.

Every day I had scarcely cut my chop in half or conveyed a chip to my lips before Mr. Isaacs would lean towards me with his elbow on the arm of the chair. He pouted his lips, shut one eye, and wagged his forefinger slowly in my general direction. The newspaper was always open across his knees as a general indication that what he was about to say was not only topical but hot. His delivery was slow and authoritative, and in order not to miss a single gem I invariably looked up from my lunch and gave him my undivided attention. When, and only when, this happened, did Mr. Isaacs give me the confidential benefits of his morning's study. "All this bother in CZECHOSLOVANIA – MUSSALOONI'S to blame!" I was not in a position to challénge this profound observation, so he went on, "And that HILTLER isn't much better." I nodded approvingly, so he added "And another thing, what would 'appen if they let 'em all out of these CONSECRATION CAMPS?" What indeed!

Not every day was as serious as this – Friday brought lighter relief in the form of the local paper, which usually announced something in which he could take pride. One such happy piece of news was – "Last week they opened some new Baths in Rhos-on-Sea, with separate CRUCIBLES for dressing in." And another item which made his lips curl with something like contempt – "You musicians think you're clever but there's a little girl here in Llangollen, 5 years old, has been conducting one of these CONCUSSION BANDS". One other choice piece of gossip lowered his voice to a whisper, and instead of wagging his finger at me he nodded his head in the direction of the Rhododendron bush outside his kitchen window. "They've had a terrible SKELLINGTON in their cupboard next door – a divorce – but in this paper today it's all right now: it's just been made OBSOLETE!"

Mrs. Isaacs had bought him some socks one day, in a sale – "they were cheap because they were SUBSTANTIAL", and I think that was the occasion when she ascended to the upper floor of the store riding upon an 'OSCILLATOR'. On one occasion he read out from his local paper a number of motoring offences "for speeding on these AERIAL roads".* There was one sad item of news – "the winger on Colwyn Bay's football team had fallen and DISCOLATED his collar-bone".

Finally, he had taken Mrs. Isaacs the previous Sunday on a trip to Chester (in his taxi) – "Ooh, there's a beautiful CATHREDRAL in Chester". This one does not fall lightly off the tongue, and I had to practise pronouncing it before I could relate the story: a compliment to this remarkable man.

---

* At this period of history motorways were referred to as Arterial roads.

Chapter XI

The rumours which had circulated among the more discerning members of the Manchester public that efforts were being made to persuade Sir Hamilton Harty to return to the Hallé came to naught. None but the tone-deaf or musically insensitive members of the Hallé Society could deny that such a move would have rescued the Orchestra from the gradual decline into mediocrity which it had reached before the second World War. Although Beecham began the 1937–38 season with a performance of Rimsky-Korsakov's 'Antar' Suite, which was new to the orchestra, and at a later concert gave the first performance of Rachmaninoff's 3rd Symphony, there was a 'run of the mill' content of Brahms, Beethoven and Sibelius in all the eight concerts he conducted in Manchester. Denis Noble was soloist in 'Sea Drift' at Beecham's last concert of the season in March 1938, which had in all other instances been purely orchestral programmes. He repeated 'Ein Heldenleben' at one of his January concerts, without the usual fire and brimstone which had distinguished previous performances, in fact he said and did very little above the ordinary during the whole season except sack Raymond Meert (the 1st Horn) for making a false start in the Schubert 'Great' C major Symphony (February 3rd, 1938).

In complete contrast to the ever-so-slightly 'dilettante' Beecham, eleven of the season's concerts were entrusted to Sargent, who niggled his peevish way through a seemingly interminable number of rehearsals teaching us the rudiments of music and breaking down phrases into bars of semi-quavers, quavers, dots, dashes and dynamics with an occasionally contrived ritardando. The great danger (apart from the inevitable boredom and sulks) of breaking down the music at rehearsals lies (as Humpty Dumpty well knew) in the simple fact that all the King's Horses and all the King's Men cannot put it together again at the performance.

The main interest for me during the season was a fine array of soloists playing superbly – Egon Petri played Rachmaninoff's 3rd Concerto; Casals the Elgar and the unaccompanied Bach C major. Henry Holst played the Busoni Violin Concerto (on December 16th, 1937) before it was finally put back on the shelf; Catterall played the Sibelius on January 20th, 1938, and this was the last occasion we met. Thomas Matthews, who played in the orchestra, was given an opportunity to prove his vastly superior talents by playing the Elgar Violin Concerto on January 13th, 1938.

The best orchestral playing during the season was evoked by Weingartner (on March 3rd) conducting a Beethoven concert. The main work was the 'Eroica' Symphony, complemented by a fine performance by Edwin Fischer of the C minor Piano Concerto.

Great performances which had been regular and exciting events in my early days with the Hallé were becoming exceedingly rare in the late 'thirties. Beecham's disenchantment with the Hallé Society and Manchester audiences, which were notoriously difficult to please, was probably a reaction to the astonishing success he was enjoying with the London Philharmonic Orchestra, which was now the finest orchestra in England, perhaps in Europe. Pierre Monteux (whose genius was never appreciated by any except orchestral players) took a permanent post in the United States of America and was absent from the Manchester scene for nearly thirty years.

The dearth of available conductors of comparable stature to Harty, Beecham and Monteux was becoming increasingly apparent and my interest in the Hallé Orchestra became a routine apprenticeship of learning the 'business' (a lay term for acquiring technique and experience). Real enjoyment and edification sprang almost entirely from the soloists who were internationally famous, and appeared in the late 1930's to be in more plentiful supply than adequate conductors.

Flawless performances are rare events in a musician's life, and by some miracle there were two within weeks of each other in the season 1937–38. On February 17th, 1938 Kreisler played the Brahms and on March 10th Rachmaninoff played his own Paganini Variations and the Beethoven Concerto (in C) No. 1. Both concerts, in quite different ways, were unique examples of the modesty of these great artists. Rachmaninoff rehearsed the Beethoven almost to the point of totally neglecting his own piece (there was just enough time to play it through without comment) with the inevitable result that the concert was an unbelievable contrast of styles. The Beethoven was immaculate in classical simplicity and the Variations played with disarming brilliance and restraint, which endowed performances of his own works with rare dignity.

There were all the elements of surprise, relief and delight in Kreisler's appearance at the Hallé on February 17th. Huberman, who was at best unpredictable, and often unreliable, had cancelled the engagement at short notice: Kreisler, in the country on a recital tour, accepted the booking without fuss, and the concert was a sell-out within a few hours of the announcement in the press. The programme was altered to include the Brahms Violin Concerto, Beethoven's Romance in F Op. 40 and the Rondo Capriccioso by Saint-Saëns.

When I arrived early for the morning rehearsal, Kreisler was already established in the band-room, showing his two violins to a very

Fritz Kreisler

interested audience of fiddle players who had never before been at close quarters with either him or such magnificent instruments. His cloak was hanging on the communal hat racks and his violin-case was open (along with many others of less distinguished pedigree) in the middle of the long table which almost filled the room: he played a few passages, not from diet of the day, and his only comment was regarding indecision about which of his fiddles he would play today!

The rehearsal bell rudely interrupted the demonstration and we were summoned to the platform to rehearse the insignificant pieces which made up the rest of the programme. Sargent, who was the conductor for the day, eventually sent a porter in search of Kreisler (whom he had not yet seen) to inform him 'that he was waiting'. Kreisler came onto the platform to spontaneous applause from the orchestra: after a benign smile and a brief tune-up, the rehearsal began. The respect which the orchestra had intuitively felt for this great artist, and already shown on his appearance on the platform, continued like a spell throughout the rehearsal. No-one dared to make an unmusical sound, and there was abundant proof, as the rehearsal progressed, 'that the art of orchestral playing is listening'. The first movement of the Brahms was in every respect a performance, and Kreisler played his own cadenza in its entirety in order not to mar the sublime moments when soloist and orchestra are almost unperceivably reunited in the Coda. There was nothing during the brief interval between the first and second movements beyond a murmur of relaxed breathing and minimal tuning: the slow movement began and the atmosphere of this memorable occasion was soon restored by the serene Oboe solo which Alfred Livesley (who was a comparative newcomer to the Hallé) played superbly. The movement ended as serenely as it began, but it was Kreisler who broke the spell by putting up a cautionary hand to Sargent, preventing him from charging into the Finale. He turned to Alfred Livesley and addressed him in warm sincerity – "I have never in my whole life, anywhere in the world, heard that movement played so beautifully".

Sargent, who was incapable even of thinking such a compliment to an orchestral player, was in no great danger of choking himself by giving expression to it: he merely grinned.

The ovation Kreisler received at the concert he also shared with Alfred by inviting him to stand – a memory which Alfred must treasure, although, during the twenty years of intimate friendship we enjoyed after the war, he never mentioned the incident.

Alfred Livesley was a genius who passed through this world in obscurity and finally into oblivion, without the comfort of Dr. Johnson's invaluable information on 'distinction' and the ease with which it can be obtained.* He was a man of many parts – an accomplished painter who either became disenchanted with Art or was absurdly unaware of his own immense talent. He reached his early thirties before he aspired to play the oboe, which he mastered in an incredibly short time, and although he was regarded as the finest player in the North he remained impervious to praise and hypersensitive of critical comment regarding his sometimes shabby appearance or introvert Bohemian life. During the years when I was closest to Alfred he turned his boundless creative energy almost willy-nilly into a wide variety of unrelated skills and crafts: one of these – the art of violin making – he admitted had taken a great deal of time to study and acquire. In all, Alfred made eight very fine violins which he gave away – in only one instance can he remember to whom they were given: Philip Whiteway (who at one time was leader of the B.B.C. Northern Ireland Orchestra) was in Manchester in 1946 and played in the B.B.C. Northern Orchestra on Alfred's *seventh* violin, which he later gratefully accepted and took with him to Bristol.

In only two of Alfred's many and diverse enterprises did he not excel – playing the violin, in spite of relentless practice, and GOLF, at which he has never succeeded in making any impact on the handicap of the maximum 24 given him 35 years ago by the Withington Golf Committee. Alfred, in his retirement, is still sustained by the belief (having mastered everything else in which he ever dabbled) that a miracle will happen on one of his lonely daily rounds, and he will look up from the little white ball and say "There's nothing to it". In this, the fondest of all his aspirations, Alfred has long had my best wishes and encouragement, but never my confidence.

Immediately after the War, in the summer of 1946, I joined the B.B.C. Northern Orchestra and formed with Alfred what was considered to be an unusual friendship, which lasted for twenty years. In the words of Maurice Johnstone (Regional Director of Music) "I'm glad you've taken him in hand: you're the only one who can do anything with him". Alfred's eccentricities were often hilarious, sometimes tragic, but always fascinating. Although artistically inactive he is still alive, so I will restrain myself into relating one instance of his remarkable talent and generosity.

One day in the summer of 1948 we were hacking our tedious way around Withington Golf Course when Alfred relieved the depression (into which we regularly sank whenever we played the game) by saying, quite casually, "I haven't put brush to canvas for years – but I'd like to paint you". I readily agreed to sit for him, partly to encourage his whim to paint again, and partly to escape for a while from wasting our mutual time and strength on the unrewarding game of golf.

---

* Dr. Johnson begins the second paragraph of his essay 'Dick Minim the critic' with the words "I hope it will give comfort to many who are passing through the world in obscurity, when I inform them how easily distinction may be obtained".

Alfred had recently bought a new semi-detached house in New Mills and within a week of acquiring the keys, quite surprisingly announced that he was already living in the house and ready to start painting: he met me at New Mills station on the morning of our next free day at the B.B.C. and by his brisk conversation all the way to his new work-shop studio, I felt heartened by his eagerness to 'put brush to canvas'.

The house had all the external appearances of being not only new but unoccupied: there were splashes of white-wash on the windows, which I believe (in the building trade) is a way of indicating to other tradesmen that the frames 'now have glass in them'! I was not expecting to see curtains at the windows or fitted carpet in the hall, but I was taken aback when Alfred unlocked his front door and hung his shabby cap on a 4" nail which he had strategically driven into a wooden post at the foot of the stairs. This nail was the only improvement which Alfred had made during a week of occupation: the hall and staircase, like the rest of the house, showed all the traces of the speedy evacuation of the work-force – bits of plaster, the marks of hob-nailed boots, wood shavings and sawdust – which would have offended anyone but Alfred.

The living room, next in line on the conducted tour, was a revelation: there wasn't a vestige anywhere of carpet, linoleum or matting, and the furniture consisted of a table, upon which stood a 2lb. bag of sugar, a ¼lb. carton of tea (gaping open) and – a relic of the War – an R.A.F. pint mug which had in it the dregs of a 'brew of tea', probably three days old! The rest of the furniture could be appraised at a glance – a deck chair was strategically placed in front of a television set which was safely but inelegantly standing on an empty 12-compartment beer-bottle crate. To own a television set in 1948 was a symbol of splendid living to anyone but Alfred Livesley, whose philosophy in this life was to have about him only those utilitarian objects which satisfied his immediate needs. Unlike Socrates, who remarked as he strolled idly through the Market Place, "I had no idea there were so many things in the world I do not need," Alfred would never have wasted his time in the Market Place unless he had specifically wanted something – urgently!

The walls of the living room were beautifully shiny bare plaster for the most part, but one of them had been covered in a hideous daffodil-coloured emulsion paint, and the one in which the fire-place stood had been partially covered. It was obvious from the brush marks, which had petered out in all directions, that the 'decorator' had been interrupted in the performance of his duties. Alfred explained that he had walked casually into his unfinished house and 'caught him at it'!! "I soon despatched him and his vile paint!" Over the fireplace, in a space which had escaped the emulsion paint, were two examples of Alfred's handiwork – one was a beautiful free-hand pencil sketch of a young girl's head, her soft hair floating away from it in an imaginary light breeze.

This 'instant Pygmalion' had the spontaneity of a Schubert song, created in a few minutes for no better reason than – "I just HAD to do it!" The other example of Alfred's free-hand pencil drawing was also the other extremity of his amazing philosophy – that everything in his frugal life had a material purpose: he scoffed at any utensil which designers or manufacturers had attempted to make decorative or attractive. Alongside his dream girl was a 24-hour timetable of the train services between New Mills and Manchester Piccadilly – "for easy reference", he explained. There was no easy explanation for the next oddity I saw in the kitchen – there was only one pan on the stove, but *three* bags of coal – in the PANTRY! "I can't be bothered to go *outside* for coal!"

Alfred began to show a little impatience at my interest in his living conditions and he rather brusquely prodded me upstairs to his studio – and the first of my sittings for the portrait, which lingered on through the summer months. The violin which I am holding in the portrait was a recently finished instrument (his eighth) which he took from his work-bench and handed to me – "Here, give your hands something to do" – and it was from this bench that the camera (with a timing device) took the composite photograph of the sitter, the portrait and the artist.

After my marriage in 1950 I perhaps saw rather less of Alfred Livesley than in our single, carefree days, but our friendship has continued and of all the great musicians it has been my privilege to meet, or know intimately, I have regarded Alfred as the genius who, unaccountably, could not sell himself.

The 'Kreisler' concert, described in some detail earlier in this chapter, was followed on February 24th by the first (rather patchy and under-rehearsed) performance of William Walton's B*b* minor Symphony, which Sargent conducted. There was another first performance (at a Hallé concert) on March 10th – this time of the Haydn Symphony in E*b* No. 103 – the 'Drum Roll'. Another rarely-heard work was included in this programme – the third of Debussy's 'Nocturnes' – 'Sirènes' with wordless female voices. 'Nuages' and 'Fêtes' have become familiar orchestral pieces since they were detached from their expensive, unrewarding and unexciting 'Sirènes' and I was grateful to have as my first experience of 'Nocturnes' a complete performance.

The soloist at this unusual concert was Rachmaninoff, who played yet another performance of his Paganini Variations and also Beethoven's No. 1 Concerto in C major. It was the Beethoven which dominated the rehearsal – Rachmaninoff insisted on every minute detail being observed and (what was far more important) purging the work of 'tradition' and 'personality' – particularly his own. I have never in my whole life spent more time rehearsing the Beethoven than on this occasion, but neither have I since heard a performance which compared with it.

It was very apparent at the rehearsal that Rachmaninoff had set his heart on an immaculate performance of the Concerto and he stayed on the platform merely to go straight through his own work, the Paganini Variations: he waved his hand to Sargent, and looking around the orchestra said, "You all know this piece," as if creating the impression that his own music was undeserving of appearing in the same programme with Beethoven.

Chapter XII

The season began on October 20th with a Beecham concert which, included the Sibelius Symphony No. 2 in D, a work which he never conducted consistently, but to be kind to some of his wayward performances, this particular symphony 'took shape' in different ways each time it appeared. At the rehearsal we were through the reading session very early and came back from our interval to listen to what was usually a boring recitation of what he required from the flutes two bars after the letter C, or 'less' from someone else in bar 65. But he did enliven the morning by a most unexpected remark at letter E in the Sibelius: having talked us drearily through the first movement until he arrived at the development section (with its endless meandering quavers) he looked up over his half-moon spectacles and in his inimitable, whimsical manner observed, "Gentlemen, at the letter E ... this movement will pursue its course like an AMIABLE TAPEWORM" (referring to the forty-three bars of continuous quavers between letters E and H).

The second concert of the Winter series was conducted by Eugene Goossens (enjoying a working holiday from his permanent post in Sydney, Australia). His manner was gentle and persuasive and the concert, which included Debussy's 'La Mer' and the 'Symphonie Fantastique', was excellent.

Sydney Coulston (the recently appointed 1st Horn in the orchestra) had to wait but a short time for his baptism – on November 10th in a performance of Bach's B minor Mass he acquitted himself brilliantly, with the inevitable feeling of relief to all concerned, and has continued to do so throughout a long and distinguished career in Manchester.

The concerts which Beecham conducted during this, the last Hallé season before World War II, were, with one exception, purely orchestral, and contained nothing more enterprising than symphonies by Tchaikowsky, Schubert, Mendelssohn and César Franck. One work which he introduced to Hallé audiences for the 'first time' was Handel's Concerto Grosso Op. 6 No. 1, and never before in the history of this piece has the contrast between 'concertino' and 'ripieno' been more pronounced. The soloists (Violins I and II and 'Cello) were competing rather uneasily with a lusty 'ripieno' string orchestra of about 60 players.

There was one delicate concert which Beecham had obviously intended from the first few bars at the morning rehearsal to be superlatively good. The programme was 'typical' – the 'Jupiter' symphony, 'Appalachia' and the Dvorák 'Symphonic Variations'. He worked seriously without a trace of the wit, humour or relaxation which usually characterised his rehearsals, and although the concert was a great success I left the Free Trade Hall that evening with an impression that he had spent the whole day trying to 'prove himself'.

The only concert Beecham conducted at which a soloist appeared took place on March 16th. R.J. Forbes played the Delius Piano Concerto and the final concert (which was the annual 'Pension Fund') the following week, March 25th, was the only one at which Beecham, in an explosive tantrum, gave vent to some of his lofty, contemptuous feelings toward the Hallé Society.

The date of this concert had been changed from Thursday to Saturday in order to accommodate his own busy schedule and the programme, of his currently favourite pieces, included the Good Friday Music from 'Parsifal' and also the Liszt Hungarian Rhapsody No. 2 in D minor.

Before the rehearsal began Harold Ball (the Hallé librarian of 'singular' fame) distributed Tommy's carefully-marked orchestral parts, which he invariably brought with him on guest engagements. The single exception on this occasion was the Hungarian Rhapsody – in a moment of aberration Beecham had committed the supreme blunder of relying on this well-known piece being available from the Hallé Library. It was, but he could never have foreseen (as he nonchalantly sprawled on the rostrum) that the tattered copies which could scarcely stand upright on our desks were probably the parts Charles Hallé brought with him when he founded the orchestra in 1842!

Tommy began the rehearsal, in the best of good humour, with this piece and it soon became evident that generations of despairing orchestral players had given up the task of 'inking in' the notes, or making accidentals legible, or correcting 'rests' which faced the wrong way, or joining into groups the individually printed semi-quavers, or guessing what had appeared in the last few bars of every page which a hundred years of sweaty thumbs had torn off in fumbling to see what was in store for them on the next page. The primitive plates used in this unique edition had embossed some incredibly faint signs on soft, dirty, cream-coloured blotting-paper, which over the years had absorbed a great many other stains besides wrong notes – probably beer, or tea without milk.

Even with clearly legible parts in the newest edition, Liszt's Hungarian Rhapsody No. 2 would have been the last piece in the repertoire I would have entrusted Beecham to perform and, in spite of the screaming and cracking of his whip (to which he invariably resorted when normal conducting did not produce any tangible results), nothing remotely resembling the Rhapsody No. 2 emerged from what appeared to be a product of Caxton's Printing Press. He flopped into his armchair, legs and arms akimbo, and puffed a few times as he slowly and very deliberately put down his baton and tore the hallowed full-score into two pieces before tossing them into the stalls. This time, the pronouncement he made could not have been rehearsed or premeditated – "Gentlemen – this Society runs a very grave risk of becoming utterly overwhelmed and submerged in a torrent of ignorance and imbecility." After a short pause he announced 'Meistersinger', a piece which held pride of place on his list of 'emergency items'.

The concert on February 2nd, 1939 was devoted entirely to Brahms – the 'Academic Festival' and symphonies Nos. 1 and 3. Weingartner, who conducted with a minimum of gesture and speech, re-created the huge, sonorous, vibrant sounds which had characterised Harty's performances of these works almost a decade before. This concert was outstanding and quite isolated in a season of otherwise unmemorable and sometimes anxious experiences.

A concert which Constant Lambert conducted on December 1st, 1938 came very close to being a disaster, for the obvious reason that the statutory three-hour rehearsal was grossly inadequate to prepare a programme which included the first performance of the 'Checkmate' Ballet Suite by Sir Arthur Bliss and Balakirev's Symphony No. 1 in C. Egon Petri was the soloist in two piano concerti (by Mozart and Liszt) which deserved more attention (at the rehearsal) than the short shrift they received. Constant Lambert made the fundamental mistake of niggling at great length over the 'Checkmate' Suite, leaving time only for a cursory glance at the two piano concerti (the Liszt being particularly neglected). The Balakirev received what is known in the profession as a 'top and tail', which meant that great areas of this unfamiliar work were left to the mercy of the Gods, who that day appeared to have far more pressing problems elsewhere: the concert was unforgettable – for the wrong reasons.

The concert on March 9th was sadly, for me, the last time I made music with Rachmaninoff, and the only occasion in my experience that he played his second concerto (in C minor) with the Hallé Orchestra. Sargent was the conductor, and it was apparent that the orchestra was playing from his orchestral parts (which were stamped with his name on every page). The rehearsal of the concerto proceeded quietly and attentively until Rachmaninoff played the cadenza in the slow movement and the orchestra rejoined him before the re-statement of the opening theme. In the bar before Adagio Sostenuto (Tempo I) the two Flutes broke the spell by 'stealing in' with their passage in thirds (as flute-players all over the world had been doing since 1902 and still continue to do).

Rachmaninoff allowed them to play as far as the pause against his own trill on A natural, then he put up his hand and broke the spell completely by saying "No, no, I DID NOT WRITE THAT." He then went on to say that "the passage is too low for the 2nd Flute to play (pp) with certainty of intonation: I wrote the passage for 1st Flute and Clarinet – it is an editing mistake" (1901).

There was a pause whilst the Flute II and the Clarinet I parts were corrected and Sargent made a blue-pencil note in his full-score.*

The editing mistake first made in 1901 has persisted for 78 years and is unlikely to be rectified. Sydney Coulston, (the new 1st Horn) who was present at this rehearsal and concert had, the previous season, played with the Hastings Municipal Orchestra conducted by Julius Harrison. Sydney related that this 'alteration' had been the centre of a great rumpus which had taken place between Pouishnoff and Julius Harrison at a rehearsal of the work in Hastings the previous season. Pouishnoff pointed out with some heat that he had talked with Rachmaninoff and had been given the great man's blessing to put this matter to rights wherever he performed the work, but he had no joy with Julius Harrison, who retorted that "If Rachmaninoff had felt so strongly about this mistake he would have done something about it himself". It was self-evident on March 9th, 1939 that Rachmaninoff was 'working at this problem' quite diligently: it is equally clear, forty years later, that his efforts were singularly unsuccessful, and it is now unlikely that the correction will ever appear in the numerous 'pirate' editions of his works which have followed the lapse of copyright.

The two concerts which followed on March 16th and 25th were conducted by Beecham, and proved to be the last depressing remnants of a Hallé season overshadowed by Hitler's 'Anschluss' in Europe and

---

* In August, 1978 I was enabled to examine this score, which is now in the library of the Royal College of Music, London. A blue-pencil cross is the only indication that anything was ever amiss at this point. The only orchestral parts into which the alteration was so carefully written were later acquired by Boosey & Hawkes Hire library and – according to Mr. Malcolm Smith, in charge of the Hire Department – subsequently 'wore out' and were destroyed.

Five sets of parts in current use in the Boosey Library and three sets at Yelding House, for the exclusive use of B.B.C. orchestras, show no traces of the composer's wishes ever reaching the numerous publishers of this popular piece. One score and set of parts (in the B.B.C. Manchester Music Library) is correct – I confess to borrowing them (about 25 years ago) for a performance in Todmorden and quite unashamedly making the alteration!

the inevitability of the war which erupted in the following September.

The short season from Easter to Whit I spent happily at Llandudno with George ('as it were') Atkinson and then moved on to Buxton and the promise of 'bigger and better things' as the leader of Tommy Matthews' 'Swift Serenade' for the summer season at the Pavilion Gardens. 'Swift Serenade' was the title of a series of regular half-hour broadcasts from the B.B.C. Manchester Studios. The programmes consisted of tunes from Jerome Kern, Irving Berlin, Gershwin and others, dressed up beyond recognition in sophisticated (and expensive) special arrangements and played in the pseudo Paul Whiteman 'concert style'. The reaction of an unseen audience to an occasional half-hour of these tit-bits cannot reliably be assessed, but the response to daily four-hour doses by a handful of people bewildered, harassed and depressed by the threat of war was unmistakable.

In spite of the white jackets we wore on the stage and the professional, artificial gaiety we infused into 'The Way You Look To-night' we were singularly unsuccessful in creating or sustaining anything resembling a holiday mood. Audiences, such as were snatching a few days 'close to home this year', were restless and rarely stayed at any performance long enough to applaud anything. A great deal of coffee was consumed by those who quickly tired of trying to find the tune whenever we played 'Smoke Gets In Your Eyes', and the music from the Pavilion would bring in a few people from the Gardens who were caught in the rain. Regular patrons at our concerts were non-existent, and I became increasingly bored with the soul-destroying arrangements of the music I was obliged to play, and increasingly apprehensive about the future. The season was enlivened in July and August by some excellent performances of plays by J.B. Priestley given in the adjacent Opera House by the Northampton Repertory Company. Access was easy from the Gardens and I confess to sneaking into their daily rehearsals, and also many of their performances. It was refreshing to see so much enthusiasm for the job, and endless patience for getting things right: 'Dangerous Corner' may not be the greatest play ever written, or the most difficult to produce, but I can still remember several first-rate performances by the Northampton Rep. Perhaps I admired their dedication to work, which was in sharp contrast to my own during the miserable summer of 1939.

I can remember meeting Constance Cummings and Robert Donat on the streets in Buxton late in August and attending one rehearsal of Goldsmith's 'She Stoops to Conquer' by the Old Vic Company, but I have no recollection of a public performance taking place, in fact the Old Vic Company, in common with Tommy Matthews' Orchestra, assembled in the Gardens at 11 a.m. on Sunday, September 3rd to hear the Prime Minister declare a state of war. There was no-one, not even an usherette, to answer the question on everyone's lips "What happens now?"

After the Prime Minister's announcement, the Buxton Municipal Orchestra did not exactly flee in all directions, but in the absence of anyone in authority, or indeed with the remotest idea of what ought to happen next, we drifted to our lodgings, packed our fancy costumes, and without ceremonious farewells, left Buxton by the first available train.

be confused with puke!) until the right combination was eventually settled upon and he left the stage to its one miserable pilot light and, presumably, went back to the Midland Hotel. I sat for some time recovering from this charade but at 10.25 a.m. he tripped onto the stage to begin the rehearsal, passing the outside layer of 1st Violinists on his way to the rostrum: he had completely changed his clothes and, as he looked around the theatre, he said quite nonchalantly "Oh, so this is where we're playing to-day!"

I was informed later in the day that a small welfare committee had been formed of older members of the Hallé Orchestra who had seen service in the first World War, and were firmly (but naively) of the opinion that the course of this one would follow the same static lines as the first. Motivated by these generous thoughts, those members left behind were contributing 5/- a week for the duration of the war, in order to send parcels of cigarettes, socks and scarves to its absent members. Syd and I were the only two members in uniform on this occasion and were asked by the treasurer, Ted Heaton, to keep him well-informed of our whereabouts. He also told me that he had invited Sargent to contribute to the Fund (since he was conducting the Orchestra regularly) but he was either not quite in sympathy with the cause, or extremely optimistic that hostilities would end in three-and-a-half days: his only contribution to the Fund was a miserly 2/6d.!

After the performance I returned to Padgate by a train from Manchester Central Station at about 6 p.m. The sirens were busy as the train left the station and, long before I arrived in Warrington, it was apparent from the sky-line, and the sounds of bombing, that Manchester was the target for yet another hammering. Syd was caught in it (as I discovered the following day) having decided to steal a few extra hours at home: he was also taking my fiddle along with his own instrument to a safer hiding place than RAF Padgate, having recent and vivid recollections of the disappearing 'mug and irons', or indeed anything which wasn't firmly screwed to the ground.

A few days before Xmas, Syd and I were posted to our respective training courses and lost touch with each other for the duration of the war: in fact we next met in the Spring of 1946 when I joined him in the B.B.C. Northern Orchestra.

The Equipment Training School to which I was posted was based at Cranwell: I passed through the concentrated seven-week course with sufficient interest in it to do well, and well enough to be retained on it as an Instructor. Promotion to Sgt. was rapid and, soon after, the school was transferred to Bridlington in the Spring of 1941. I was vetted by the C.O. and dispatched to Air Ministry in London for an interview. In June I found myself at school again, first of all at Gosforth, learning about channels of communication and how to be a 'leader of men', and later at

Grange-over-Sands for another seven-week course on the Equipment Procedure. This course was devoted entirely to forgetting the first one (which was the peace-time procedure) and could have been summarised in one brief sentence "Get on the 'blower' if you want anything and let the paper-work go to hell!"

Grange is ideally situated on the fringe of the Lakes and the Grand Hotel (in which the Equipment School was comfortably accommodated) still retained many of its peace-time recreational facilities, not the least of them being a nine-hole golf course which the Physical Training Instructor (Sgt. Spencer) had, with great skill and professional zeal, converted into a cricket field.

Sgt. Spencer's main concern (now that the 'square' was showing the fruits of his mowing and rolling) was finding a sufficient number of junior officers to take an interest in his sport, or to make up none-too-friendly sides to meet the villagers.

Seven weeks is a very long time to spend learning how to use the telephone in order to dispense with accounting 'in time of war' and it was soon apparent that we were being schooled for overseas duty: there were a great many tedious lectures on enemy aircraft recognition (even one on battleships – just in case Bismark steamed into Barrow to re-fuel!) and many more on survival. The interesting lectures on improvisation and initiative led to several Field Exercises into the delightful countryside in search of the perfect site for storing 'equipment' in 'advanced positions on mobile fronts' – presumably with the invasion of Italy in mind. We were well aware of the exact location of the site (having been informed by 'bush–telegraph') but there were many delightful excursions to be enjoyed, during the first few weeks, avoiding finding the spot!

The Instructors enjoyed the game too: whenever classwork dragged on, or the sun shone, we were told to "Get lost!" which was the command to make another abortive search for the 'site'. Eventually, of course, we found it and were rewarded for our initiative by being posted overseas. Cats are rarely bitten by kittens!

Sgt. Spencer, and the cricket I played at Grange, have remained the most pleasant of my war-time recollections. Thirty-eight years elapsed before I met Sgt. Spencer again and then only because I summoned enough courage (during a prolonged stoppage for rain at a Yorks. v Sussex County Cricket match at Headingley) to ask the Yorkshire Secretary (Joe Lister) if T.W. Spencer O.B.E. Test Umpire "had ever served as a P.T.I. at Grange-over-Sands?" "Wait here a minute, I'll ask him" said Mr. Lister, and off he went into hallowed places and returned with the answer "Yes", and the man himself, who seemed to be delighted to have a chat about old times. When we parted he said "I'm glad you came to see me, in fact, quite flattered – do you know that you are only the THIRD person I met during the war who has spoken to me since?" I can honestly say that Tom Spencer was the only man I met during the war I ever wanted to see again!

The remainder of my brief service in England was uneventful, and early in January, 1943, I sailed from the Gladstone Dock in Liverpool in the good ship 'Duchess of Richmond' for some secret destination: all the troops going aboard were carrying pith-helmets and I had been issued with tropical kit!

The 'Duchess of Richmond' survived her war-time convoy duties and in the immediate post-war years was re-fitted and re-named the 'Empress of France'. She was intended for service between Liverpool and Canada but never sailed under her new name. The 'Duchess' died of shame, and capsized, probably from some explicable cause, in Gladstone Dock – a total wreck.

About the middle of January the 'Duchess of Richmond', with 5,000 men aboard left the Clyde and sailed around the North of Ireland and into the North Atlantic – or so I was later informed. The cabin I shared with 3 sadists was three decks above the water-line and as an indication of the gale-force winds, 40 ft. waves and blown spume, the port-holes and hatchways on Decks 1, 2 and 3 were battened and padlocked until we had been at sea for ten days.

My three companions, who were obviously descended from good maritime stock, went below three times a day and not only ate three hearty meals but reported the variety and quantity of food to their nauseated, dying comrade, who spent five whole days strapped to his bunk. My position could be decribed as basically horizontal but I experienced every kind of rocking motion, head to foot and side to side, as the good ship left the water and settled uneasily down again: the sounds of groaning plates and creaking timbers were as nothing compared with the roaring propellers as the stern came out of the water. It was difficult to distinguish between night and day: from 9 a.m. until 3.30 p.m. it was perhaps less dark, or just possible to see wild, stormy grey clouds merging with, and swallowed by, a merciless ocean. In that helpless condition I was singularly unconcerned with navigation and the skills of those upon whom our lives depended, but when we were allowed on deck and the sea was sufficiently calm to observe the rest of the convoy and its escort vessels, I was amazed at the planning and coordination involved. The troop-ships and supply-vessels were six abreast and seven astern, in perfect formation, escorted by one aircraft carrier, several cruisers, and more busy destroyers than I could, at any one time, count.

The convoy stayed as an entity for about four weeks zig-zagging across the Atlantic (which had long lost its interest and charm for me). It broke up, one calm, beautiful day, and all the heavy armour escorted all but a few of the troop-ships to Gibraltar and into the Mediterranean.

We crossed the Equator a few days later and put into Freetown for a brief stay. The voyage to Cape Town was continued in monotonously good weather with nothing to relieve the tedium except watching porpoise, dolphin, flying-fish and the occasional whale. There was a flutter of excitement one afternoon, when a message came down to us from the bridge, actually raising a cheer – "We're having company – the ship 'Queen Elizabeth'". It was a very brief visit she announced her approach belching smoke, said 'hello' as ships usually do, and was gone.

We docked in Cape Town in the late afternoon, seven weeks after leaving the Clyde, and we were 'let loose' on the town until 23.59 hours, to look around and 'find our land-legs'. Late February is harvest-time in the Southern Hemisphere and South Africa grows an abundance of luscious, exotic fruit. Cape Town had never experienced even a practice black-out, and George Street, which was brilliantly lighted, presented a sight to be remembered for life.

On both sides of the long, straight, fashionable boulevard were thousands of troops sitting on the edge of the kerb, with their legs sprawling in the roadway, spitting out peach stones, grape pips, pineapple skins, banana skins – in fact the whole assortment of fruit none of them had seen, or tasted, for three years. Every left hand held a bag and every lap supported another in reserve: the prices being asked, and eagerly paid were ludicrous – peaches the size of tennis balls were 1d each, huge bunches of black grapes 4d., and whole pineapples (with the inedible cores removed) were 4d. each. Nothing was weighed (there wasn't time) and 4d. appeared to be a standard price for everything handed out to an extremely orderly, if untidy, shipload of vitamin C deficient troops. There were probably a few cases of tummy-ache the following day, but I left the ship early and was transported in comfort, but at great speed, to a transit camp about fifteen miles down the Cape Peninsula where I stayed for three weeks.

There was nothing transitory about this camp – the buildings were permanent, the accommodation luxurious, and there was minimal confinement except for those on the duty roster. The Officers' Mess resembled, in every way, a country club, and the civilian staff urged us to take advantage of the many tit-bits of entertainment and offers of hospitality displayed on the notice boards. There was a fast, frequent, and absurdly cheap electric train service from the camp through the rich, sub-tropical sheltered side of the Cape Peninsula: the naval base of Simonstone (the least attractive) and the beautiful residential suburbs of Rondebusch and Wineberg were leisurely stops on the scenic railway which finally made a circuit of Table Mountain before its arrival in Cape Town. The British Clubs in Cape Town displayed welcome notices (to commissioned officers) and in the dining-rooms there was a ceiling charge of 2/6d. for grills and 1/3d. for a bottle of wine! This standard charge also applied in Hildebrands (Cape Lobster) Restaurant in George Street.

I hope that I may be forgiven for dwelling too long on fruit, food and wine in this land of plenty, or enjoying the hospitality thrust upon me by the British residents. Although World War II was 3,000 miles away, it was soon apparent that the Boer War was still lingering on in South Africa. The warmth of the hospitality shown by the British minority was offset by the hostility publicly demonstrated by the Dutch: I was twice spat upon in the street, and many times shouted at, quite venomously, to 'get on with the war'.

One of the first persons I visited was Col. Hart, M.P. for Rondebusch, who not only filled me in briefly on the political climate, but took me to a session of Parliament in order to listen to General Smuts make an impassioned speech (in an incomprehensible language) TO KEEP SOUTH AFRICA IN THE WAR! (It must be remembered that in one of our sieges of Tobruk, which changed hands many times in the North Africa campaign, the South Africa Corps lost 25,000 men, killed and captured.)

Apartheid was then, as it is now, the least of South Africa's internal problems, and in the short space of three weeks I became acutely aware that the British, in their over-demonstrative friendliness towards their kinfolk, were enduring a harrowing period in the smouldering, never-ending struggle with the Dutch. One of the blind invitations I accepted, which I believed would be free from political overtones, came from Dr. Grant, Professor of Music in the University of Cape Town. The Music Department was well endowed and equipped for music-making, from chamber music to opera: there was an orchestral class about to begin its regular rehearsal when I arrived on the campus, and it was no surprise to me, or to them (when I was introduced), that Dr. Grant invited me to rehearse them for nearly two hours. On my second visit to the University I found Dr. Grant much more communicative, although I had an intuitive feeling that, in spite of his success in building and extending the Faculty, he was homesick, lonely and disenchanted with the country. The rather pathetic and unconvincing manner in which he tried to sell his Music Department (and the Land of Opportunity) to me, was ill-adapted to succeed in persuading me to emigrate after the war, especially in view of the inflexible impression I had already formed.

The 'sailing order' which suddenly and unexpectedly appeared, late one afternoon on the Mess notice-board, threw some of the officers into confusion – many of them had 'social engagements' which young men find hard to get and harder to give up, and since the camp had no perimeter fence there were a few 'absent without leave' the night before we sailed.

The vessel, in Cape Town Docks, which was to carry us to the Red Sea was an absurdly small, smelly, shabby little steamer which had probably never been out of sight of land since it was launched. Of the many characteristics it undoubtedly shared with other ships, the one which immediately appealed to me was the fact that it floated! In the course of the morning some dock-hand gave it a push, and we bade farewell to Table Mountain and chugged, not very majestically, round the Cape to Durban where the little horror put in for four days, either to refuel, or to rest, or both. I knew it was Durban, because we were greeted at the end of the longest sea-wall in the world by a lusty 'Brünnhilde' dressed in a Union Jack, howling 'Land of Hope and Glory', with the assistance of a superfluous megaphone.

The Egyptian crew of our pleasure steamer were either ignorant of, or indifferent to, producing any edible or recognisable 'English' food, and, like Jane Eyre, 'the first edge of hunger blunted, I perceived I had got in hand a nauseous mess'. It was impossible anywhere on the ship, to escape the heavy, musty smell of curry, vanilla, and exotic spices which intensified in the hot, airless, sub-tropical evenings.

The small lounge, appropriated as the officers' mess, was, from Durban to Port Tewfik, monopolised by the M.O. (a man without charm and possessed of a squeaky, piping tenor voice) who, inspired by the lusty lady on the jetty, considered it his duty either to preserve our sanity, or to hasten losing it, by giving us excerpts from his repertoire of ballads. The repertoire, which was limited, was no deterrent to our determined songster, who repeated every item without encouragement or provocation from the select band of senior officers clustered around the tone-deaf O.C. Troops. The bridge-school, of which I was one, sitting as far out of sight (and earshot) as possible, endured the torment, and played some disgraceful bridge. Long before we reached Port Tewfik I was lost in admiration for 'Maud', who twice nightly, for three weeks, had resisted all entreaties to 'Come into the garden'!

On the balmy evening of March 28th (a date I well remember) I was leaning on the boat-rail looking at the lights and the dim coast line of Madagascar, when my depressing thoughts were interrupted and further saddened by the Radio Officer, who came on deck to announce that he had just 'caught' a news flash – 'Rachmaninoff had died in California'.

On arrival at Tewfik we were whisked unceremoniously to a transit camp which wasn't near anywhere except the middle of a hundred miles of desert: I slept for two nights on the sand in a mosquito-net as the first line of defence against a very special species of insect – the Egyptian fly. This bold and brazen pest breeds in countless millions in arid areas which might with difficulty sustain a couple of celibate midges.

When our contingent arrived at Group H.Q. in Heliopolis, the German threat to Egypt was over and Rommel's forces were in full flight towards Tripoli: it was no surprise that very few of us were posted to units in the Cairo area, the remainder were immediately despatched to Libya, presumably for the build-up to the invasion of Sicily and the

Italian mainland. For no apparent reason I was posted to III Maintenance Unit situated at Tura-el-Asmant on the eastern bank of the Nile, about ten miles south of Cairo. 'Tura-el-Asmant' literally means 'mountain of cement' and adjacent to III M.U. was the biggest, busiest and ugliest cement works in the world, taking the fullest advantage (for 24 hours daily) of just another of Mohammed's great general prophecies 'that Allah will provide' – free! – a rash promise which presumably in this case did not include the bags.

One of the fringe benefits of this hideous factory was its rail-link with Cairo. The proximity of the camp and the frequency of a cheap, express service to Babeluk Station (Cairo) provided RAF personnel with easy access to that city's dubious pleasures – on pay days.

With the exception of a ten-month posting to an army camp near Aden, I spent the whole of my overseas tour at Tura. The Egyptian Government and the RAF occupied a mountain of solid rock, horse-shoe shaped and beautifully camouflaged by centuries of fine, white, powdered sand. The road which led into the Waadi (valley) separating the open ends of the mountain, had been constructed by British engineers (who never before in their lives had had building material more conveniently to hand). The 'Burma Road' as it was inappropriately called, was shaped like a serpent's tongue, each section of it connecting the mouths of caves hewn out of the solid rock by Pharaoh's stone-masons 5,300 years ago.

The indeterminate number of caves occupied and heavily guarded by Egyptian security forces on the opposite side of the Waadi housed all the treasures from the Egyptian Museum, which included Tutankhamun: before the end of the war the treasures were gradually restored to their original places and once again on public exhibition.

The RAF occupied 62 caves, (after they had been cleared of centuries of rubble) which housed workshops for the repair and re-channelling of aero-engines and propellers recovered from the Western Desert, and the storage of radar, radio and all the equipment necessary to support the aircraft employed in the Middle East.

The cave in which I spent the major part of my tour of duty at Tura was the longest (496 yards) and in it was stored the radar and radio equipment. Although the length, width and height of all the caves varied enormously, the entrances were identical in shape and the ceilings bore the clean, symmetrical chisel marks, uneroded by 53 centuries of time, left behind by the stone-masons who cut the cubes of stone with which the great Pyramids of Giza had been built.

For ten hours of every working day at III M.U. I had a very handy ledge at my elbow, left beautifully carved by the Pharaohs, upon which stood a very expensive radio-receiver, on trial from stock: I heard almost every note broadcast by the B.B.C. Northern Orchestra in the latter stages of the war.

In the evenings, I had the opportunity, from my tent in the Waadi, of watching a big red sun set behind the Pyramids on the western bank of the Nile. Having had daily experience of 'where' the stone came from, with just a notion of 'how' it was procured, and for 'what' purpose, I was mystified at first, and later (when I visited Giza) staggered by the immensity of the undertaking. In spite of my insatiable appetite for questioning the mining engineers, who frequently inspected the caves, (particularly mine, the longest) I got nothing from them beyond admission that 'those masons had instincts for stresses like spiders building a web'.

One of the caves was aptly named the 'Cathedral Cave' because of the perfect symmetry of the pillars of rock cunningly left by the masons to support the 'nave' as they dug (and abandoned for no apparent reason) little 'chapels' to the left and right of the main span: the other 61 caves had similar characteristics, but the tunnels off the main shaft appeared to be willy-nilly affairs varying in depth from 10 to 50 yards.

My first sight-seeing trip to the Giza Pyramids was more in the nature of a pilgrimage than an excursion. Having speculated for so long on how the huge quantity of precisely-cut stone ever reached the mouths of the caves, how it reached the Waadi hundreds of feet below was yet another 'imponderable' as was its transportation to the Nile (a mile-and-a-half away): it was then, presumably, floated down that ancient waterway and again hauled up the left bank to the plateau of blue granite upon which the Pyramids were built. At the foot of the plateau stands a very fashionable Hotel, which only a few weeks before had played host to one of the summit meetings between Churchill, Stalin and Roosevelt. It is impossible not to be impressed by the first sight of the Pyramids, which can only be approached by a two-mile stretch of perfectly straight dual-carriageway road and tramtrack from the Giza bridge in Cairo. I travelled by tram, which is a unique experience in Cairo: they resemble two bee-hives linked together, with hundreds of natives jumping on and off the running boards, avoiding the conductor, whose hopeless job it was to collect the fares. The only space I ever saw on a Cairo tram was that immediately surrounding the nimble, cursing conductor. The trams were without windows and doors: some would say they were unnecessary because Egypt enjoyed the perfect climate, others, including myself, were of the opinion that it was vitally important to be without them, because Egyptians may, in some circumstances, just about tolerate the sight of one another, but they cannot stand the smell.

In consequence of the custom of fare-evasion, I found it easy to get a seat on the tram to Giza by looking for the conductor and surprising him by paying the fare. As the tram eventually came to the end of its tortuous wriggling about the busy streets and turned into the straight, the Pyramids appeared like a picture postcard – but at a distance of two miles they were of incredible proportions. My amazement increased with every hundred yards of the journey – one of the Pyramids (the Chephren) appeared to have withstood the ravages of time with perfectly smooth surfaces, like a bedroom ceiling. The Cheops (in the foreground of the group) was, when viewed for the first time and from such a great distance, less perfect than the Chephren, but what at first appeared to be natural erosion gradually revealed the miracle of how the Great Pyramid had been built. Despoilers had over the centuries stripped the outer casing of the Tura limestone and removed several courses (and capstone) from the apex. The jagged edges of the casing began to take shape and symmetry, as if the pyramid had been built of sugar cubes which grew in size to kiddies' building bricks with every breathtaking mile of my approach to the realisation that the smallest block of stone weighed 2½ tons. An estimated 2,300,000 of them weighing up to 15 tons had been used in constructing the outer casing of a monument 755 feet along each of its four sides, rising to a height of 481 feet at its apex, and occupying an area of 13 acres.

The missing capstone, and the 31 feet at its apex which are barely noticeable would, as I have been reliably informed, accommodate a substantial pair of semi-detached houses: that is if the tenants could live and breathe at the height of Blackpool Tower.

I quickly abandoned the idea of scaling the mountain of stone – each stepping stone was well over 4 feet in height and although I managed the third layer at great risk to my bare knees and shoe-toes, one glance at the remaining 700 feet of the climb in a sun temperature of 120° was all the deterrent I needed – I walked around it instead.

Tourists were in short supply at Giza and the Dragomen (official guides) outnumbered the few service-men who were there that day. The Dragomen (like Pooh Bah in the Mikado) are all 6 feet in height, weigh 16 stone and wear long green galabeers tied at the middle with a yellow sash: they are entitled (like Tommy Cooper) to wear the red fez of exalted rank, and they all brandish an evil-looking fly-swatter which serves the dual purpose of disturbing the flies and flaying the living daylights out of the unofficial guides who outnumber them by ten to one, threatening to share the easy pickings which Allah so generously provided for them at all the Pharaohs' burial grounds.

I, like half a dozen of my colleagues, fell for the oldest trick known to this cunning breed. The Dragomen do not undertake to guide anyone to the sacred Cheops burial chamber by means of the Robber's Hole – they loftily delegate their authority to one of their less distinguished (and much thinner) colleagues, for the obvious reason that none of the Dragomen could have squeezed his fat belly through the first hole on the tortuous and very dangerous 200 feet climb through jagged solid rock! Before the appointed scraggy little worm would begin the guided tour (which none of us dared to miss) there were certain conditions which inevitably had to be met – the price was fixed at 10 piastres (in advance), which was cheap (to begin with) but in order not to invoke the wrath of the Pharaohs, or because of firerisk, we had to relinquish all matches, torches, cigarette lighters or other means of ignition – and so the six lambs went very meekly to the fleecing of their lives! The guide wriggled his way through the first hole and made sufficient headway to allow the last of his victims to bid farewell to daylight or any chance to be heard if any of us should make a futile cry for help. The only advice we had from our guide was "Assib-a-shwier" – "Take a little care", quite unnecessary in our predicament since we were able to stand upright for only brief spells: the rest of the eerie journey was spent squirming through cracks and holes and up short rickety ladders but always with the terrifying thought that above our heads were 12,000,000 (give or take a few thousand) tons of rock. Any feelings of relief we may have experienced at being able to stand up or to be reunited as a group were quickly dispelled by the guide, who extinguished his light (a magnesium tape) at every one of them, to re-negotiate his fee! I would gladly have given £5 for a box of matches at any of our resting places.

We eventually arrived, much wiser and poorer, at the Burial Chamber. The empty Sarcophagus was the only thing in it, as we expected, but this time there was some real purpose behind the guide extinguishing his light. At an angle of about 45° a tiny shaft of brilliant sunlight shone from the polished granite wall of the tomb onto the head of the Sarcophagus, like a laser beam. The air-shaft (which archaeologists tell us allowed the spirit of Cheops access to the outside world) was cut through 200 feet of solid rock: it is also an astronomical miracle. On one night only in mid-summer and then only for a few minutes, there can be seen from the Chamber the new crescent moon, cradling (as it were) three stars exactly as they appear on the white emblem on the green background of the Egyptian flag. When this astronomical phenomenon occurs (I have forgotten whether or not it is the new moon of June or July) the Muslims begin their annual Feast – or is it Fast? – of Ramadan, which lasts a month.

When I reached safety again and escaped the threats of the guide who, in spite of taking all my money, screamed that he had been robbed and all his chicos would starve to death, I resisted becoming involved again that day and taking one of the many camels offered to me 'to see the Sphinx'. I left that pleasure for another time.

The trips I made to Sakkara, Memphis and Luxor were spread over a period of three years and were in many cases organised by the Welfare Officer at III M.U. with transport and a knowledgeable guide provided. The guide, whether knowledgeable or not, was essential on all sight-seeing trips in Egypt to warn off, fight off and protect us from the swarms of persistent natives (like the flies) who regarded a tourist as a gift from Allah.

At Memphis I lingered for too long in a cave, classified in the guide book as 'The Tomb of the Sacred Bulls'. The rest of our party had taken a cursory glance at the 24 empty blue granite sarcophagi (with the lids ajar) and moved on to look at statues of Rameses II and what remained of his ruined city. If my memory serves me correctly, the sarcophagi (which were huge), were ranged in a circle like a 24-hour clock, and only those near the mouth of the cave were clearly visible. My curiosity was richly rewarded, and my amazement increased with each one I examined, until I could no longer see. The coffins, which were identical in shape, appeared at first to have been assembled from slabs of beautifully polished marble approximately 6" thick, but to my astonishment there were no joints – they had been miraculously carved (coffins and lids alike) out of solid hunks of granite. Nowhere, after minute examination, inside and out, could I find a scratch or a blemish: the inside corners were perfect right-angles, as if cut with a blade and polished into each recess with needle sharpness. The lids had fitted the coffins so snugly that they were originally air-tight and to suggest that the craftsmen who built them worked to a margin of a thousandth of an inch would be an insult – they appeared to have been moulded out of glass by a machine which the mind of man has not yet conceived.

I left the Tomb of the Sacred Bulls as I had previously turned my back on the Pyramids at Giza, with the same unsolvable problem – how was it done? This time, I was perhaps more impressed by the patience and skill of the ancient craftsmen who produced such beautiful (although useless) works of art than I had hitherto been with the colossal monuments at Giza which were constructed, according to the fatuous speculation of countless Egyptologists, with nothing more tangible than a length of fibre rope, a few copper chisels, some rollers, an inclined plane and the sweat of 100,000 slaves. The credibility of all theories concerning the monuments of Ancient Egypt were finally put to flight (in my mind at least) when I returned from the last of my brief sight – seeing trips to Sakkara and Aswan.

As on previous trips, I left the official party who were engrossed in the bits of official information about uninteresting bits of ruined sculpture and wandered off to a rocky plateau half hidden by loose, shifting white sand: I was intrigued by seeing heads and shoulders of native 'guides' scurrying about in pursuit of a few tourists – a certain indication that there was something worth investigating, which proved to be the case. I scrambled up the slope and joined in the excitement: the plateau consisted of a narrow perimeter of fine sand which was very slowly, like a gigantic egg-timer, sifting (at an angle of 45°) into a rectangular hole about 40 yards long and 8 yards wide cut perfectly symmetrically out of solid rock. The angles were square and the walls of the stone grave still showing the familiar chisel marks were perpendicular to a depth of 160 ft. The last piece of information was provided by the 'guides' who were willing to hold the feet of any inquisitive tourist for 10 piastres – 'just to have a peep over the edge'. For another 10 piastres they would have been willing 'to let go'. Any approach to the edge would have been suicide and having had previous experience of the integrity of native 'guides' I had to forgo the thrill of looking into the pit. Two blocks of stone, each weighing approximately 200 tons had originally been cut and lifted out of this grave: one of them ultimately became Cleopatra's Needle which now stands on the Thames Embankment and the other, I believe, is in New York.

Cleopatra's Needle, after it had been suitably trimmed and cut to its present size and shape now weighs 140 tons: it took a year of involved and advanced 19th Century technology to transport this monument from Alexandria to London – how long it took the masons (4,000 years ago) to dig two such monsters from a depth of 160 ft. and haul them to the surface is of little consequence beside the imponderable question of 'How was it done?' and 'With what equipment?'.

The organised sight-seeing excursions described in detail were restricted to four half-days early in my 'tour of duty' in the Middle East and perhaps stimulated by inescapable daily contact with the amazing 'diggings' in the Tura caves and the spectacle of the Giza Pyramids which I could see, across the fertile Nile Valley, from any part of the camp. Within a few weeks of becoming established at III M.U. I joined with any escapist group of junior officers who preferred an evening out in Cairo to the nauseating rounds of losing at 'bridge' and drinking oneself silly in the C.O.'s 'School'. Transport, on repayment, was available every evening from the Officers' Mess, or there was the fast electric train service from Tura-el-Asmant to Babeluk in Cairo: there was safety in numbers on the trains since well over a thousand 'other ranks' were nightly in search of whatever diversions Cairo had to offer – and there were plenty.

The present TV series 'It ain't half hot Mum' had its counterpart in the Army Barracks at 'Kasa el Nil' in Cairo in 1943, except that the Sgt. Major was trying, in this case, noisily and unsuccessfully to instil some discipline into a band of professional musicians who could never have been taught to use firearms against the enemy, or trusted to handle them amongst friends.

In this army-band (which scarcely ever had a parade, or a roll-call, or a rehearsal, or a concert) was Cecil Beattie, a member of the B.B.C. Symphony Orchestra. On one of my early 'evenings out' in Cairo I met him, and Wilf Collinge, a colleague in the Hallé Orchestra, in the Café Riche in Suliman Pasha Street and discussed the ambitious plans which were already well advanced for the formation of the Cairo Symphony Orchestra, of which we were to become the principals.

Group Captain Stubbs (head of RAF Welfare in the Middle East) was the organiser of this venture, which had the blessing of the A.O.C. in Chief Middle East. The build-up of forces, of all nationalities, for the Western Desert conflict (not yet over) was enormous, and entertainment for the restless troops awaiting re-deployment in the Italian campaign was a priority in the minds of high-ranking officers in Cairo, with the single exception of the C.O. III M.U. who resented his instruction from High Command to release me 'for the more important duty of playing with the Cairo Symphony Orchestra'!

He made his views quite clear to me before I played my first concert in Cairo and his displeasure lasted for well over a year: it was no surprise to me to be 'posted' at a few hours' notice to a tiny scrap-metal dump about 20 miles from Alexandria. I spent only three days in exile (long enough to be missed in Cairo) and my posting back to III M.U. was accomplished by driving an empty 3-ton truck along the (fortunately straight) desert road to Cairo and the transport yard at III M.U. I learned from the Adjutant that the C.O. had had his fingers rapped and was feeling rather sore at the failure of his ruse to rid himself of the 'fiddler'! Some little time later the A.O.C. (Sir Sholto Douglas) returned to England and the following day, ironically, I was duty officer to receive at the hands of the orderly-room corporal the signal marked 'NO APPEAL' and 'IMMEDIATE' posting me to Aden! I returned to III M.U. for the third time after the war in the Far East ended in the Autumn of 1945, but this time I was 'boarded' out of Aden for medical reasons. A condition known in the medical profession as Furunculosis (incurable boils) had not in my case responded to the new miracle cure of penicillin, and I was flown back to Cairo (via Luxor) where my 48 boils disappeared without a scar in the more humane Egyptian climate. The 'atmosphere' at III M.U. was less explosive on my return to duty. The vindictive C.O. had been replaced and the reasons for his resentment were no longer remembered by the personnel I found on the Camp. The Cairo Symphony Orchestra no longer existed and the smaller combinations in which I had formerly made a great deal of music were breaking up – the war was over and the exodus back home which had already begun was gaining momentum.

Chapter XIV

The meeting with Wilf Collinge and Cecil Beattie at the Café Riche in Suliman Pasha Street in the spring of 1943 was the beginning of a two-year period of involvement in almost every aspect of music-making, from the R.A.F. Dance Band (where I first met Hugo Rignold) to weekly broadcasts with the Forces Network and regular symphony concerts with the Cairo Symphony Orchestra.

I may have created the quite erroneous impression (in the last chapter) that I was officially 'released' from duty at III M.U. in order to play music in Cairo. In truth, I worked in the Tura caves from 7 a.m. until 5.30 p.m. daily (except Sunday) and 'released' myself from the ribaldry of the Officers' Mess in the evenings, by escaping into Cairo, where, for the first time in four years, I had the opportunity to hold a musical instrument in my hands and talk 'shop' among friends. The choice of which instrument I was destined to play for the next two years was made at the first 'get together' of service personnel flown into Cairo by R.A.F. Welfare and seconded to H.Q. for fulltime duty with the Symphony Orchestra.

The most likely person to play the viola among the distinguished group of string players already established was Hugo Rignold, who had, until the outbreak of war, spent his whole career playing the viola in Jack Hylton's Dance Orchestra. He was a 'natural' to direct the R.A.F. Dance Band in Cairo and he was conducting this combination when I first met him but, in the light of his subsequent meteoric post-war success as a conductor with the Covent Garden Ballet and the Liverpool Philharmonic, it is not difficult to appreciate his reluctance to play the viola and banish himself to the obscurity of that section in a modern orchestra, when fame could be more readily achieved by playing the violin. When it became known that I could swell the existing ranks of the Cairo Symphony Orchestra, I, quite truthfully, answered 'Yes' to the question 'Do you play the viola?' and was immediately pitchforked into the position of Principal for the duration of my stay in Cairo.

Of the violinists already assembled for exclusive musical duty in Cairo were Joseph Shadwick and Charles McKeown (leader and sub-leader of the Covent Garden Opera House Orchestra), George Deason, an Australian (leader of the B.B.C. Concert Orchestra) and a young Palestinian recruit, Zvi Zeitlin (a virtuoso pupil of Heifetz).

Hugo Rignold, in spite of his comparative inexperience in the field of serious music, and in the teeth of distinguished opposition for the post, had been appointed leader of the newly-formed Cairo Symphony Orchestra for the inaugural concert on Saturday, April 3rd, 1943, at which Lance Dosser played the Grieg and Joseph Huttel conducted. The first concert at which I played was on Thursday, June 17th. Having volunteered to play the viola, there arose, in my mind at least, the insuperable problems of where such an instrument could be obtained and how its safety could possibly be guaranteed, either at Tura or in transit in this land of Ali Baba and his forty million well-trained thieves!

My dilemma lasted only a few days: R.A.F. Welfare provided a beautiful instrument for my exclusive use and Wilf Collinge (Double Bass) took upon himself the responsibility of its safe custody, and also (which was invaluable to me) became the only means of communication I had with E.N.S.A. and R.A.F. Welfare. The working arrangement was simple: at 6 p.m. almost every evening Wilf met me at Babeluk Station, with the viola and the minutest details of where I was required to play it, or without it, in which case, to brief me on my next commitment. I was thus enabled to lead a double (although busy) life; one, irksome and often unpleasant in the Tura Caves from 7 a.m. until 5.30 p.m., and the other from 6 p.m. until midnight in Cairo, pursuing a wide variety of musical activities, often surprising, but always with immense pleasure.

One of the first 'surprise' encounters with Charles McKeown occurred at Babeluk Station when Wilf Collinge greeted me with the words "We're playing with Charlie to-night," and handed me the viola! We hauled ourselves into a 30 cwt. army truck with painted signs "N.A.A.F.I" and "E.N.S.A.", driven by a service-man: it was obviously a well-organised and authenticated trip. Inside the vehicle I was introduced to Charles McKeown, George Deason, Jimmy Sherran (pianist at the Stratford Memorial Theatre) and Cecil Beattie (B.B.C. Symphony Orchestra), whom I had already met before. I cannot remember precisely what was said, but 'Charlie' made it quite clear that a 'viola player was a luxury' – 'I was most welcome' – and 'I should be very busy from now on'. After a few pleasantries all round, the truck stopped at the Continental Hotel in order to pick up a young soprano and we sped off to Tel-al-Kabir, where Charlie's sextet (and soloist) gave a rather smooth concert to a most appreciative audience of troops. Charlie's remark 'You're going to be busy from now on' was an insidious one – 'You're going to be very useful to us from now on' would have been nearer the truth. The sextet was extremely versatile – easily transported as an entity in a 30 cwt. truck with stands and folios of music, and E.N.S.A. was able to arrange camp concerts at a few hours' notice. It was also adaptable enough to provide incidental music in the pit at the Cairo Opera House whenever 'Plays' were flown out from the

Hugo Rignold conducting the Cairo Symphony Orchestra

West End of London: it also complemented the skeleton orchestras which sometimes arrived with West End 'musicals'.

Being as busy as the rest of the sextet would not have created problems for me, but Charlie 'landed' a contract to broadcast a programme of light music from 7.15 p.m. to 7.45 p.m. in the Forces Network (under the auspices of Egyptian State Broadcasting) every Friday evening. We were to have a 'resident' singer, this time a baritone – Jack Higginson, who was to be featured in the 'centre-spot', singing in a wide variety of styles from Jerome Kern to opera.

I had very good reasons for not flying quite so far 'over the moon' as my colleagues: Charlie, with great diplomacy, pointed out the obvious fact that 'We cannot expect the soloist to sing his songs with piano accompaniment – not in a show like ours' and he went on very slyly to add 'and we need some special arrangements for ourselves'. Looking straight at me, he gave me what he considered to be the good news: 'There are no copyright laws or performing rights to worry about in this series and E.N.S.A. will provide all the manuscript you need!'

Admittedly the combination for which I made the 'special arrangements' was small, but time was a commodity in very short supply in my double life: my nights off from playing the viola in Cairo were spent in my tent at Tura, writing out manuscript parts for the sextet. Orchestrating the songs and ballads in Jack Higginson's repertoire was a

The Charles McKeown Sextet – on tour and in the studio

tedious duty, and converting the Kreisler violin solos (published by Schotts) into small orchestral pieces required very little imagination, but I make no apology for the arrangements I made to feature Jimmy Sherran, the pianist. He was a charming, modest, introvert chap, disinclined to make conversation on our trips to camp concerts and equally disinclined to complain about the dilapidated condition of the N.A.A.F.I. pianos he was obliged to play. Not until we began the series of broadcasts and I heard him doodling and practising on the Bechsteins in the studios was I first made aware of his enormous talent: he played Chopin Etudes and Preludes brilliantly, and it gave me a great deal of pleasure and musical satisfaction to provide a string background to the Chopin pieces he chose to play in the programmes. (Musicologists and Historians have, for the last hundred years, dismissed Chopin's two piano concertos as being sonatas with crude orchestral accompaniment.)

The arrangements I made, (between fifty and sixty) without fee and by the light of two torches in my tent at Tura, were of no commercial value: they continued to be used by the sextet after my posting to Aden in September, 1944, but on my return to Cairo in August, 1945 the fighting was over and the sextet disbanded – what became of my manuscripts I shall never know.

When I arrived in Cairo in April 1943, the newly-formed Cairo Symphony Orchestra had given only two concerts: at the third I was agreeably surprised by the standard of performance and amazed at the incongruity of this ad hoc combination. Egyptian State Broadcasting sponsored the C.S.O. and provided its own resident orchestra consisting entirely of Bulgarians, Hungarians and Rumanian refugees (all brilliant but highly volatile players): this contingent appeared in uniform – shapeless shirts and slacks of drab khaki cotton, adorned only by badges of rank. The remainder of the hotch-potch orchestra (mainly wind players) appeared by kind permission of H.M. King Farouk – his Palace Band, resplendent in shining buttons and rows of medals, no doubt earned for bravery in battles unrecorded in the history books. To add the final touch of distinction to this comic ensemble each player wore a red fez (like Tommy Cooper) throughout the performance!

The conductor (Joseph Huttel) was the well-established director of music for Egyptian State Broadcasting and had, during decades of residence in Cairo, acquired fluency in Arabic and English: the problem of communication at rehearsals did not exist for this remarkable man. He was a prolific composer and several of his large scale works were included in the early concerts of the C.S.O. As a composer he had not acquired a distinctive style because much of his work, fundamentally rooted in late 19th century Romanticism, was marred by half-hearted, uncourageous experiments in the 'new music'. Unfortunately for Mr. Huttel there have been many radical changes in 'style' in the last hundred years, and composition has little merit, or hope of survival, if it sits comfortably astride the fence and occasionally takes a 'lucky dip' at modernity.

It was certainly not as a composer that I found Mr. Huttel remarkable: he was a very good conductor who commanded respect and achieved disciplined, lively performances. In spite of his advancing years he was by no means senile, and there was no reason to doubt that his tenure of office as conductor of the C.S.O. would endure for years, except perhaps that Mr. Huttel had already spent too many of his years in Egypt. The devastating combination of sun and climate (with perhaps a little assistance from the gin bottle) had brought him to the sublime

Some members of the Cairo Symphony Orchestra

condition which can only be adequately described as 'Allakeefik', a delightful Arabic word of infinite subtlety, which means 'let the world go by' or 'never do anything today which can be put off until tomorrow' or 'never do anything likely to disturb the blood pressure or increase the pulse rate' or 'never stand up to do anything if it can be done sitting down' or 'worry causes ulcers – don't do it!' The state of 'Allakeefik' into which Mr. Huttel had gently subsided was in many ways similar to Stage III of the System referred to on page (ii) where the victim is soundly asleep, with his eyes wide open, and at the same time looks intelligent!

Mr. Huttel arrived at the Ewart Memorial Hall for the performance on Thursday, June 17th, 1943 in a little deeper 'Allakeefik' than usual, and quite incapable of conducting the concert: he had also forgotten – or lost – the score of Dvorák's 'New World' Symphony, which occupied the whole of the second half. A small group of Principals met to discuss the minor crisis into which Mr. Huttel's condition (and the missing score) had thrown us: the meeting was brief – I offered to conduct the Dvorák from memory, which brought a very sharp retort from Hugo Rignold – "If *you* conduct, any Tom, Dick or Harry will want to do it!" And that is precisely what happened – HE did! – but with a hastily changed programme. On his own admission he didn't know the 'New World', but having seized the opportunity of conducting the orchestra he relentlessly held on to the position for the duration of the war, and further enhanced his reputation by short spells of guest conducting in Palestine, Johannesburg and Cape Town. Charles McKeown succeeded him as leader of the C.S.O., and in the routine concerts which followed, the celebrity soloists aroused most attention. They were invariably 'birds of passage', caught, as it were, in transit and engaged at short notice to play with the C.S.O. Gina Bachauer, who in 1943 was young, dark and very beautiful, appeared at two of the concerts playing the Grieg and the second Rachmaninoff concertos.

There were two concerts on the 13th and 14th of November, 1943, which brought me into close contact with a brilliant young Palestinian violinist who had volunteered for non-combatant duty in the R.A.F. and was attached to H.Q. Cairo in order that his unique talents could be utilised in the C.S.O.

Zvi Zeitlin had returned to his native Palestine from the U.S.A., where he studied the violin with Heifetz: the results were obvious, although in the early days of our acquaintance he irritated me by 'showing off' in the bandroom and doing nothing at all on the platform, where his inexperience as an orchestral player and irrepressible bravado led him to make mistakes. By the time we appeared together in the Quartet of the 'Introduction & Allegro' by Elgar I had learned to forgive his showmanship and admire his playing. During one of our rehearsals for the Elgar, Zvi Zeitlin became extremely communicative about Heifetz as a teacher and went on to relate a quite remarkable 'session' which he (and two other pupils) had experienced in Heifetz's New York apartment. There was nothing unusual about the lesson which Zeitlin and his two colleagues had received in the morning, but as they were about to leave the flat, Heifetz invited them to return at 6 p.m. that evening and "sit in the window-seat as quiet as three mice! – you will probably learn something."

The prospect of 'learning something' may not have appealed to Zvi Zeitlin, but the mystery certainly did. He arrived in good time and established himself in the window-seat: the rest of the evening's entertainment is best told in his own words. "It soon became apparent that we were about to hear a session of 'quartets', and a long one, by the size of the pile of music thrown on the floor next to the chair where, presumably, the First Violin would sit. Heifetz set out four chairs and carefully placed three music stands in front of three of them: instead of looking for another stand he took out his violin and practised, whilst everyone waited for the quartet to assemble. Kreisler was the first to arrive, followed by Feuerman: not far behind them came a 'little fat man' with a jovial face and a huge moustache – he carried what must have been a viola under his arm, but I didn't know him. After a few brief pleasantries they sat in their well-accustomed places and tuned their instruments – the little man at his place without a music stand: parts were handed out to those who required them and agreement was soon reached on which quartet they would play. The session lasted about five hours and although there was a serious application to the actual playing there was a relaxed atmosphere and NO BOSS – Heifetz and Kreisler played First Violin alternately and little was said as they 'dipped' into a wide variety of quartets, from Haydn and Beethoven to Debussy, Ravel and Bartók."

Zvi Zeitlin's amazement at the little man with the viola not requiring music was quite genuine – it had obviously happened many times before, and was taken for granted that whatever was played, Pierre Monteux (as he later discovered) would not require a part.

Another aspect of Zeitlin's vivid description of the unique quartet session was the conversation between Heifetz and Kreisler during the short periods of relaxation and enforced stretching of legs. The subject of the conversation was the Mendelssohn Violin Concerto and the ease with which this wonderful piece was introduced appeared to Zeitlin to be a continuation of discussions they had previously had many times. "I used to finger it like this," said Heifetz, playing a passage for Kreisler, "but now I find this better." "I tried that for a while, but now I find this better," said Kreisler, and so the conversation would be dropped and resumed intermittently throughout the evening. Zeitlin was of the opinion that the passages sounded marvellous however they were fingered and he wondered why the two greatest violinists in the world should be 'bothered' by the niggling difficulties of the Mendelssohn Violin Concerto.

I found the story extremely interesting: the Mendelssohn deserves to be well-played, but rarely is, in fact, I have never in my life heard a performance approaching perfect. It is regarded in most 'Academies' as a useful teaching piece which slots conveniently between the Max Bruch and the Beethoven in order of difficulty: it is universally played in public with an over-sentimentalised slow movement leading to an irresponsible, hell-for-leather last movement which hurtles to self-destruction!

Kreisler died a short while after the 'session' which Zeitlin so vividly described to me, but on two occasions since the war I have had confirmation that Heifetz still continues to be 'concerned' about the Mendelssohn. Clifford Knowles, who, like myself, is a great admirer of Heifetz, attended one of his rare concert appearances in this country at the Royal Albert Hall on June 5th, 1949. Sitting with Clifford at the rehearsal were three other distinguished violinists: Raymond Cohen, Albert Sammons and Alan Loveday. Albert Sammons was the only person who had been permitted to see Heifetz in the green-room and he joined his colleagues in the stalls having been paid the greatest compliment of his life! In his presence, Heifetz had seriously asked the impresario who arranged the concert, "Why do you engage me to play this piece when Sammons is available?" Throughout the interview he practised the Mendelssohn relentlessly, until the moment when the steward knocked on the green-room door to announce that he was 'wanted on the platform'. Heifetz walked resolutely up the stairs, TO PLAY THE ELGAR!

In another instance, as recently as 1972, Clifford Knowles (who was at the time leader of the Royal Liverpool Philharmonic) had further proof of Heifetz' continuing anxiety about the Mendelssohn. The soloist at one of the Philharmonic's concerts was Joseph Sivo (one of the leaders of the Vienna Philharmonic Orchestra) who had recently been leading the Orchestra at a concert in Los Angeles. The main work in the programme had been 'Ein Heldenleben' and Sivo, who had obviously acquitted himself exceedingly well in the difficult violin solo, had received a visit back-stage from no less a person than Heifetz (who had been unnoticed in the audience). "He was very complimentary about my playing," said Sivo, "and the conversation drifted to the problem of nerves." "Of all the pieces in my repertoire," said Heifetz, "I am always nervous when I play the Mendelssohn – it is VERY NASTY!!"

I met Zvi Zeitlin many more times in Cairo but we never again had an opportunity to talk: after the war he visited England three times without renewing our Cairo acquaintance, and it is unlikely that we shall meet again – he has settled in a teaching post at the Eastman School of Music in Rochester, New York.

Chapter XV

Although I gradually became involved in many aspects of music-making in Cairo between April, 1943 and October, 1944, I remained indebted to Wilf Collinge for his patience in meeting me at Babeluk Station; taking the responsibility of the borrowed viola and providing every detail of the engagements which (as a part-timer) I was able to fulfil.

With the Charles McKeown sextet, only the camp concerts within a radius of 30 miles from Cairo were hastily arranged by E.N.S.A.: the appearances in Cairo were well organised and soon settled into regular Sunday evening open-air concerts or the Friday broadcasts already described. There were no 'clashes' with the Cairo Symphony Orchestra, for the obvious reason that the members of the sextet were 'Principals' in the C S.O.

One other activity in which the McKeown sextet became wholly involved was the provision of incidental music for short seasons of Repertory and to augment the 'skeleton' orchestras accompanying the 'West End' musicals regularly flown in from England. The shows were lavishly staged at the Cairo Opera House and one of them, a superb presentation of 'The Merry Widow', packed the theatre for a three-week season. Act III – 'Maxim's' – utilised the considerable facilities of the Cairo Opera House stage (which equals the auditorium in size) and the effect of depth was further enhanced by a row of six brilliantly-lit chandeliers, cunningly diminishing in size from front to rear. At every performance, there was an involuntary gasp of astonishment from the audience when the curtain rose, and the applause, which was quite spontaneous, temporarily stopped the show! Other 'musicals' which followed intermittently ran for one week and proved to be so uninteresting that I can remember the title of only one of them – 'Rose Marie'.

The season of Repertory was particularly enjoyable for me: the sextet was involved in a few minutes of incidental music before the curtain and between the acts. Two National Anthems were played at every performance, which meant staying until the curtain fell: this was no hardship in my case – I enjoyed every word and inflection and after eighteen repetitive shows I began to admire a great many of the tricks, and appreciate the technique of acting.

The first play in the series was 'Night Must Fall', in which Emlyn Williams played the part of Danny with great relish since he had written the part for himself. The other parts were superbly played, particularly the terrified old lady, whose name has, to my shame, escaped me. I cannot recall the second play, which I believe was by J.B. Priestley, but the third was a sparkling bit of Chelsea froth by Noel Coward – 'Blithe Spirit', of which I can remember only two typical lines, (at the breakfast table) – 'Anything interesting in the Times this morning?' 'Don't be foolish, darling!'

In spite of the regularity of the sessions of plays and musicals at the Cairo Opera House I never became familiar with the tortuous labyrinth of corridors between the stage door and the orchestra pit. Repeatedly losing my way brought some singular rewards: the Stage Director was a friendly soul who in the early days, and with great patience, guided my erring steps to the pit. Later, when I strayed – perhaps deliberately – into forbidden areas, he explained some of the mechanical wonders of his switchboard, which resembled the signal box at Euston Station. He was certainly not boasting when he told me that the stage could be set in a few seconds for every opera in the repertoire. Above the stage were layers of neat rolls of backcloths and scenery of all shapes and sizes, numbered and catalogued. Locked at each end in an elaborate system of runnels, they could be released at the touch of a button, presumably the right one and in the right sequence.

The 'Sorcerer's Apprentice' crossed my wicked mind every time I passed the switchboard!

The opportune moment did eventually arrive when I mentioned (with some temerity) the date Christmas Eve, 1871, and the great occasion of the first performance of Verdi's 'Aida'. The Director was agreeably surprised at my interest in this historic event and with little or no encouragement led me to a remote corner of his vast storeroom to display the 'props.' used in the original production. The chariots were beginning to look rather tatty and the 'stones', which had buried Radames and Aida alive in the final scene, appeared to be losing weight rapidly, but I nevertheless spent a long time in euphoria, re-creating the triumphal procession of 300 Arabs, and all the crowd scenes which the enormous stage would that night have engulfed with such effect.

The auditorium of the Cairo Opera House was as traditionally built as any Opera House in Europe, except perhaps for the presence of the two very grand Royal Boxes on opposite sides of the stage overlooking the orchestra pit. At least once a week King Farouk attended (having arrived punctually) and occupied his own box. Queen Farida, who was distractingly beautiful, exquisitely dressed and bejewelled, attended regularly but *never* on the same night as King Farouk, and occupied the opposite box. Each Royal Box (when occupied) was cunningly illuminated by a spotlight on the royal occupant throughout the performance. Needless to say this greatly enhanced the effect of Queen Farida's diamonds and beauty: half the orchestra, fortunate to be facing her direction, were less than efficient on these occasions. My position in the orchestra pit (playing the viola) faced the opposite direction and I was singularly unimpressed with what I was obliged to look at!

The Opera House was one of many fine buildings in Cairo surrounded by boulevards and gardens. The stage door was the vantage point, particularly on leaving the theatre at midnight, for a tantalising panoramic view of Cairo's Clubs and Cabarets, expensive and strictly out of bounds to 'other ranks'. Beyond the facade of glittering signs was an area of indescribable squalor, filth and smells which was voluntarily out of bounds to anyone who gave a 'hoot' for his health, his money or his life.

One of the more respectable of the neon-signs – Café Badia – aroused in me the urge to peep inside this particular den of Middle Eastern profanity, but none of my 'other rank' colleagues emerging from the Opera House would have eluded the keen eyes of the S.P.'s as they crossed the road. I thought it wise to solicit the company of a fellow officer from III M.U. in order to make my initial excursion to the Café Badia. The interior was designed much like an amphitheatre with shallow tiers wide enough to accommodate tables and chairs: each set of chairs and table was enclosed in a box with a high back and low front, resembling a family pew in the balcony of a Methodist Chapel. In front of the stage was a semi-circular space in which a liberal supply of austere light chairs could be moved about willy-nilly by the groups of ogling Arabs more interested in a worm's eye view of the belly-dancers than in the food and drink supplied in the 'pews'.

The stage was merely a bare platform illuminated by one oil-lamp which was the brightest light in the building. The Café was not dingy but dimly lit and the atmosphere (which could be set to music) could only be described as a thick, exotic blend of vanilla, French cigarettes, Persian aromatic tobacco, curry, other Oriental spices and anything else which might be wafting by on the evening breeze.

The show, when it began, was a dreary procession (at 15 minute intervals) of solo belly-dancers who writhed, twitched and contorted until exhausted, to the obvious delight of the 'promenaders' who cheered, leered and smoked through the most boring antics my companion and I had ever seen. Any ideas we may have entertained that we were about to see a Windmill Theatre show were quickly dispelled when the first dusky beauty appeared on the stage. (Those Bathing Belles who had brazenly displayed their ankles and forearms on Brighton's beaches in the 1890's were naked by comparison!) Each of the dancers was heavily veiled and every part of her anatomy which could possibly betray her femininity was protected by rows of beads: her ankles (on which pretty bells tinkled) were barely visible and her fingers, which were covered in rings, also performed with great dexterity on the castanets. The only part of the dancer's anatomy exposed to view was a strip of midriff, and since all members of the human race possess a remnant of their umbilical cords it was no surprise that the dancers should choose to adorn their navels with a solitary jewel. How the jewels were fixed was of little concern to me, but it transpired in the course of the evening that the climax of each dancer's routine was the ease with which each jewel performed a set of gyrations – north-south, east-west and circular motions which I can only describe as ludicrous. The response of the 'promenaders', who cheered their favourites, and patronised the beginners, seemed to depend entirely on the size of the ridiculous gyrations: the remainder of each set would have been put to shame by any teenage 'jiver' any Saturday night at the Hammersmith Palais.

Two 'tenets' of the Moslem faith which puzzled me during the war years were concerned with alcohol and women. Allah permits every male to have four wives and guarantees to provide for the astronomical number of children (although he does not throw his provision into the nest). He also allows the males to ride on small donkeys to market, carrying a parasol to shield their delicate eyes from the sun, whilst their numerous wives walk in single file behind them covered from head to foot in black muslin and balancing on their heads huge shallow baskets of melons and fruit from the fields. Women are not allowed in any public place in Cairo unless accompanying their husbands and segregated from other families in boxes or stalls, where the husband sits in front (quite by himself) and his wives in a neat row behind him.

The rules which apply to alcohol are more flexible: Allah does not permit his faithful to make it, look at it, sell it, serve it or taste it! – but in times of war there is so much money to be made at the expense of the infidels that Allah turns his face away (in shame) from an insidious beverage called Lager, which tastes like onion water, and a spirit called Zibeeb, which tasted, at the Café Badia, very much like aniseed.

In deference to the wishes of my companion, who had no stomach for either the dancers or the drink, my first visit to the Café Badia was a brief one. I went back on several occasions and stayed very much longer for reasons which only a musician could possibly comprehend. In one corner of the stage sat a small group of musicians playing instruments which bore a family resemblance to their western counterparts. The drummer played with his fingers on the skins of two 'tabors' which he held between his knees. Another played the 'cimbalon' with soft-headed sticks, but with a difference: the wooden blocks were arranged in two rows and he played the instrument vertically instead of horizontally as is usual. The 'bass' was a one-string affair which looked very much like an old-fashioned bed-warmer. The melody instruments were two in number: one of them was a double-reed bulbous pipe which belonged somewhere in the oboe cor-anglais family – the man playing the contraption looked suspiciously like a glass-blower having great difficulty in extending the size of his bulb. The wailing sound his instrument emitted was akin to a Welsh lamb calling for its mama across Snowdonia. The other melody maker fascinated me and was the real reason for my repeated visits to the Café Badia – he was a left-handed fiddle player, who, if he ever had acquired the subtleties of legato, staccato and other aids to expression, had long since abandoned them in favour of the uncomplicated up and down, back and forth method which gives music only two dimensions – starting and stopping!

The intonation of the Café Badia Ensemble was excruciating, and the music, which appeared to be shapeless, interminable improvisation was, at first hearing, without any recognisable repetitive feature. But I was premature in my judgment: the dancers followed a regular routine and the accompanying music (although I never became familiar with the idiom) acquired recognisable 'landmarks' which I could, with some degree of success, anticipate on my third or fourth visit to the Café. The intonation which had at first offended my ears proved to be my initiation into 'quarter-tone' music, or a system of tonality alien to our western civilisation, in which the octave has for 2,000 years been divided into 12 (more or less) equal semitones.

I apologised to my left-handed fiddling friend (under my breath, of course) for misjudging his putrid playing: he was out of tune consistently, by the same number of vibrations each time he repeated a figure, which suggested that his ear was better trained than mine and that his heritage went back a little further than Bach's 'Well-Tempered Clavier'. In any event, I was fascinated by his prowess in playing the fiddle, left-handed!

The only date which I can remember disturbing the daily routine of cave-dwelling and music-making in Cairo was June 6th, 1944. The Adjutant at III M.U. (presumably on the C.O.'s instruction) began at 8.30 a.m. to inform all the officers in charge of the 62 caves that the invasion had started – and was going well! Why he imparted the news in a confidential whisper I shall never know, but he issued further bulletins later in the day with a boldness which implied that he was beginning to believe the news himself!

The Normandy landings very quickly influenced strategy in the Middle East. The build-up of arms, equipment and personnel for the defence of the Suez Canal began to disperse to the fronts in Europe and the Far East. The A.O.C. Middle East (who had been the champion of the Cairo Symphony Orchestra) was posted back to the U.K. and within two days of his departure I was banished to Aden by the C.O. of III M.U., who presumably had resented the 'protection' I had enjoyed during my double life in Tura and Cairo.

The irony of my posting was the timing: I was duty officer for the night and had inspected the guards in all the caves – they were Nubian giants with sparkling eyes, who couldn't speak a word of English, and sprang out from behind every rock with fixed bayonets and 'one up the spout'! The password was 'nadgermimi' and woe-betide any duty officer who forgot it or stammered – the risks were quite alarming!

On my return to the orderly room at about 2 a.m. I was handed a signal, with the remark "You won't like this one – Sir." It was my own posting notice, which ended with the venomous words "IMMEDIATE. NO APPEAL." I was on my way very early next morning, without taking leave of the C.O., but I have, nevertheless, been searching diligently for him for 35 years, with disdainful disregard of Francis Bacon's philosophy that 'A man that studieth revenge keeps his own wounds green, which otherwise would heal and do well.'

The flight to Aden by way of Khartoum was an eventful ride in a service Dakota on its way to the Far East. The only freight on the plane consisted of two 500 lb. bombs lashed to the sides as ballast: they also provided the only seating accommodation. I sat on one of them and a Flight Sergeant (in transit also) sat as uncomfortably as myself on the other. We were situated amidships, or just aft of the wings, and there was a tiny porthole window which gave us a fine view of the Sahara whenever we chose to screw our necks through an angle of 180°, or sit astride our bombs and ride them like racehorses. There was nothing particularly attractive in the view of white, powdery sand in blistering, sub-tropical sunlight, so we chatted for a little while, mainly about our discomfort, until the navigator thrust his head through an incredibly tiny hatchway and uttered an unbelievable warning "Hang on boys – we're running into a shit-storm – it MAY be a bit bumpy!!" The sound of his chirpy voice was the only comfort I had for the next 30 minutes: he piped up at regular intervals with the inane remark, "Still with us?" to which he did not expect a reply. I have never known the distinction between gale-force winds and a hurricane, but all I could see was a wall of sand howling horizontally past my window, lit up by exhaust flames and sparks from the engines which were flat-out. The bumps were frightening and could only be described as 'lurches' of 100 ft. in every direction, from nose-diving to near looping-the-loop. It was far too dark to see the wing-tips but I could well imagine, from the creaking rivets, that we were fluttering like a helpless bird. The storm eventually lost its intensity, and 'sunshine' made the announcement which brought a little colour to my cheeks and some use to my petrified limbs – 'Khartoum in 2 minutes," and signed off!

From my porthole I could see the rows of mud huts, sophisticated hotels, offices and the welcome sight of an air-strip: and so for the second time in the war I had good reason to be thankful for the miracle of 'blind' navigation.

The night I spent in Khartoum was a curious mixture of service discipline and civilian luxury. At the air-field the crew and two passengers were picked up by the usual open jeeps and deposited according to rank in two widely separated hotels in the town. The pilot and navigator were sergeants and together with the other passenger (whom I never saw again) were dropped off, with many cheerios and first names, at one hotel, and the other air crew officers and myself were taken to another, which was obviously run by a civilian staff as an officers' mess for transit personnel. The food was good and the beer cold: the bed was extremely comfortable and I slept like a man reprieved until the arrival of the jeep next morning to carry us off to the air-field.

The flight to Khormaksar via the Cameron Islands was not particularly interesting, neither was my first sight of Aden, as I looked down the throat of its extinct volcano in which 'Crater Village' (and 26,000 native inhabitants) lived a perilous life. Aden has a unique climate of insufferable heat and humidity, in which not a flower or a green shoot will grow except in a tub of imported soil, neither is there any justification for humans to sweat their lives away in the 20th century, defending a pile of cinders which may have been part of some colonial empire-building strategy in the 19th.

Khormaksar, when I eventually arrived, was everything I expected it to be: all the regular Air Force personnel I had previously met spoke of their 'tour of duty' in Khormaksar as 'years spent on Devil's Island'. My tour of duty lasted just long enough to requisition transport to H.Q. Aden (about four miles away) where I learned to my immediate discomfort that I had been seconded to the Army, in order to relieve the Captain-Quartermaster, who had not seen his family in England for six years.

The unit to which I had been banished for a year was the Aden Protectorate Levies and the camp was about 12 miles from Aden (or any other vestige of civilisation). There was no reason at all why the camp should be situated precisely where it was; there was nothing to see in any direction but an arid, perfectly flat desert with the inevitable heat-haze rising from it, through which it was possible to see a mirage of the Yemeni mountains (about 60 miles away). The camp consisted of hideous rows of hot, bleached concrete blocks of permanent barracks and married quarters which stretched for half a mile. Surrounding the camp was a flimsy wire fence supported at regular intervals by short concrete posts, as useless in keeping marauders out as it was in keeping the Arab troops in! There was a heavily-guarded gate through which those who wished to be seen entering and leaving the camp could pass: it was good sense for the 38 British ranks to use the front door to everything on the camp and to sign in and out of the guard-room when off duty.

I was incarcerated for 12 months in this benighted place, doing nothing which could possibly be construed as useful, necessary, or even remotely connected with the war effort. This outpost of the British Empire was an unbelievably non-operational, non-functional, peace-time holiday camp, where 1,500 native warriors from the Yemen could learn how to fire a 303 Enfield rifle, before 'borrowing' it and deserting to the mountains, where they might make a more positive contribution to their own endless tribal wars.

One very effective deterrent was devised which made desertion an embarrassing experience – even for an Arab. Married quarters were cunningly provided on the camp, where two of their wives (and the inevitable broods of chicos) could be housed and fed at the expense of the British taxpayer! There were seven Companies of roughly 200 men, each of which was commanded by one British major, one Hindoo officer (of the rank of captain) and one British N.C.O. Each Company (on a seven weeks rota basis) was despatched to the uninhabited island of Socotra (in the Indian Ocean), ostensibly to patrol and guard a volcanic rock against unlikely German occupation. Needless to say, there were no deserters on this tour of duty – the sharks patrol the Indian Ocean in great numbers!

My responsibilities as Quartermaster on this incongruous Army Camp were well-defined and inescapable, but the inadequacies of my previous training in the Equipment Schools of the R.A.F. soon became apparent when I was called upon to maintain a herd of goats (to feed the Arab population) and provide stables and fodder for 16 thoroughbred Arab race-horses! The diversity of my duties was an endless source of anxiety during the year I spent in Aden, in spite of the Adjutant's early reassurance that "the Bimbashi knows everything. Leave him alone!"

The Bimbashi was a regular Indian Army Officer, of the rank of Captain, who was approaching the end of his service life and looking forward, with some trepidation, to enjoying the rewards of his labours in a return to his native Nepal – a pension and a promised acre of land. My predecessor (who was also a regular officer) had trusted the Bimbashi implicitly and had placed the camp storehouse in his sole charge. With this delegation of responsibility also went the distribution of rations to the native population and the arms, ammunition and equipment (on inventory charge) to the Company Commanders. The Bimbashi had obviously thrived on army procedure: very soon after my arrival on the camp he proudly showed me around 'his' stores and demonstrated his immaculate book-keeping and the efficiency of 'his' staff! He was a huge fellow of not very prepossessing appearance, and at our first meeting I was at a loss to understand his nervousness: 'Sahib' was on his lips every second word and whenever my eyes rested upon any harmless pile of equipment he found it necessary to stammer out, in great detail, the answers to questions I had never asked. My presence on the camp obviously embarrassed him but it was some time before I learned the reason for his suspicions – the Bimbashi was seriously disturbed at the arrival of a new Quartermaster – particularly an R.A.F. man, and so near his own retirement – he must be a spy sent by the Air Ministry to uncover all the petty swindles on the camp and deprive him of his pension and his precious acre of land!

Swindles there certainly were, many which the Bimbashi had knowledge of, but was hardly likely to have complicity in: he was blameless in all aspects of storekeeping except one – the issue of rations to the civilian population, not as one would expect in the dead of night 'when evils are most free' but in the dead of tropical afternoons when all British ranks were panting on their 'charpoys', deluding themselves that the fans which wafted hot air onto their bodies were a boon.

'Weights and Measures', 'Customs and Excise' and other guardians of right and wrong would have had a field-day in the Bimbashi's private market place. According to my reliable informants (the two Hindoo sergeants who worked in my outer office) the Bimbashi had his own primitive scales and a selection of graded 'pebbles' which represented the entitlement of each family in weight of grain and other unidentifiable stuff which formed their daily diet! In these circumstances it was not surprising that the Bimbashi (like Pooh Bah in the Mikado) accepted a few bribes for a few favours, and there was nothing I could do to stop the practice or even prove it ever happened.

The handle-bar moustaches worn by the Company Commanders, and the presence of Hindoo officers and N.C.O.'s were not (as the labels of Camp Coffee Essence would suggest) the only lingering relics of our conquest of India: there were the horses to remind us of the famous deeds of the Cavalry. These handsome, temperamental, irresponsible beasts were an entitlement for the officers who retained the status of Cavalry and possessed enough courage to ride them: they were rarely seen outside the stables and then only on the occasions when a newcomer to the camp was eager to show off his horsemanship – for the first and last time! The regulars derived a great deal of sadistical pleasure from watching the beasts stand still, barely long enough for the 'junior' to mount, before streaking off with him across the desert at upwards of 45 m.p.h.

The expense of maintaining so many fine but useless animals was on my conscience for months after my arrival on the camp: the boring, idle conversation in the Officers' Mess never included a passing reference to the stables, which intrigued me. The C.O.'s regular Friday morning camp inspection (with all its pomp and ceremony) never passed within 50 yards of the stables, or indeed within sight or sound of a neighing horse, and the Bimbashi (who was suspicious of every move I made) blushed and stammered whenever I mentioned harness and fodder. My two Hindoo sergeants, who haunted my outer office and chattered endlessly about book-keeping and accountancy, usually fled to make tea at any reference to the horses. The mystery, or swindle, as it turned out to be, was yet another of those palpable frauds perpetrated under my nose, which my superior at Group H.Q. (like the proverbial ostrich) chose to ignore. I was ultimately posted (for the second time) out of harm's way, but since there was no place on earth worse than Aden to which I could be banished my lot was greatly improved by being flown back to Cairo.

My suspicions that there was something to hide in the stables of the Aden Protectorate Levies besides manure were reanimated one afternoon in late May by attending a Race Meeting in Khormaksar organised by the British Colony and attended by a most enthusiastic Arab population. All my life I have loathed and abominated horse-racing, fox-hunting, hare-coursing, boxing, or any other form of barbarous entertainment, but on this occasion, partly out of boredom, I allowed myself to be dragged to the meeting. The printed programme of events proved to be quite captivating – in two of the main events there were entered horses OWNED and RIDDEN by Majors O'Halloran and Pelham who were Company Commanders at A.P.L. The animals were in the peak of condition, as well they might, considering the training, grooming and fodder they were receiving on the camp: the miraculous aspect of their immaculate condition was the fact that they had both 'been shot' two years before this event and written-off as a charge against the public on Form 34* which was filed in my office, and very sheepishly presented on my desk the following morning! "We wondered how long it would take you to find out," said my two sergeants (in unison), and they were greatly relieved, as was the Bimbashi later, when I absolved them all from blame. The pressure of 'rank' had obviously been put upon them: it was later imposed upon me too when the scandal broke, and I was put on a charge (an indignity for an officer) by O'Halloran, for refusing to salute and stand to attention in his office. The C.O. took no action and the incident was not recorded on my documents, but the atmosphere in the Officers' Mess was heavily charged for the remainder of my tour of duty.

The absurdity of 'playing at soldiers' in this obscure part of the world became a constant source of amazement to me, and the only reminders that there was a war still in progress were occasional letters from home

---

* Form 34 was a convenient R.A.F. document for 'getting rid of' or getting equipment 'off charge' or 'off someone's responsibility' for its safe custody; e.g. aircraft, lost by enemy action, were 'written off' by Form 34. In the R.A.F. 'imperishable' equipment must be 'accounted' for at all times. 'C' class stores, of which the best-known examples are soap, petrol and paint, are totally consumed in use and are accounted for only at the initial issue.

and the incessant noise of American aircraft ferrying men and equipment to the Far Eastern front from a hastily constructed air-strip about two miles to the east of the A.P.L. camp.

The organisation of the American 'war machine' and the speed at which this air-base appeared in the desert was incredible! I had no knowledge of its existence until I received a phone call from the Quartermaster of the Staging Post, inviting me in the warmest tones to pay him a visit and take advantage of all their facilities, which included entertainment, the cook-house and complete freedom in the P.X. Stores. The Base was fully operational: the pre-fabricated buildings had been erected in a day and every Dakota landing at the post was laden with equipment of every kind, from war material and fuel through the whole spectrum of planning and organisation down to the luxuries of turkey legs, frozen cans of beer and 'coke' – often to be consumed whilst watching the latest films from Hollywood (on 36 mm) in the open air on balmy tropical evenings.

The cinema was the centre of the evening relaxation, and I persisted in my visits to the camp open-air theatre long after the novelty of buying ridiculously cheap cigarettes and tobacco (and the cook-house food) had worn off. The 'theatre' boasted a stage and a very orderly array of benches in semi-circular tiers: the audience was a very disorderly, dishevelled bunch of half-naked men with pot-bellies, which they were maintaining at full stretch with canned beer and chicken legs, followed by the inevitable cigar. Besides the elaborate sound equipment for the 'movies' there was also a microphone on the stage which was used extensively by the Entertainments Officer, or Master of Ceremonies, to infuse some discipline into the proceedings, or to introduce a 'personality' who happened to be in transit overnight. The evening began always with a few cards of the American national game of Bingo, or 'House' (as they called it), an exhausting intellectual exercise which still flourishes in England in such cultural centres as Barnsley and Rotherham: there was no charge for the stimulation of playing the game and everyone who played got a prize or consolation gift. The object of playing at all appeared to be a process of gradually settling the mob until it no longer resembled Heathrow Departure Lounge on Bank Holiday Monday!

The next announcement was either the introduction of the celebrity (if any) or the title of the 'movie', which was always a surprise pre-view, in fact some of the films I saw were not generally released until years after the war. I was, on all but one occasion, singularly unimpressed by American stars of stage and screen (they had, in 1945, more nonentities than we had) but I was rewarded one evening when the Master of Ceremonies introduced Mel Blanc, who stepped up to the microphone and, with no other equipment but his hands to his mouth, gave us a riotous 20 minutes of impersonations of every Disney character, animal and bird, re-creating whole sequences of comedy in which the voice changes were unbelievable. The art of the theatre is the ability to identify oneself with characters and situations. I sometimes wonder why I have never identified myself (in my affinities with characters on the screen) with anyone except Donald Duck, who, in every episode in his life, sets out with the best intentions in the world (like Siegfried) of doing good, and ends every brief exercise in frenzy and frustration with his feathers flying. I am eternally grateful to Mel Blanc for making Donald Duck such a plausible character and sympathetically playing down his frailties.

The miraculous appearance of the Staging Post, in a matter of days, gave a credibility (especially in Arabia) to the romantic tales of Aladdin and the Genie of the Lamp, who satisfied his every wish. Planning permission had evidently not been sought, or the whole exercise so craftily concealed from the C.O. of the Aden Protectorate Levies, that I was (within a week of the first plane landing) abruptly brought face to face with the most ludicrous example of Army 'Bull' I experienced playing toy soldiers in Aden.

Every Friday morning at 6 a.m. was the C.O.'s camp inspection. The procession formed outside the C.O.'s office and consisted of Colonel Jones (who was fat and 5' 2" in height) followed by the second in command (who was skinny and 6' 3"). Then, in order of importance, and still in single file, came the Adjutant, the Quartermaster (myself), the Medical Officer, several Hindoo Army Officers and an interpreter. The comic safari was preceded by a very loud and not too proficient bugler, who announced our arrival at every strategic point on the camp, and as the morning wore itself tediously away, so did his lips, the 'cracked notes' eventually outnumbering the ordinary ones, to the torment of my sensitive ears. As noon approached, so did the safari arrive at the extremity of the camp and 60 miles of purple desert, the colour of which matched Colonel Jones' face as he broke into a trot, stopping only to wave his cane at an object of American engineering which had certainly appeared since the previous Friday's inspection! "Q.!!!" he howled, (waiting until I broke ranks with my little book to attend to his every whim) "WHAT'S THIS?!!" (There were many occasions during my service life when confronted with similar acts of lunacy that I bit my lip and chose a few careful words, but this one took the first prize.) Instead of blurting out "You bloody idiot, what does it look like?" I calmly replied, with extreme cunning and control, "An electricity pylon, Sir." "WELL, MOVE IT!!" yelled he, and he stalked off towards the camp.

I stayed behind long enough to make the cryptic note in my tablets – 'Electricity pylon – move it!' – and to examine the monument which was standing on 10 tons of concrete and which rose to a height of 30 feet: there was a conspicuous notice (in English) warning the Arab population of the 'Danger and Death from 20,000 volts' should they fly their 'kites' in the area. On the way back to my office I had a few more serious problems upon which to ruminate, so I went to lunch and returned to my office in the afternoon when the rest of the camp was taking 'siesta'!

Camp construction, and the erection and maintenance of permanent buildings, is the responsibility (Army and R.A.F. alike) of the Department of Works and Buildings, affectionately known to the Equipment Branch as 'Works and Bricks'! The man 'in charge' at the Aden Protectorate Levies was, as at every other station on which I served, a civilian contractor, and completely aloof from military discipline and 'bull'. I rang Works and Bricks on my return to the office in the dead of afternoon, and was surprised to hear the sound of another voice. Very soon, an extremely courteous, well-dressed Arab civilian walked into my office and assured me that any problem I had would be dealt with immediately – before I uttered a word of my silly tale! I was perfectly safe in addressing him as 'Mohammed', as one, or all three of his names was bound to be inherited from his father or grandfather: he smiled and bowed graciously during my narrative and then assured me that Allah, in his infinite wisdom, could work miracles, and I must put this trivial incident completely out of my mind! He left me, with my profuse thanks, although I did not, at the time, share his confidence. Within half an hour of his departure a gang of about sixty bare-footed Arab soldiers (from the 'Glass-House') marched past my office bearing picks and shovels and pushing rubberwheeled hand-carts – the whole silent cortège disappeared in the direction of the pylon, and, like the Pied Piper's children, was never seen again. I went back to my billet, rather sadly, and resolved to leave Mohammed to his miracle and not show my anxiety by asking for progress reports or listening for 'bush-telegraph' gossip among the natives. The week passed very slowly in routine matters connected with the previous camp inspection, and the entry in my 'tablets' remained unresolved – "Electricity pylon MOVE IT!".

The Friday parade began as inevitably as every other, with a rejuvenated bugler blaring dulcet tones at all the strategic places and provoking me (with my heavy heart) more than usually to choke him. Whenever the parade moved into open country I cast many furtive glances in the direction of the pylon – which was still there! At last we arrived, and the C.O. howled "Q.!!", and waited for me to approach to receive sentence – "VERY GOOD!!" said he, and stalked back to camp, leaving me to contemplate the pylon (which was now standing 15 yards *outside* the perimeter-fence) and Allah's miracle or Mohammed's ingenuity or whatever had contributed to my salvation. I, too, hurried back to my office for a consultation with 'Works and Bricks'. Mohammed, who was expecting my call, chuckled and said "My friend, it never was a problem – WE MOVED THE PERIMETER FENCE!!" Air Ministry (or the War Department) lost 20 yards of Yemen Desert as a result of this incident, but there have been no repercussions since my repatriation, and I have implicit faith in Mohammed's ability to cope with any which may have arisen in Aden.

Colonel Jones remained blissfully unaware of what had happened and continued happily to play at soldiers in the desert, surrounded by Company Commanders who could race dead horses and a Quartermaster who could move electricity pylons!

The predominant wish of my heart remained my eventual escape from Aden's abominable climate and its wild dogs and poisonous snakes, but I was to endure a great deal of physical and mental discomfort before I was finally dispatched to Cairo (by a Medical Board) at the end of August, 1945.

The interesting trivialities of life in the tropics I now vividly remember – my first shower, and my first leap to safety from the boiling water which gushed from the only water tap! My Arab servant, who rushed in to warn me (a little late) said, most apologetically, "Take care, Sahib, the water comes from the water-tower 100 yards away in pipes 6 inches under the sand – it gets a little hot – let it run for 10 minutes." I did: it was then luke-warm!

One phenomenon which was especially interesting to me was the absence of twilight and the intensity of both sunlight and darkness. Tennis was the only game the British ranks were able to play on the camp, and then only in the setting sun between 5 p.m. and 6 p.m.: it was common practice to gather all our equipment together in great haste, when the sun (which appears to be huge in the tropics) began to dip over the horizon, otherwise we would arrive at our billets, in just a few minutes, in the dark. The night sky in the tropics is wonderful and incomprehensible: my knowledge of the stars is abysmal and I shall never understand why 'Orion' is bolt-upright in Yorkshire, upside-down in Cape Town, and horizontal in Aden!

Whatever the climate on any Army or R.A.F. Camp in the world, 'treacle pudding and custard' will be introduced into the diet, and 'football' into the daily life of every man in uniform, whether he likes it or not. The Arabs did not take kindly to 'Air Council Instructions' on suet-pudding, but they revelled in the unarmed combat called 'football' and were not too nice about the rules or the precise numbers who were permitted to play. They marched with great discipline to the touch-lines, where they took off the army boots (which were crippling them) and dashed bare-footed onto the field where they surged about like a swarm of bees, kicking hell out of the ball and each other for the permitted 25 minutes. The British ranks sometimes played, in order to demonstrate to the natives that, if there was little skill in the game, at least it had some purpose – to get the ball between the goal posts, preferably at the other end of the ground.

Taking part in one of these mock-battles resulted in a few knocks and scratches which turned septic and nasty enough to justify my transportation to the Military Hospital in Aden where I spent a month in considerable discomfort. There developed, as a complement, or complication, to what I already suffered, a complaint known in medical circles as 'Furunculosis', which means, in lay terms, more 'boils' than anyone can cope with at any one time. I had 48, which made sleep difficult to induce in spite of counting them over and over again. One memorable afternoon, the matron (who was a regular Amazon) arrived at my bedside with a small troupe of underlings, and, after drawing the curtains round the bed, began a very bossy speech, which I at first thought was a premature post-mortem examination! I was relieved to find that she was explaining in great detail the unfortunate condition I was in (using the present tense) and that I was about to become a guinea-pig for a new miracle drug which had arrived that very day, and would not be available to the world in general for some time. She then held aloft a phial of the life-giving stuff 'Penicillin' and proceeded to administer it according to the instructions which couldn't possibly have been printed on the bottle. I was scrubbed without shame in carbolic soap; hypodermic needles were pushed into the most unlikely places of my anatomy at 3-hourly intervals, day and night, for 5 days until my boils subsided.

Within a week of my release from hospital, the M.O. at the A.P.L. received a Medical Board report from Aden which he brought to my office and translated for me in simple terms – "This climate is no good for you (or anyone else) and you cannot be cured here. Pack your bags, young man – you are on your way to Cairo tomorrow." The flight to Heliopolis was by a small civil aircraft which called at several interesting places, among them Jeddah (in order to drop off a pair of terrified, air-sick Sheikhs on their way to Mecca for a routine march around the square). Other places were the Cameron Islands in the Gulf, and Luxor, where the passengers were forbidden to disembark until 2 officious gentlemen had douched us with some obnoxious spray, muttering, "Mosquito, mosquito!".

Chapter XVI

On arrival at Heliopolis I was soon at Group H.Q. and posted to III M.U. where I rejoined some of the friends I had left almost a year before. The war in Europe was over and that in the Far East nearly so: the atmosphere at III M.U. was decidedly explosive with frustrated and impatient men (some of whom had been overseas for four years) eager to be home and pick up the threads of a normal civilian life. 'Demobilisation' and 'Rehabilitation' were major problems for High Command in Egypt: the former, though orderly, was extremely slow, and, consequently, the latter became a prolonged conversion course designed by Air Ministry to 'Educate' and 'Entertain' the restless animals in order to divert them from perhaps more sinister ideas of mutiny and desertion. The magnitude of the problem gave rise to the creation of a new class of Commissioned Officer in the R.A.F. – The Education Officer (holding the rank of Flight Lieutenant) – and also the publication and worldwide circulation of a new pamphlet called 'Current Affairs'.

The first Education Officer to arrive at III M.U. brought with him the first editions of his pamphlets and tremendous enthusiasm for his missionary work, but the pallor of his skin (particularly his knees) betrayed the fact that Lincoln was the nearest point he had ever previously been to the Equator, and did little to endear him to the airmen who were not only brown, but 'browned off'!

The Education Officer flung himself into his work with great courage (or foolhardiness), and many of his fellow officers, myself included, who went along to assist at his first mass-meeting had his protection in the forefront of their minds when he embarked on Guessing Games, Brains Trust Panels, and the crushing ignominy of handing out paper and pencils and giving the audience a Spelling Test! How he escaped being pelted to death with beer-bottles I shall never know, but the spelling test was a 'corker' and deserves quoting – "A harassed Cobbler met an embarrassed Pedlar in a Cemetery, gauging the symmetry of his Uncle's ankles, eating desiccated Pomegranate with unparalleled ecstasy". The test was perhaps a master stroke: it proved to be a humiliating experience for all who tried it, and the attenders at subsequent meetings, although diminished in numbers, began to show a lively interest in conditions at home and their prospects of survival when they returned to it.

On my return to III M.U. after the miserable year spent in the Aden Protectorate I found great difficulty in picking up the threads of my previously busy double life, or even making contact with Wilf Collinge and Charles McKeown, who had for two years been responsible for my carefree involvement in music-making in Cairo with the Symphony Orchestra, Egyptian State Broadcasting and E.N.S.A. The C.S.O. had already evaporated for the obvious reason that demobilisation was decimating its ranks and the morale-boosting purpose of its existence was no longer of interest to anyone. Charles McKeown was the first of my friends to be repatriated, and his departure marked the final dissipation of the Sextet. Wilf Collinge followed him a few weeks later and my visits to Cairo became less frequent and confined to souvenir hunting in the 'out-of-bounds' areas of the Bazaars.

Having lost a few friends in the repatriation exercise, I too became impatient to be home, and sought the company of the Education Officer whenever possible in the Officers' Mess after dinner, when conversation of any kind was at a premium, and the only diplomatic thing one might otherwise do was to lose consistently at the C.O.'s 'Bridge' table. My newly acquired companion was well aware that, by the nature of his non-combatant duties, and the ultimate failure of his temporary mission, he was 'the man in the middle' – mistrusted by those who knew nothing of what he was trying to achieve and held in varying degrees of contempt by those who did. Two weeks before his posting abroad, Flight Lieutenant Baker had served on an R.A.F. Station in the low country in England – the name is unimportant, but the attitude of his superiors and the grand old R.A.F. game of 'passing the can' provided Baker with a most hilarious story which he related to me one evening with great relish, and one which is best retold in his own words:–

"The Adjutant at Manston sent for me one morning and threw a signal across the table in my direction, and, with some disgust, shouted 'This is your department, Baker! What will the buggers at Air Ministry think of next? They're sending an Oxford Don down here tomorrow to give a lecture on KEATS! Do something about it!!'" (I vividly remembered only three months before, having to move an electricity pylon!) Baker went on with his intriguing narrative – "I first of all thought of ways and means of postponing the visit, and then of the safety of the Don in the unlikely event of his reaching the second paragraph of his lecture – there was always the possibility of him slipping quietly away if there was no audience at all – and so on until I decided to 'pass the can' for the second time and invoke the assistance of the Station Warrant Officer who was a 'regular' and the personification of 'bull'. He strode into my office, threw up a salute, and said 'Sir'!' in such a manner as to imply 'Pig!!', and waited for my pathetic story. At the end of it he threw up another salute and said 'Leave it to me, Sir!' and marched out. The following day I passed the parade-ground at 2.15 p.m. on my way to the N.A.A.F.I. and saw a sight not unfamiliar on the square at any time of day. The S.W.O. was drilling and bawling at about 60 airmen whose misfortune it was to be in 'jankers' or on permanent fatigue-duty. He halted the tired wretches and addressed them sneeringly – 'Now, yew lot, this arternoon in the N.A.A.F.I. there's goin' to be a lecture on Keats, an' there in't one o' yew higorant shower knows what a KEAT is, so now yew're goin' to find out – left turn! at the double! pick 'em up!!" The S.W.O. didn't attend the lecture, so he was the only one of the 'higorant shower' who went through life bereft of the knowledge of what a 'KEAT' is!'"

My posting back to III M.U. had been one of the non-events of the war, and I was greeted on arrival by a casual remark from the Adjutant, "Glad to have you with us – see Wing Commander . . . the Chief Equipment Officer he will find you something to do!" The C.E.O. was equally not overjoyed to see me and said "Grab yourself an office – I'll send you a 'File' in due course." It was inevitable that, having found an office (this time in 'R' Group – radar and radio equipment), I should soon become involved in the R.A.F.'s second most popular game (after 'passing the can') of 'passing files', with memos attached which always read "I believe this is your pigeon – comment, please." After 4 years' experience in the game I became expert in all its ramifications, and on my desk were always 4 trays, conspicuously marked, to avoid confusion – 'IN', 'OUT', 'PENDING' and 'TOO DIFFICULT'. Files in the latter tray were always dealt with by the Corporal, who was invariably the only person in any department who knew what he was doing. Corporal Jones in 'R' Group was no exception, and became a staunch ally, after quickly becoming Sergeant and enjoying the privileges of the Sergeants' Mess for the first time in his life.

A very busy man in the Middle East in the closing stages of the war was the M.P.O. (Master Provision Officer) and the bulk of correspondence with him concerned disposal, dispersal and transfer of equipment, particularly instruments in 'R' Group still regarded as being on the 'Secret List'. Standing at the mouth of 'R' Group and looking into a cave 496 yards long crammed with equipment was a daunting sight at any time, but it presented a depressing picture to the handful of personnel involved in the task of cleaning-up. Very soon after my arrival, and certainly before I felt established in 'R' Group, the 'phone rang and the C.O. announced nervously that the A.O.C. in C. was coming round in the afternoon on a 'lightning inspection'. "Tidy up, for God's sake, Horsfall!" said he. The overseers cracked their whips and 43 Arab slaves set up clouds of fleas and dust which took weeks to settle down. For yet another time in my service career was a trumpeter engaged to signal the approach of a V.I.P. – he also signalled the departure, in some haste, of every living creature in 'R' Group. I was left alone to greet the most imposing array of ribbons and medals I had ever seen in one place and at one time – the lowest ranks were Group Captains (with four rings and scrambled eggs) and the A.O.C. was at least Air Vice Marshal – I lost count. The introduction was a very brief one, and the A.O.C. stalked off into the cave at a brisk pace, as though he intended to see everything, but either his courage gave out, or he couldn't see the end of his journey for dust and fleas: he stopped in his tracks and pointed to a pile of packing-cases near the entrance – "What are these?" – in a tone which suggested that I had better know! "Redundant equipment, Sir, which I put up for disposal to the M.P.O. Those cases are going back to U.K. next week, Sir!" There was a little pause and then he said, quite quietly, "Very good, Horsfall," and turned, and the whole glittering cavalcade marched out of the cave and into the next one (from the sound of the distant trumpeter).

After my very convincing speech about the 'Redundant equipment, Sir', the A.O.C. might very well have asked "What redundant equipment?", but he didn't. Someone 'up there' was looking after me that day, or perhaps it was Sergeant Jones, whose face just bobbed up from behind one of the packing-cases and said (as soon as the way was clear) "That was a near thing, Sir: all this 'redundant equipment' you seem to be so keen on sending back to the U.K. next week is the very latest from America – it only came in yesterday!!"

One evening in the Mess I was feeling particularly 'down': I had opened an air-mail letter-card from home in which my Father had, with great difficulty, broken the news of the brief illness and sudden death of my Mother, whom I hadn't seen for 3 years. I received the letter the day *after* the funeral, which distressed me even more. The Adjutant assured me that compassionate leave and a flight back to the U.K. could have been easily arranged a week earlier. The general conversation about 'leave' brought the Adjutant eventually to the subject of my 'documents' in his office, and the fact that in them he could find no evidence of my ever having taken leave since I had been commissioned nearly 4 years before. He then suggested taking advantage of a 14-day conducted tour of the Holy Land, based in a holiday-camp for officers in Tel Aviv with 2 nights in St. David's Hotel, Jerusalem. There was to be plenty of leisure for bathing in the Mediterranean (which didn't appeal to me at all), a guide for every trip, and a first-class return rail ticket from Cairo to Tel Aviv – the inclusive price of the holiday was £10, which was approximately half of my basic pay.

It would be untrue to say that I enjoyed the visit to the Holy Land: it was an experience I shall never forget, and an education in the phoney problems and confrontations which have beset Jews, Arabs and Christians for 2,000 years: I could very well have missed out on the 2 days I spent in Jerusalem! There is a great deal less piety displayed in Jerusalem at any time of the day or night than there is in Blackpool's Central Beach peep-shows on August Bank Holiday Monday. The narrow streets and alley-ways were cluttered with the Catholics doing their daily ritual of the Fourteen Stations of the Cross – there were Arabs jostling them (and the tourists) with carcases of goat-flesh, and vendors selling ice-cream and cool drinks. The Arab guide assigned to us was a 'fifth columnist' to our Christian beliefs, muttering words of doubt at regular intervals: his favourite argument concerned the location of Calvary and the Church of the Holy Sepulchre. Each and every time we passed the Well, which, he asserted with some spirit, had not changed its location in centuries, he said, "If Calvary was outside the City Walls, and the only well for miles is *there* – do you think the Romans were so dim as to build fortifications and be besieged within them, and leave the only water supply outside?" He also took us, one morning at 7 o'clock, to the parapet overlooking the Wailing Wall, where we witnessed another of Jerusalem's insoluble problems. The participants in this charade wore coloured scarves thrown over one shoulder (not unlike football supporters). At this point our guide excelled himself by explaining that the colours changed every week according to the tribes or sects which were in charge of the wailing. The game was played by rolling about backwards and forwards with their shoulders on the Wall, letting out the most hideous howls at unpredictable times and then pausing to bang their heads on the Wall, which obviously inflicted great pain, and then, finally, pushing little bits of folded paper into crevices in the huge stones of the Wall, which is all that remains of King Solomon's Temple. The 'Wall' supports the plateau upon which now stands the Mosque of Omar.

The 'Blue Mosque' is very beautiful and contains nothing dearer to the heart of every Muslim than a little shrine in which there are 3 whiskers from Mohammed's beard! He may have been the last of a long line of Prophets, but he quickly acquired the sole rights to every yard of ground in Palestine sacred to Jew and Christian alike. The Mosque of Omar, which stands firmly on the sacrificial stone of King Solomon's Temple, will not deter the Jews from ultimately re-building their shrine, and the Christian pilgrims may one day visit their Holy Places without greasing the palms of eager Arab 'dues' collectors. The visit to the Church of the Holy Sepulchre was, for me, the most tawdry, expensive and irreverent experience of the entire tour of the Holy Land. Our Arab guide, having delivered his usual jibes of disbelief at the door, abandoned us to a Coptic priest who was waiting inside, assembling the required number of pilgrims, to begin just another tour. At the time I was there, the Greek Orthodox Church and the Catholics jealously guarded their respective rights to a week in turn to 'administer' the needs of, and retain the revenue from, services, collections, sales of souvenirs, and indeed everything we were persuaded to pay for at every turn. The glass bowls, which were strategically placed at intervals of only a few yards, intrigued me: they were filled with tawdry 'junk' which, at the end of the day, would have stocked an average-sized Woolworths' store with fountain-pens, cheap strings of beads, rings, ear-rings, brooches, watches, combs and trinkets, which would have supported Woolworths' famous slogan at that time – 'Nothing in this Store over 6d.'!! We were hustled eventually into the crypt where we were met by Archbishop Makarios and told to kneel for his Blessing – he prattled on at great length about our pilgrimage being now at an end, and that we would remember it to the end of our days – I shall remember the end of his blasphemous speech to the end of mine! Without pausing a second, or introducing a comma into his galloping jargon, he rattled on "through Jesus Christ our Lord Amen they're a shilling each!!" Before we had time to get off our knees, his minions were at us with 'certificates' which he had previously signed, bearing witness to our pilgrimage: but the crowning piece of moneyspinning odd-jobbery was the appearance of quantities of postcard-sized pieces of stiff paper upon each of which was glued a small chunk of concrete, with the assertion that it was once a fragment of the hallowed stone which was rolled against the entrance to the tomb of Jesus! The number of souvenirs sold to the gullible pilgrims that day stimulated my irreverent mind to processes of mental arithmetic, and two quite illogical answers emerged that over 10,000 'genuine' tombstones had been discovered since the year 33 A.D., and that the profits from the 'racket' had now exceeded £3,000,000.

A few hours later I passed out of the city gates into the valley and began the fairly stiff climb to the Mount of Olives, which I failed to reach: I halted my weary limbs at the Church of the Twelve Nations and the Garden of Gethsemane, where I did something which greatly angered two monks who proved beyond doubt to be men of wrath after all – I was hauled out of the Garden for daring to have a closer look at the Olive Tree! I was also escorted to another souvenir shop where I could actually obtain and take home one of the sacred leaves, stuck on a card, for the same nominal charge of 'a shilling each'. If the Olive Tree had shed its leaves twice a day this little industry could not have survived without enormous supplementary supplies!

Our conducted tour of Jerusalem concluded with a visit to the Mosque of Omar, when, needless to say, our Arab guide could not disguise his partiality for Mohammedan dogma: neither could he stand aside (and risk his fee as a guide) and see us all 'fleeced' as we had hitherto been by the Christians. The 'faithful' (as they all well know) may enter barefooted, but the 'infidels' (as we obviously were classed) were only permitted to enter if divested of our own shoes and were wearing some special sacred sandals which could be hired at an exorbitant fee from a host of noisy, haggling vendors on the steps of the Mosque. We were, of course, helpless – we either paid, or spent the rest of our lives regretting having missed the opportunity. We took off our shoes (the first mistake), paid the fee, and put on the sandals, which were tatty bits of shapeless cloth tied with endless lengths of filthy tape. The little monsters made an elaborate show of *not* tying the tapes, and sending us on our respective ways.

Two steps inside the Mosque was as far as any of us managed, in fact it was one step beyond the point they expected us to reach, before the sandals fell off. The hullabaloo which ensued is still ringing in my ears – the wrath of Allah was invoked spontaneously on the infidels who had dared to profane their holy place, and the only way that our lives would be spared was to pay another fee (this time double) to have the sandals tied on again. We then had the dubious pleasure of boring a passage through throngs of smelly Arabs to look through some iron railings at a box (in the shape of a minaret) in which, it was alleged, were 3 whiskers! The experience was not yet over. When we reached the fresh air and the sunshine again, our shoes, and the custodians, had vanished! but not too far away was our Arab guide, with the whole cluster of them. Our relief at recovering our shoes was immense, but I suspect that the relief on the face of our guide stemmed more from desire to retain his job than any scruples of morality.

The following day we bade farewell to 'Las Vegas' and, in complete contrast, visited a place nobody wanted – the Dead Sea! It is a desolate place over 600 feet below sea-level, where the sun relentlessly evaporates the shallow sea-water, leaving miles and miles of common salt for anyone with sufficient energy or enterprise to shovel it up. There were no souvenir shops, but some of our party walked a considerable distance into the sea in order to prove the point that submersion in the heavily-salted water was impossible: there were several snapshots taken and later developed, showing men sitting in the water reading books – with their feet in the air.

I cannot remember the sequence in which other excursions were made from the camp at Tel Aviv, but they were certainly to gentler places than Jerusalem. Bethlehem was beautiful and did much to restore my faith, but the Sea of Galilee was showing unmistakable signs in 1945 of commercial enterprise. The Churches and Mosques were there side by side, but there also were the cafes and well-advertised boat-trips: the only things lacking were the signs – 'Devonshire Teas' and 'Back in time for them!'

I returned to Cairo without regret: I may have derived some physical benefit from the change, but spiritual uplift was there none, in fact the whole trip was a great disillusionment.

The remainder of my tour of duty at III M.U. was boring, and relieved by only one incident which shook me temporarily from the lethargy of waiting for my repatriation. The Entertainments Officer at III M.U. came to me in the Mess one evening with a notice announcing an E.N.S.A. 'coup'.

T.E. Matthews and Eileen Rolph were coming to III M.U. the following week to play the Three Brahms Sonatas for Violin and Piano! "Like hell they are!" said I, and, the following day, I set out for Shepheards Hotel in Cairo on a life-saving mission. Tommy Matthews had been a colleague of mine in the Hallé Orchestra for 10 years (until the outbreak of war) but he had, for some reason best known to himself, escaped military service: his wife, Eileen Rolph, I had met on one or two occasions, but I had lost touch with both of them for 6 years. When I found them, eventually, they were staying at the 'Continental', next door to Shepheards, and looking hot and exhausted after their flight and non-adjustment to the sub-tropical climate. They listened with some impatience to what I felt it was my duty to tell them of my experiences in and around Cairo, entertaining the troops in conditions far less hostile than those in which they now found themselves. Hissing and booing were the *gentler* forms of non-acceptance by troops in transit camps, particularly those in which Colonial – Australian, New Zealand and South African – troops were, with difficulty, confined. I went on to explain that the McKeown Sextet, playing the lightest music, had been obliged to abandon dangerous missionary trips, and I ventured to suggest what *their* reception would be if the Brahms Violin and Piano Sonatas were 'on offer' to restless troops awaiting repatriation. I further explained that the Cairo Symphony Orchestra concerts in the Ewart Memorial Hall had satisfied a cultural need and had attracted large audiences of troops and civilians alike, who were eager to listen to good music. "Thrusting Brahms down the throats of an unwilling audience is a rash enterprise at the best of times, but a highly dangerous one in these circumstances," and so I went on without shaking their resolution or scepticism.

After exchanging a few pleasantries I was about to leave when I casually mentioned a visit to III M.U. and the fascinating things which could be seen there (and nowhere else in the world) including the N.A.A.F.I. piano! I knew this remarkable instrument very well – just over half the ivories were missing, revealing an odd assortment of glue and wood, distinctly uncomfortable to sensitive finger ends: strings which had broken over the years had never been replaced (which made a mockery of trying to tune the damned thing!) and about 10 or 12 of the hammers had been broken by insensitive performers who had never in their lives been concerned with the niceties of the 'Matthay Touch'. Its crowning glory was the endless variety of jangling sounds which it used to emit at the slightest jar. These sounds fascinated me, and on many occasions I investigated them. I never discovered fewer than 5 empty beer bottles lurking in its innards!

What it was in my narrative which influenced their decision I shall never know, but Eileen Rolph was the first to lose interest in playing Brahms Sonatas at III M.U., and Tommy Matthews, who couldn't bear to lose the engagement, soon gave up the idea of playing Bach Partitas, unaccompanied, in place of them. I advised them to escape from Egypt while they were still safe – which they probably did. I never met Tommy again. Soon after the war he gravitated to London and eventually became the leader of the Covent Garden Orchestra. The last news of him reached me from Melbourne, where, after taking up a post with the Symphony Orchestra, he died.

My repatriation was uneventful: nameless American 'liberty-ships' plied between Alexandria and Toulon, carrying cargoes of uncomfortable and badly fed service-men across the Mediterranean to an equally painfully slow rail journey across France to Dieppe. Dieppe to Newhaven was not without anxiety – we wore life-jackets as a precaution: mines were not yet completely cleared from the English Channel. Special trains at the quayside at Newhaven conveyed us to demobilisation centres located (and isolated) at strategic places around the country – I arrived at Retford in the late afternoon and began a clearance operation which lasted a week. Becoming a civilian involved a great deal of 'documentation', and in the space of 3 crowded days, having satisfied the M.O.'s that I was not a carrier of the 'plague' and other horrific diseases, I heard much of the word 'entitlement' which embraced a ration-book, clothing coupons, a suit of civilian clothes (or sports-jacket and trousers) tokens for chocolate, free issue of cigarettes (because I was still on overseas service) and overseas pay until I was demobilised. I cannot remember at what stage of the proceedings I received the 'gratuity', but one of the 'hand-outs' mystified me and irritated the clerk to the point of 'shooing' me out of his office as the oddest creature he had been called upon to deal with.

The 'thing' which caused the rumpus was an 'Unemployment Card', partially covered in stamps. The inane conversation which ensued went something like this – "I have never seen one of these before in my life – what is it?" "Well, we've been stamping it ever since you joined the Services: you can 'sign-on' and draw unemployment benefit." "Like hell I can," said I, "I am not in an insurable job, and I have never seen the inside of a Labour Exchange." "Ah, well, now that you've got one – you can put your own stamps on it and sign-on." "But I can't sign-on," said I, "and I have no intention of subscribing, for life, to charity." "Ah," said he, "if you put your own stamps on you get free 'doctoring'." "But I don't want free 'doctoring'!" By this time a little heat was being generated, and he played a trump card. Not knowing what to do with the Card if I didn't accept it he slyly handed it to me with the soothing words, "When you get home, just register with your Doctor. You are 'entitled' to free medical treatment for two years after leaving the Services." I did, and a fine pickle I found myself in for the next 22 years!

In 1948 a grand Utopian scheme was started in which everybody, musicians included, was entitled to free medical treatment, free dentures and free spectacles. The scheme was called 'National Health Service' and there was great joy among the members of the B.B.C. Northern Orchestra (myself included), that, for the first time in history, musicians had been included in a contributory scheme and accepted, in law, as human beings who might contract normal ailments. The joy, in my case, was short-lived – I received a dirty little note from Newcastle demanding £42 arrears of contributions. I refused to pay them, and was curtly informed that if I remained in full employment (i.e. 52 stamps on every card), 2 of my stamps would contribute to wiping off the arrears of £42, but it would be 22 years before I was 'clean' enough to be 'in benefit'.

Douglas Houghton, who initiated the National Health Scheme, was also M.P. for Sowerby Division, and I once responded to his invitation to meet him at the Constituency Headquarters. He listened, and also laughed, at the penalty I had paid for 6 years in the Services. "There is nothing I can do about it (the typical answer at Question Time in the House of Commons) – you must be the only one in the country – what a pity!"

Chapter XVII

My homecoming in mid-January, 1946, was sad. I found my Father beyond consolation, and although it was now three years since I had said 'good-bye' to my Mother, she was everywhere in that empty house. The tears, which ought to have flowed, filled our hearts, and the words remained unsaid, yet, by the Grace of God, we shared each other's grief and were closer at that moment than either of us realised.

A few days sufficed to get over the first batch of meaningless – "Eh, hello, you don't look a day older," and "What are you going to do now? Something useful this time, I hope?", and so on. What I intended to do was quite clear, but there were several schools of thought as to its usefulness. I first met Professor Procter-Gregg in the Department of Music at Manchester University to solicit support for my application to read for the degree of Doctor in Music. The Board of the Faculty approved the application and I began the statutory three years of residence for the degree. Earning a living, preferably one which did not involve travelling, was the second priority: the B.B.C. Northern Orchestra offered the perfect solution to my problems. Maurice Johnstone, who was the North Region director of music and Manager of the Northern Orchestra, was expecting a visit from me (so he said) having been made aware of my existence, and availability, by stalwart friends in the persons of Syd Coulston, Reg Stead (the leader) and Charles Taylor, who were already established members of the Orchestra. The interview with Maurice Johnstone was extremely amusing – he was a shining example of decision makers at the B.B.C., who never made up their minds about anything. He began, "I can't do anything for you at the moment, but there is a distinct possibility that the 'establishment' of the Orchestra *may* be increased within the next twelve months. In the meantime, I will bear you in mind if we should ever require any deputies or extras. If you call next door, and leave your name and address with Mrs. Roberts (the orchestral secretary) she may be able to use you – good morning!" I did as I was instructed and went up into the Canteen where several of my friends were waiting to hear the outcome of my interview. They laughed, and said, "It went well – see you in a few days." In this respect they were also right – I deputised regularly until the beginning of July, 1946, and was then offered a permanent contract which I held for 18½ years.

Promotion was rapid. I was very soon sitting at the Second Desk with Charles Taylor and eventually at the First Desk with Reginald Stead, as subleader. The conductor in those early post-war years was Charles Groves, to whom I had good reason to be grateful in the later stages of the 'practical' examination for my Mus.D. degree. He and I gave three Violin and Piano Recitals in the Jubilee Hall at the University to which the public were admitted. In the finals, Sir John Barbirolli and R.J. Forbes (Principal of the Royal Manchester College of Music) were invited to act as external examiners for a recital programme in which Maurice Aitchison (Reader in Music in the University) accompanied me. I remember both the external examiners 'requesting' the E.J. Moeran Violin Concerto: the work was a particular favourite of Sir John's (since E.J. was a friend of his) and R.J. Forbes, who was responsible for the published 'piano reduction' of the work, had a lively interest in Maurice Aitchison's ability to cope with its difficulties! We both 'passed' although I must confess that I, in the end, had more to show for it than Maurice. The 'practical' was a minor part of the Finals: there were written examinations in Fugue (in six parts), Counterpoint (in eight parts), Composition in a variety of styles including a Choral Prelude (for choir and orchestra) on a modal theme devised by Maurice Aitchison – I later forgave him for this subtle piece of devilment! Although the Degree was not conferred until December, 1948* the examination results were published in the 'Manchester Guardian' in July.

I arrived one morning for a rehearsal with the B.B.C. Northern in the studios in Piccadilly, Manchester, to find (to my surprise) a reception committee consisting of Charles Groves, Maurice Johnstone and Mr. Salt, the Regional Administrative Director. To my embarrassment they all made suitable noises of congratulation, to which I responded by quoting the Aesop Fable of the chicken which stuck a Peacock's feather in its tail and strutted for a little while in the wrong pen, until the fraud was discovered. When it was eventually thrown back where it belonged, its own kind would have none of it either, and it was thrown over the fence to the wolves!

There were two very significant remarks made at the conclusion of the speeches. The Regional Director asked me "What do you intend to do now?", and Maurice Johnstone said "I've got a 'Rare Bird'† in my orchestra – I don't know what to do with him!" In answer to the Regional Director's question, I applied for 17 vacant posts at the B.B.C. for conductors, music assistants, programme pickers, timers, librarians,

---

* until the statutory 9 terms of residence had been completed.

† hence the subtitle of the book.

tea-makers! – anything, in fact, without ever, in 16 years, getting as far as an interview! After every unsuccessful application, Maurice Johnstone solved his own problem ("I don't know what to do with him!") by consoling me with the soothing words – "You are doing a much better job here."

Being useful, in oblivion, became the story of my life until 1962. I shared, during this period, a Lectureship with Clifford Knowles at the University. The part-time appointment in the Department of Music at the University was mostly concerned with under-graduate teaching in the 'skills' of counterpoint, canon and fugue, and the flexible tutorials with small groups of students were easily arranged in the free time from duty at the B.B.C. As an Internal Examiner in the University, and committed to a rigid timetable for the June examinations, I experienced little difficulty in being released by the B.B.C. when clashes occurred: by curious coincidence these were rare – the first of the B.B.C. Northern Orchestra's staggered holidays invariably fell during the period of the examinations.

The years between 1946 and 1962 slipped away in comparative security and busy boredom.

Since this book is 'mainly concerned with interesting people' it would be difficult to write about the hundreds of applicants for places in Music at the University who chose a career in music 'with a pen', or their parents who thought that music was a 'nice clean living', especially for a girl! Industry and application without aptitude are not enough to sustain students embarking on a music course at University level! The only student in those early years who subsequently made a mark in the profession was Maxwell Davies but he learnt nothing from me, and very little from the other members of the staff.

The 'interesting people' at the B.B.C. were mainly fascinating, unstackable nonentities who were promoted out of sight provided that the standard of its saleable product – 'transmissions' – did not attract criticism from an undiscerning public rapidly becoming satiated with entertainment on numerous wave-lengths from 6.30 a.m. until midnight. The policy of spreading culture and providing young composers with the unique opportunity of having their works well-rehearsed and performed led the B.B.C. to establish 13 Staff Orchestras on permanent contract. Lofty as these motives were, the immediate effect was economic disaster for the already well-established, self-supporting Symphony Orchestras such as the Hallé, L.S.O., R.P.O., Birmingham City, Liverpool Philharmonic and the Scottish National, who were driven to the extremity of offering yearly contracts to players in order to prevent massive migration to the B.B.C. The provincial orchestras which managed to retain players against more attractive salaries offered by the B.B.C. were obliged to 'create' work for them during the summer months, and have since survived only with huge subsidies from City Councils and the Arts Council.

The surfeit of music relentlessly turned out by the B.B.C. and unwillingly aided and abetted by the provincial orchestras has, like the Sorcerer's Apprentice, produced a seemingly uncontrollable flood of concerts in this country that the Magician himself would have had the greatest difficulty in stemming, or in recreating a climate in which fewer and better concerts were 'events' worth making the effort to attend. One of the most fallacious precepts of the B.B.C.'s post-war expansion programme was the 'unlimited' supply of public money which could now be spent on unlimited rehearsal time – the inevitable result hopefully being a steep rise in the standard of orchestral playing! In my experience, between 1946 and 1963, the reverse was the case. The creation of new jobs, and security of tenure in them, was warmly welcomed by the Musicians' Union, who gladly endorsed the new contracts of service and salaries with the B.B.C. and eventually with the provincial orchestras, and so began the New Era of boredom, disinterest and mediocrity with the greatest disincentive of all – no 'differentials' in pay between the responsible, experienced players at the front desks and the raw student recruits at the back. Unlimited rehearsal time made experience, ability to read at sight, and conscientious private practice superfluous to requirements: it also, by interminable repetition (to use up the time) produced a hitherto unknown terminal disease rarely recorded on death certificates of being 'bored to death'. This disease was quickly followed by another, even more deadly; that of being 'bowed to death'.

'Bowing' is the greatest sacrifice British orchestral players have ever made to the ego of conductors who wish to impress upon audiences that the orchestras they conduct are well-trained and disciplined if the bowing in the strings goes 'up and down' like a well-drilled regiment of soldiers. Every professional string player knows that if there was any distinguishable difference between the sounds he or she made with an 'up' or 'down' bow they are in the wrong business! Yet every string part of every piece in the B.B.C.'s music libraries in London and Manchester are disfigured with the signs 'V' (up) and '⊓' (down) which have taken years to write in, and were regularly changed, from one to the other, at every rehearsal according to the whims and caprices of the Principals with the blessing of the Conductor (if he had the time to spare – and he had!).

'Bowing' became the bane of my life at the B.B.C., and has remained so ever since: on the other hand there were those who were so devoted to duty, and so anxious to impress the conductors, that pencils and rubbers dangled from their music-stands and they found it impossible to play any piece until every note in it had been suitably branded with the signs 'V' or '⊓'. The Principal Viola in the Northern spent more time playing his pencil and rubber than his instrument, and there were caustic remarks passed by members of his own section, who were obliged to stop playing and copy the changes into every part at every desk, and also by other

Principals whose time was also being wasted. He remained impervious to all comments, even to one I made when I was driven to the point of screaming at his constant interruptions – he took up his rubber and pencil for the thirty-fourth time and said to the Conductor, "Some damn fool has bowed this part!" Said I, "The trouble with you, Paul, is that when you rub out one damn fool's bowing you write another's in!".

Not all the stoppages ended in bitterness and wrangling – one in particular was laughed out of court by the Orchestra's chief wag, Norman Cunliffe, who was a long-suffering member of the viola section. After a very long spell of lifting instruments up to their chins and playing a couple of bars, putting them down and writing 'up' bows and 'down' bows incessantly for half an hour, Norman Cunliffe exploded, and at the top of his voice appealed to the Conductor, "I don't know why there's all this fuss about 'down' bows and 'up' bows – Tony is just grateful if you BRING a bow!!" The spontaneous laughter which greeted this remark put a stop to bowings for the rest of the day. 'Tony', as everyone in the Orchestra well knew, was a reference to Anthony Hopkins (harpist in the winter season with Julius Harrison at Hastings), who had for many years conducted the North Pier Orchestra at Blackpool with great success during long summer seasons: he also epitomised the general public's image of what a musician 'ought to look like' he bore a remarkable resemblance to Franz Liszt, and could 'sell' anything in 'light music' to the public. He had several attributes which attached him to the happy members of his Orchestra, the principal one being that he never rehearsed! He said, "Hello!" on the opening day, and "hoped they would have a happy time," and after the closing concert thanked them for their loyalty and help and hoped to see them all again next season! Norman Cunliffe chose this adorable character well when he cried from the heart "Tony is just grateful if you BRING a bow!"

Not all the orchestral parts used by the Northern Orchestra were available in its own music library – extensive as it certainly was. Frequently it was necessary to borrow from the Central Library at Yelding House, London: these parts carried warning 'stickers' announcing that, "The 'bowings' and 'fingerings' have been approved by Paul Beard and the Musical Director, and must not, in any circumstances, be altered." The best 'fingering' for the difficult technical passages which abound in the string parts (particularly first violin parts) of the orchestral repertoire since the mid-19th century has evolved by the cumulative practice and experience of generations of orchestral players. Awareness of the existence, and the acquisition of, the fingering to cope with the difficulties, distinguishes the professional from the amateur (who, alas, plays wrong notes with such conviction that difficulties do not exist!). In pre-war England it was necessary for survival, as an orchestral player, to get the passages 'up one's sleeve' – a maxim not perpetuated in the B.B.C. post-war orchestras. Days of rehearsing from parts 'bowed' and 'fingered' invariably produced insipid performances from robots.

The new invective on fingering stirred Norman Cunliffe eventually to make two outbursts (in response to promptings from me, I must confess) which rendered the whole thing ridiculous. In the early 1950s the intake of students and young inexperienced players into the Northern Orchestra had brought with it a new-style conversation into the bandroom – 'Schools of Violin Playing' and 'Methods' and 'Systems' superseded all else, and the older generation, myself included, would give a disdainful sniff, and walk away from it. After one of these high-brow tea-intervals, when we were back at work, the viola section got into one of its rare difficult corners which brought the Orchestra to a stop – the time was ripe for a comment, so I said, rather archly, to Norman "Which 'system' are you using for that passage, Norman?" "The 'Hoover'* System," was his prompt reply.

To his credit, I never heard Norman repeat a wise-crack, and it was some time before I prompted him again on the subject of fingering. The violas did get into further difficulties with a chromatic passage and I couldn't resist a little prod – "Doesn't the 'Hoover' System work with this one, Norman?" "Oh, no," said he, "I'm using the 'Anything-which-happens-to-be-passing-at-the-time' fingering!" He could, with consummate ease, give a ridiculous answer to a serious question – with a straight face. On one occasion there was a great confusion about a little piece having a mixed bag of publishers: some of us had Boosey & Hawkes' parts on the stand, and others parts by Chappell & Sons. Stanford Robinson, who was conducting, asked Norman Cunliffe, "Is your part Boosey & Hawkes?" "Oh, no," said Norman, very seriously, "it's Marks & Spencer's!"

It was usual for soloists (in the 1950s) playing concertos in broadcast programmes to write their own cadenzas, and on the occasion Max Rostal played the Max Bruch violin concerto, Norman made a little aside during the announcer's introduction, which fortunately was not heard over the 'air' – "With cadenzas by Max Factor!"

The moments of light relief were scarce, and the efforts of Maurice Johnstone to take the Orchestra 'out and about' and to bring new faces on to the rostrum were not always successful. Some of the nonentities (to whom I have previously referred) were unbelievable in their inexperience, and one of them – Michael Mudie – was introduced to the Orchestra as 'the next permanent conductor'. The 'dignitaries' stayed

---

* 'Hoover', of course, is the trade-name of a famous brand of carpet-sweeper, which once carried, on every advertisement, the startling news that "It beats, as it sweeps, as it cleans!" – a reference, we all knew, to Norman's new system of fingering.

long enough to listen to him rehearse an excerpt from the first act of 'La Bohème' which he obviously knew very well, since he cried out, many times, "Have you blown your candle out yet?" On his way out, Maurice Johnstone made the comment (to Reggie Stead and myself), "I've found you a JEWEL!" He *had*, as the next day proved! The programme for Michael Mudie's second broadcast was the Bach 3rd Brandenburg Concerto and the Dvorák 'Cello Concerto in which the soloist was (I think) Michael Bunting. The Orchestra had, the previous day, (with the infallible intuition all professional orchestras have) arrived, after five minutes, at the decision "We've got a right one here!" Michacl Mudie was, unfortunately, in the last stages of Multiple Sclerosis: in conducting Puccini from memory he had not betrayed the fact that he was nearly blind, neither had his retarded movements proved his inability to turn over the pages of a score.

The morning's rehearsal began harmlessly with the Bach, but when the wind joined us for the Dvorák, there was near pandemonium in the Milton Hall. Otto Pearch (the 3rd Horn) was an old Hallé player, and regarded by us all as an institution within an institution: he began the proceedings by standing up and waving his music in the air, shouting (in a stage whisper) "Oih, oih," in the direction of the rostrum. He put his music and his instrument down, and walked all the way through the Orchestra, saying quite audibly "He's as blind as a ruddy bat, this one! I'm going for lunch!", and he did. Minutes before the end of the rehearsal Otto came back as noisily as he went out, saying, as he resumed his place "Are you at it yet?" Michael Mudie had not missed either his presence or the notes he ought to have played. The actual broadcast was a near disaster – the two link bars between the movements of the Brandenburg, which had been carefully rehearsed, were omitted, which surprised everyone except Mudie, who galloped from one movement to the next as if they never existed, and, in the Dvorák, his tremor was such that he managed to twitch at about twenty loose pages of the score and scatter them all over the place! Reggie Stead put down his fiddle and spent an interminable time picking them up, sorting them into page-order and replacing them on the rostrum (the Orchestra and soloist in the meantime played about thirty bars of the piece without the useless conductor). Reggie, quite unceremoniously, found the right bar and pointed to it with his left hand (like the 'moving finger … having writ …') and, with his right hand at the back of Mudie's head, slowly bent it down to within ten inches of the music: he resumed his seat and the performance continued without further incident, but not without anxiety.

The Orchestral Committee made very strong, and not unreasonable, protests to Maurice Johnstone against Michael Mudie's appointment, but he was inflexible, and it was other influences which eventually changed his mind – we were relieved not to see Michael Mudie on the rostrum again.

The rear windows of many motor-cars belonging to members of the Musician's Union now carry conspicuous 'stickers' appealing to the public to 'Keep Music Live'. This cry in the wilderness is thirty years out of date. The broadcasting of orchestral music never has been a 'live' musical experience for the unseen audience, and in order to remove all traces of human frailty (wrong notes, bad balance, faulty intonation, wrong entries and the like) from its transmission, it became the policy of the B.B.C. to pre-record most of its programmes. The Recording Engineers or Studio Managers or Balance Controllers (or whatever name was currently given to them) became highly skilled in all the ramifications of recording, and, as their importance grew with their responsibilities, so did the 'knob-twisters' (with their never-ending adjustments of microphones in the studio) take over from the conductors the problems of nuances and internal balances which were now artificially created in the 'listening box'. Not until the Studio Manager was satisfied that a recorded programme was free from blemishes was the orchestra released from the studio; the tapes were meticulously checked, and, if necessary, suspect passages re-recorded and 'cut-into' the tape: thus began the insidious practice (now completely out of hand in the gramophone business) of selling to the public superhuman performances which are compilations of the best bits of many.*

---

* It never crosses the mind of anyone devoting a life-time, and a fortune, to collecting 'perfect' recorded performances that they eventually become the yard-stick by which he or she assesses all 'live' music. Recently, I was playing in the Yorkshire Sinfonia Chamber Orchestra at a concert in Leeds Town Hall where the very expensive soloist was Ricci, who played the Mozart A major Violin Concerto, and (as was expected of him) a group of Paganini Caprices. For the Paganini Caprices the orchestra was requested to disperse, leaving the platform free for Ricci to display his phenomenal technique. I retired to the back of the choir benches on the platform, occupied by the overflow of a packed audience, and sat next to a 'fanatic' who told me, with great pride, that 'he had everything that Ricci had ever recorded'. In spite of a lapse of memory in the Mozart (he inexplicably, in the exposition, began the 2nd subject in the tonic key instead of the dominant) and one or two tricks in the Paganini which didn't quite come off, I was amazed at his technique and his stamina (he gave four recitals in the space of five days in Los Angeles, Leeds, Rome and Amsterdam). But not so my connoisseur of records, who grunted, as I left him to take my place in the orchestra, "He's gone off – I wish I'd saved my money!"

Stanford Robinson, who was not the most popular Staff Conductor the B.B.C. ever had, was a frequent guest conductor with the Northern Orchestra: he was a slave to pre-recording, and, from the first bar of music at the first rehearsal, the Studio Manager began recording chunks of music which Stanford Robinson hurried into the listening box to hear played back to him – not to us. Although he never flinched at wasting our time I must say in mitigation that he wasted all his lunch and tea intervals listening to tapes of his rehearsals: he was dedicated and tireless, and I can well remember two of the 'potted operas' he recorded in Manchester, which I had not met before, and have not played since – 'The Two Widows' by Smetana and 'Die Feen', an early work by Wagner.

One member of the music staff at the North Region was sometimes let loose on us as a conductor, and given limitless time to rehearse the most elementary pieces. Gordon Thorne was a 'nace gentleman' who buried his head in the score and bored us into submission, not by fussing over details, but by endless, purposeless repetition. He smiled occasionally, and spoke too at the end of each run-through (and there were dozens of them), using the same phrase "It's taking shape, gentlemen – back to the beginning!" which, over a period of three-hour rehearsals, reduced the Orchestra to a state of anaesthesia, broken only by the announcements that it was 'break time' or 'coffee interval'. The Orchestra responded by groaning quietly each time we were directed 'back to the beginning', but the isolated protests of "Oh no! not again!" became less frequent as the hours wore on, and the coffee intervals, which were normally periods of animated gossip, cigarettes and tinkling cups, became half-stupefied periods of dreary silence and sagging minds and bodies. One of Gordon's programmes included two pieces – the 'Chaconne in G minor' by Purcell (six minutes in duration) and Beethoven's 'Little Symphony' No. 8 in F (28 minutes in duration) – which had occupied him (and us) in the process of 'back to the beginning' for six hours on the first day and three hours on the second. The Purcell 'Chaconne' (which had never previously been in my 'Top Ten') became a piece we all learned to hate that day, and the Orchestra, quite unconsciously, devised a ruse which we thought would defeat the constant repetitions. As we approached the last dozen bars, the playing became unbelievably cautious and quiet, and without blemish: the thought in the minds of us all was "He can't go back again!", but we were thwarted by the Principal Viola, who had, the previous day, exhausted all his opportunities of getting the bowings right. He broke the charm about three bars from the end by addressing the Conductor – "Oh! Mr. Thorne, I've got a 'hairpin' in this bar – how far 'up' does it go?". There were 64 members at that precise moment who were only too eager to tell him 'how far up' it ought to have gone!! but like the ladies and gentlemen they probably were, they restrained themselves and waited for the inevitable – "Ah! you've got a point there, Mr. Cropper – back to the beginning!!".

It made a change! The tea-break which followed this incident was exceedingly quiet: any movement was aimless meandering to the notice-board or to the window overlooking Deansgate. After five minutes of inertia I exploded with – "Do you know, I would like to do 'The Ring' sometime with Gordon!", followed very quickly with the rider "I should like to think that I would live long enough to be ABLE to do 'The Ring' with Gordon!".*

One other tiresome recording occupied two whole days, and was the only occasion I can remember in which a known blemish (or in this case an omission) in the recording was not rectified. Norman del Mar was the Conductor, and the work to be recorded was the 'Prometheus Ballet' by Beethoven (in its entirety). The overture is, of course, well-known, and frequently played, but the rest of the work was unfamiliar to us, and this performance of it was the only one in which I have taken part. There was one obsolete instrument revived for this expensive recording – the Basset Horn, and Colin Davies was engaged to play the few notes Beethoven had written for this exotic instrument (which emitted a sound like a bull-frog!). Two nights at the Midland Hotel, subsistence allowance, first-class rail-fare from London, and a fat fee for playing half a dozen notes was the price the B.B.C. paid to add a touch of authenticity to this rare performance. The rehearsals ran their allotted course to the second, as they always did when del Mar was on the box, and the recording was made as scheduled, BUT – Colin Davies lost his place, and not a grunt from the Basset Horn was recorded!

This trivial incident, not in itself worth mentioning, had a sequel about a year later when Colin Davies appeared once again in the Milton Hall, this time having begun to bloom as a conductor. The programme, I remember, included 'The Dolly Suite' by Fauré, and I also remember him breezing onto the box and looking airily around the studio, saying (as if he ought to start with a joke) "The last time I was in this room I played the Basset Horn!". "Oh no you didn't," I said, "you BROUGHT IT WITH YOU!!"

---

* The 18½ hours of music in the 'Ring' cycle would (at a rough estimate) have occupied Gordon for 350 years, or 20 re-incarnations!

Chapter XVIII

One never-to-be-forgotten occasion occurred in Leeds when Sir Thomas was conducting the Northern B.B.C.'s concert in the Town Hall. After the concert the Lord Mayor of Leeds entertained us all to a reception in the Town Hall. It was a formal occasion when distinguished members of the audience and the orchestra were met by the Civic Dignitaries and Beecham. I was last in line and when Sir Thomas shook hands with me, he said with a twinkle in his eye "I've seen you before," and then strode off majestically towards the salon. But at the threshold he stopped in his tracks – the B.B.C. Music Department had planned a surprise! and the bush telegraph once again sprang into action. At a sign from an assistant-secretary to one of the secretaries-to-an-assistant the Reginald Stead String Quartet broke out into Mozart's K.499 in D major. "Good God!" muttered Beecham (loud enough for me to hear) "I require at least 24 hours' notice for chamber-music, in order to flee the town!"

The establishment of 13 Staff Orchestras by the B.B.C. in the immediate post-war years, and the surfeit of music which they were relentlessly to pour out over the next 30 years has already been referred to. 'Deterioration' (which implies that the standard of orchestral playing had once been better) is perhaps a harsh word to describe my impressions of the B.B.C. Northern Orchestra on my return from war service: the Northern, in common with the other 12 newly-created orchestras, was entirely without heritage, character or tradition, and in spite of having a nucleus of former Hallé players, the standard of playing was markedly inferior to the halcyon pre-war days.

Among members of the profession in Manchester, the B.B.C. was affectionately known as the 'Factory', which (as the word suggests) turned out a musical commodity in great quantities, well-rehearsed and flawless, but just as exciting as a string of shining sausages: it is significant that in 18 years' association with the Northern I cannot recall a performance over which I can wax hot or cold, or describe, unless there were incidents or accidents which were complementary to the music. In fact, the responsibility of sitting at the first desk as Sub-Leader, and as Principal Second Violin (in the later stages) was the only inducement to stay awake and look interested in the job. (Stage III of the 'System'!)

Two of the older Hallé players who had escaped the war and were well entrenched in the B.B.C. Northern when I returned in July, 1946, were Don Hyden and Fred Brough (both of whom are still alive). Don, who was Principal Second Violin, held the Hallé '20 years' Gold Service Medal' and besides the reputation of being a fine player (and a great favourite with Harty) was also well-known as being a careful man, especially with small coins of the Realm: he smoked 'Woodbines', which in those bad old days were 2d. for five – but never, for health reasons, a whole one at one go. He nipped each one in half and pouted (from painful experience) when lighting each fragment, in order not to singe the end of his nose. The pouting position was maintained until the minute stub began to give him notice that unless he spat it out he would sustain painful burns. Don was obliged to give up this expensive habit when some wicked Government put up the price to 2½d. for five! He also (for the benefit of his health) walked from Slade Lane to the Studio, both ways, in order to save a twopenny tram fare! Fred Brough was quite charming, and had neither weaknesses nor habits, unless his passion for golf could be considered in either category: in spite of painstaking practice his golf never improved, and his handicap (like Alfred Livesley's) remained astronomical all his life.

Although they were dissimilar in character, they were fine players, and had enjoyed many more years of experience with the Hallé Orchestra than any of us who formed the nucleus of the B.B.C. Northern: they were also sitting at the first desks of the violins and in constant danger of saying too much, or too little, to the conductor at the conclusion of every broadcast. The frustration which arises from the non-existence of applause, comment or criticism from the unseen audiences of hundreds, thousands or millions is soul-destroying for performers and conductors alike, but the sight of players scampering out of the studio after the closing announcement (and the red studio light is extinguished) is not calculated to gladden the heart of any conductor who may be waiting for compliments. Neither is it in the best interests of future relationships for anyone to be so naive (as were Don Hyden and Fred Brough) as to linger on after broadcasts in order to tell the conductor that his performance 'reminded them of the wonderful pre-war Hallé days, and the superlative performance Weingartner had once given of *this very same* Brahms symphony'! Similar thoughts frequently passed through my mind, but I escaped from the building before I was tempted to express them!

Not until George Hurst became permanent conductor of the 'Northern' was Pierre Monteux invited to conduct: he came to Manchester on three occasions – the first and second were short studio recordings and the third a public concert in the Free Trade Hall on October 12th, 1963 (the date of my retirement from the B.B.C.). The main work in the first studio recording was Beethoven's 4th Symphony in B*b*, and the only two incidents which I can remember at the rehearsal were his opening gambit, (in not very good English) "Zis is za hundert and eight orchestra which I have conduct," and his insistence on the First Violins playing B♯ as the second crotchet in bar 119 of the exposition, and E♯ as the second crotchet in the corresponding passage in the recapitulation (bar 393). He explained in French that he had seen Beethoven's manuscript, 'and Beethoven wrote B♯'.*

The second visit of Monteux to the Milton Hall Studio in Manchester was memorable for me, because I was guilty of an indiscretion at the rehearsal and suitably rebuked by the Maestro. It was often said of Monteux 'that he had the smallest 'beat' and the biggest fee of any conductor in the profession': he also had less to say (at rehearsals) and was more highly respected (in consequence of it) than any other conductor I have ever met. The cardinal sin of which all orchestral players are guilty in varying degrees – from once, perhaps occasionally, frequently, and eventually to the incurable state – is that of continuing to play on for one note, two notes, half a bar, or (in the case of the degenerates) for a passage of music, AFTER the conductor has called a halt, in order to correct mistakes or rehearse. This nauseating practice, for which there is neither cure nor forgiveness, has in my experience wasted almost as much time as 'getting the bowings right'!

The photograph, taken in the Milton Hall, clearly indicates the Maestro holding up a cautionary finger and about to impart a few words of wisdom to the Northern Orchestra – also in the picture is my humble self (as Principal Second Violin) 'taking in' every word. I wish with all my heart that I had done so on every occasion at that rehearsal, but I transgressed!

Monteux was rehearsing 'Nuages' and 'Fêtes' (two of the Debussy Nocturnes') and we were within sight of the end of 'Fêtes' when, for no reason which was apparent to anyone in the orchestra, he stopped and was about to address someone in the Wood Wind department. I, having counted 10 of the 11 bars before the Second Violin entry, hastily put my fiddle under my chin and gave a resounding 'plonk' at something on the 'D' string which was approximately the right pitch, and nothing like the right dynamic. Monteux turned his head, looked me straight in the eye, and said very quietly, "C♯!" implying that the intonation was not the only thing wrong with my solo effort: he then turned his attention to whoever had caused the stoppage in the first place, and the incident quickly passed out of everyone's mind, except mine.

---

* Beethoven did not write B♯! He wrote an accidental ♯ sign against a 'diatonic' B*b*, which would, in effect, raise the B*b* by a semitone. The ♮ (natural) sign which Beethoven used against the E♯ in bar 393 had precisely the same effect.

Pierre Monteux in the Milton Hall Studio

The regular offenders in the Northern Orchestra were soon back into their stride after Monteux' visit, and at the end of one rehearsal which had been fairly well-cursed with little solos, I was goaded into relating a story from my teenage experiences with the Todmorden Amateur Symphony Orchestra.

The Orchestra was very good by amateur standards, and healthy in numbers by any standards: the rehearsals were held on Sunday mornings in the Sobriety Hall, an almost derelict building which was the headquarters of an already derelict society called the Band of Hope Union. This temperance institution had, with dubious success, been preaching the 'evils of strong drink' throughout the industrial revolution to the fathers of families varying in size from 9 to 13 children, who couldn't afford the stuff anyway! The rehearsals, which began punctually at 10.30 a.m., ended abruptly at 12.25 – the members dispersed in great haste (and in defiance of the teachings of the Band of Hope Union) to the White Hart, which opened at 12.30.

The principal character in the story (when I eventually get around to it) was Willie, who was seventeen years of age and a rival of mine on the fiddle at all local Music Festivals, which were numerous in the early 1920s. Willie's position in the First Violins was 'outside' at the fifth desk, which was situated in the heart of the orchestra (in fact, under the conductor's nose). I being two years Willie's junior, and considered to be a vastly inferior player, was placed 'inside' at the fifth desk, in order to 'turn over' the music for Willie. On my immediate left was Albert Starkie, a dry old stick in his late fifties, who held the position of Principal 'Cello, undisputed, for life. The only common factor which distinguished Willie, myself and Albert from the rest of the orchestra, was the enviable privilege of 'going on the train for lessons'!! (Todmorden, besides nestling in an isolated pocket of the Pennines, also nestled comfortably in the Middle Ages! Todmorden Railway Station was, to the vast majority of its citizens, the gateway to the outside world and all knowledge and enlightenment.)

Albert had led the good life, and being reasonably 'well-off' had indulged himself to the extent of having a long course of tuition (in Manchester) with Clyde Twelvetrees, who was Principal 'Cello in the Hallé Orchestra. In his forty-fourth year Albert's 'good life' changed dramatically – he was trapped reluctantly into the not-very-sublime state of matrimony by a widow (with two grown-up daughters) and any ideas he may have entertained of one day mastering the difficulties of the Saint Saëns 'cello concerto were dissipated in the steam of drying nappies and mounting matrimonial responsibilities. Taciturn by nature, and stoic by the gradual process of disenchantment, Albert had, at the time of our mutual acquaintance, become an exceedingly bitter and sarcastic character, who controlled his temper and biting tongue with varying degrees of success. Sitting next to him in the orchestra was a mildly terrifying experience for a boy of 15, and whenever Albert became restless and began to fume he invariably lifted his 'cello to a height of four or five inches and stuck the spike venomously into the Sobriety Hall floorboards (or symbolically into the heart of whatever was at that moment irritating him).

Willie, on my right, the central figure of my story, was an apprentice engineer, who, being stung with professional pride (on learning that I was being sent at great expense on the train to Blackburn, to have violin lessons from Ernest O'Malley, then number 3 in the Hallé Orchestra) was obliged to go one better, and straightway took himself off to Manchester, to have lessons from Alfred Barker – the 'leader' of the Hallé Orchestra!

Progress on the violin, as everyone knows, is painful and exceeding slow, with one notable exception: Willie, who after one or two lessons began to demonstrate his progress by becoming Life President of the Cardinal Sin Society, by continuing to play longer and longer stanzas after the Conductor had stopped the orchestra. At first there were 'murmurs' around the orchestra of 'how well Willie was getting on', but after months of tedious interruptions the orchestra and the conductor became resigned to Willie's solos, and waited with commendable patience. Albert, whose cauldron of wrath was constantly bubbling, was the first to show any signs of dissent at Willie's little moments of glory, and I was aware from his mounting restlessness and the increase in the frequency (and the height) of his spike-sticking that an explosion was imminent – it was a long time coming, but worth waiting for.

One Sunday morning a new work appeared on the music stands – the overture 'The Well of Love' by Balfe, which the conductor held back until late in the rehearsal, as 'top-of-the-Bill'. We had already in the earlier pieces had the usual spate of solos from Willie, but he met his Waterloo in 'the Well'. This piece, as its title suggests, ebbs, flows and gushes all over the place in never-ending passages of arpeggios of common chords and added 6ths, with crescendos and diminuendos to over-paint the picture. The orchestra, in common with every other cowardly bunch of amateur musicians, gradually began to evaporate: the violins, as they ran out of technique and courage, gave up the unequal struggle, leaving Willie, quite unabashed, brazenly playing pseudo arpeggios all over the remote and hitherto unexplored regions of his fingerboard – the recital was prolonged and excruciating! The wincing which it evoked was spontaneous, and the silence which followed the incident quite embarrassing until Albert, whose cauldron had by this time boiled over, stuck the spike of his 'cello into the floorboards (from an even greater height than ever before), and putting a gentle hand on my knee, leaned over in order to address Willie – 'address' is too kind an expression: he passed sentence through his teeth, slowly and deliberately in his native broad Yorkshire dialect – "Na then, Willie – tha sees th'advantage now i' choppin' orf wi' t'others!!"

This story, when I related it in the ante-room of the B.B.C. Northern Orchestra studio in Manchester, had an immediate effect in stamping out the cardinal sin – whenever anyone, at rehearsal, violated the unwritten law, there was an instant retort from someone in the orchestra of "Na then, Willie!"

One of the most unpleasant memories of my association with the B.B.C. Northern Orchestra had precious little to do with music and a great deal to do with Sargent's colossal ego, which had amazed and confounded me on each and every occasion I had been obliged to play for him.

In the early 1950s the 'Northern' was engaged to take part in the Huddersfield Choral Society's annual performance of the 'Messiah', which was in those days (and still is) a lusty affair of gigantic proportions – 400 voices, an orchestra of 65, drums (and a grand organ for good measure) ready and willing to 'raise the dead – incorruptible'!

The strategy behind the engagement of a B.B.C. orchestra to take part in a non-broadcast public performance became apparent to the players when advance announcements on the studio notice-board gave precise details of rehearsal times, varieties of dress to be worn, and accommodation for two days and nights (with B.B.C. meticulous attention to propriety) at the Queen Hotel, Huddersfield.

On Thursday the statutory 3-hour rehearsal ran its dreary, repetitive course, and the full-length performance which followed (in D.Js and short black) went off very well, before a packed house of hysterical 'believers'.

Friday was the longest day of my life!

At ten o'clock in the morning, with the sounds of a fairly adequate performance of 'Messiah' still ringing in our ears, we were called to a 'music' rehearsal in the Town Hall (with the same soloists who had acquitted themselves admirably the night before) to establish a 45-minute excerpt from this now familiar piece for a live B.B.C. Television presentation, before an invited audience, late in the evening.

In order to 'utilise' the quartet of soloists the excerpt consisted of the first 17 numbers, cutting from the chorus 'Glory to God' to the 'Hallelujah' chorus. At 2 p.m. we were 'on call' again for the Dress Rehearsal – a real one, in white tie and tails for the men and long black faces for the girls!

A resplendent orchestra assembled at 1.55 p.m., complete with instruments (in tune) amidst a barrage of spotlights, T.V. cameras and the bustle and noise of countless technicians, studio managers, and far too many assistants. The charade began promptly in dazzling light and deathly silence – the leader, Reginald Stead, was first to be heard making the long trek from the green room to the foot of the steps leading to the platform: he then walked slowly to his place in the orchestra, bowed to the empty hall, and took his seat. He was followed, at a discreet interval of time, by the soloists, stunningly dressed and bejewelled, who made the most of their entrance: they bowed in unison but remained standing. We all remained in suspense for the arrival of the 'Messiah' in person! The jaunty steps could be heard all the way from the bowels of the Town Hall – up the steps and through the corridor of the 'cello section, swishing the tails of his coat as he trotted to the rostrum – then the rhythm of the act changed. Sargent stepped very sedately onto the rostrum, advanced to the brass rail and bowed very low to the T.V. camera in the centre of the balcony. He then reared up to his greatest height and repeated the ritual to the camera on his left – and then to the camera on his right. The nauseating spectacle thus far was only the beginning – he turned to the orchestra, as if to begin the performance, but without a word of explanation hurried off the platform! The more observant members of the orchestra had plenty of time during the boring period of unemployment to unravel the problems of Sargent's 'entrance' – he had arrived at the rostrum on the wrong foot, which made it necessary for him to mount the steps left, right, left, right instead of right, left, right , left. He got it right at the second attempt, but quite unabashed he went off again and for the third time, 'consolidated'!

Looking very pleased with the progress he was making with the T.V. Spectacular, he then rehearsed what is known in the pantomime business as the 'Who's Best Bit'. Sargent gave the sign for soloists and choir to sit whilst he turned and rehearsed his final obeisances to the audience, and to the unseen millions behind the T.V. cameras. He then turned his back on the audience and painstakingly rehearsed the 'Who's Best After Me Bit' by shaking hands with each of the four soloists in turn, observing the protocol. The leader of the orchestra brought up the rear, followed by the orchestra and the remnants of the choir who had managed to 'get off' work for the occasion. Sargent left the platform, leaving all the combatants standing, but his departure was a brief affair – he returned immediately to take another bow. The soloists then followed him from the platform with Reginald Stead at a discreet distance behind them!

The members of the orchestra flopped in their chairs, muttering and groaning quietly or vociferously according to the extremities of amazement or disgust they might have individually felt during this unique 'dress rehearsal'. But those who, like myself, imagined that we had seen all, and that this must be the end of the charade, were quickly undeceived – a voice from nowhere in particular called us to order, and when silence had been restored (more deadly than before) Reginald Stead appeared, and every step and grimace of the entrance and exit procedures were painfully repeated. At 2.45 p.m. we were finally released and the experience was over.

Appalled and numbed (it would have been possible at that moment to remove my appendix with a rusty pen-knife) we dragged our weary legs back to the Queen Hotel to change into civilised clothing, take afternoon tea in the lounge and grapple with the intricacies of Culbertson for the remainder of a misspent afternoon. The Bridge team broke up in disarray about 6 p.m. and after an early dinner and quick change, we reassembled at the Town Hall for the spectacle – this time there was an interlude of 40 minutes of Handel between the acts!

Chapter XIX
by N. J. de V. Mather

When Doctor Ben Horsfall retired from the B.B.C. Northern Orchestra he continued working in the Department of Music at the University of Manchester. Originally appointed as a Special Lecturer in Music under Professor Proctor Gregg he eventually became Lecturer and played a large part in the selection of suitable students of which some were to become solely undergraduated of the University and others were to take the Joint Course organised by both the University and the Royal Manchester College of Music. Having the highest musical standards himself he was anxious that the standards of the undergraduates should be as high as possible and at times he was despondent over the general lack of musical and general knowledge displayed by prospective students. He frequently complained that at the interviews students could only discuss the music they had actually played and seemed singularly lacking in the knowledge of other composers and their works. He was always attempting to broaden the horizons of the students. In some ways he was most appreciated by the senior students and young graduates, for his approach to a subject was particularly wide and involved not only composers and their creations but also contemporary history and art. As a teacher and lecturer he spoke from a higher plane than that of his audience and often they did not appreciate his broad philosophic and scholarly approach.

Proctor Gregg was succeeded by Professor Hans Redlich the author of a book on Bruckner and Mahler. Fond of Germanic music and literature he suggested that Horsfall should learn German which he did with his customary thoroughness, and after attending a few classes at a College of Further Education with his photographic memory it amazed many of his friends to witness the speed of his learning, for he was then in his late sixties.

Redlich asked him to take over the University orchestra previously conducted by Proctor Gregg which he did, rehearsing and conducting on those occasions when Redlich did not wish to. If not conducting he played as leader of the orchestra at which he was very suitable as he was a strong player with a full tone. For some months he had led the B.B.C. Northern Orchestra when Reginald Stead the official leader was absent on account of illness.

Redlich's unfortunate death led to the appointment of Philip Cranmer as Professor, leaving the Chair in Music at Queen's University Belfast to come to Manchester. Although an academic he played the double bass and joined the other visitors to help in Horsfall's Todmorden concerts. After a few years he left to go to the Associated Board, being followed by Basil Dean who was the Professor when Horsfall retired from the University. Horsfall continued with the University orchestra. With a wealth of experience with first class orchestras he was aware of all the traps and hidden difficulties for orchestral players and the music students reached a high standard under his tuition. Redlich on one occasion told the present writer how much he admired Horsfall's musicianship pointing out his skill in producing an excellent performance of the Siegfried Idyll which he Redlich considered a very difficult piece to present well. Incidentally, Horsfall considered this composition to be the finest piece of chamber music to be written.

In 1962 Horsfall became the conductor of the Todmorden Orchestra. In previous pages there is a reference to the orchestra, an amateur society formed in the 1920s from the old Todmorden Musical Society. The first conductor had been a local man, a Mr. Mitchell who was then succeeded by Fred Leach A.R.M.C.M who had played the viola in the Hallé Orchestra under Richter. Leach was an experienced musician who welded the players together and was responsible for some excellent concerts including a performance of Elgar's 'Dream of Gerontius' in which the late Frank Titterton sang Gerontius for the first time – a part he subsequently sang often. In October 1935 the orchestra won first prize at the Blackpool Musical Festival playing the first movement of Schubert's Symphony No.8 in B minor (the 'Unfinished'), the leader of the orchestra being the young Ben Horsfall.

After Leach's retirement during and after the difficult war years, the orchestra was under the direction of a Todmorden man Vernon Foulds who had studied the viola and conducting under Leach, and the society owed a great deal to him for keeping the orchestra alive. From 1958 to 1962 it was difficult to keep the orchestra going as financial problems restricted attracting suitable musicians who obviously had to travel to the town.

However, the society was fortunate in having first a young graduate from the Royal Manchester College of Music – Oliver Broome by name – who was recommended by Frederick Cox the Principal. Originally a bass singer Broome wished to be a conductor and was glad of the experience. His spontaneity, enthusiasm and infectious optimism led to some excellent concerts including the first Manchester performance of Puccini's Messa di Gloria at the Houldsworth Hall, Manchester, on March 5th 1960 with John Wakefield the tenor soloist and John Copley the bass soloist. Further operatic concerts in Buxton and Stretford continued to enlarge the orchestra's experience and it was a disappointment when Broome won a scholarship in conducting awarded by the Italian Government and he left for twelve months to work in Italy. His successor was Rudolph Botta a violinist from Hungary who had managed to leave his country with his family at the time of the Soviet occupation. Living in Burnley, conducting the Burnley Municipal Orchestra and teaching at the Royal Manchester College of Music, he visited Todmorden for the twelve months of Broome's absence, conducting a concert on the 18th October 1960 with the young John Ogdon giving a brilliant performance of the Grieg Piano Concerto in A minor followed by a masterly exhibition of pianistic technique in the Liszt-Busoni arrangement of Paganini's 'La Campanella'. This was before Ogdon won the Tchaikowsky prize in Moscow. Broome returned to the orchestra for a short time before obtaining a post in London, and thus the orchestra were delighted when in 1962 Ben Horsfall came as the regular conductor.

At that time he was still with the B.B.C. Northern Orchestra in which he remained until October 1963. He had naturally known and played with the Todmorden Orchestra in his adolescent years but until 1962, apart from slipping into the Todmorden Town Hall to listen to occasional concerts, he had had no contact with the society. Apart from himself, the orchestra had been the breeding ground for other potential and subsequent professionals. Two horn players, Frank Taylor who first played with the Hallé and then became 3rd horn in the B.B.C. Northern, and Jack Johnson who took up the instrument when he was eighteen and subsequently played with the Liverpool Philharmonic, becoming principal horn of the City of Birmingham Orchestra both started in Todmorden. Thelma Maden – Mrs. Jack Johnson – a violinist, onetime leader, also went to the Birmingham orchestra. Geoffrey Love, trombone player running his own successful orchestra, with broadcasts and records beneath his belt, had his baptism in Todmorden. The professional 'cellist Mary Hartley – later Mrs. Clay – was also a regular member, coming back in her later years to be a tower of strength in the 'cello section. The orchestra had always had a strong woodwind section, two bassoonists Maurice Ashworth and Clarence Town playing with the Royal Liverpool Philharmonic and Hallé orchestras respectively.

Ben Horsfall's return to the orchestra was greatly appreciated and during his twenty-odd years' spell the concerts he gave were the finest in the history of the Society.

His wide experience both in amateur societies in his youth and in his professional life made him able to appreciate the problems of the amateur. Always courteous, never sarcastic, highly amusing at times, shrewd in his remarks and with perfect pitch, he, like Beecham with professionals before him, got amateurs to perform better than their capabilities. With a clear, incisive beat, absence of histrionics and great knowledge of the

Todmorden Orchestra

score he was able to conjure excellent performances of established and difficult masterpieces. He would tell the string sections how their parts should sound, play them from memory on his own violin and at times join either the violin or viola sections to enable them to feel their way in a piece. He was invariably able to illustrate certain points with true and amusing stories of incidents germane to the piece being performed.

Over twenty years his concerts were many and varied. His contacts were such that his work for the orchestra did not remain at conducting. His B.B.C. contacts enabled him to obtain orchestral scores from the library providing, naturally, that they were not in use. He had many friends in the B.B.C. Northern and such was the comradeship of those friends that they would willingly come to help in his concerts. Harry Massey the timpanist, Wilfred Collinge with his double bass, Maurice Murphy the trumpeter, Sidney Coulston Professor of the horn at the Royal Manchester College of Music, Don Hyden, Rene Pearce and Wendy Shaw violinists, Norman Cunliffe and Frank Needham violas, all these were regular visitors and happy to play for Ben Horsfall. Invariably their services were given.

The performances of the Messiah were always successful. He was particularly fond of the work and as the strings played a prominent part he was always very thorough in their preparation. One particular performance was outstanding even for him and will be remembered by all present. On this occasion, December 10th 1968, the Burnley Musical Choir had joined forces with the Todmorden Choral Society creating a great body of sound - "Worthy is the Lamb and Amen" being especially moving. All the vocalists were impressive and solo trumpet was to be played by Maurice Murphy. Murphy who subsequently went to London was justifiably considered to be one of the finest trumpeters in the country and had agreed to play if available. On the night of the performance the B.B.C. Northern was involved in a tedious rehearsal at the Milton Hall, Manchester. Although Murphy was not involved in the latter portions of the work, the conductor was unwilling to release any player. The evening progressed, Murphy in Manchester feverishly glancing at his wrist-watch waiting for the 'all clear'.

At nine o'clock precisely the rehearsal finished. Murphy leapt into his car and covered the twenty miles to Todmorden Town Hall in thirty minutes, most of the journey being through built-up areas. Horsfall dallied over Part Two of Handel's work with quick visual snatches at the empty seat. A young student playing second trumpet sat in a state of terror knowing he had to deputise should Murphy fail to appear. The fatal moment arrived. The Bass singer arose. "Behold, I tell you a mystery" was declaimed. Was it to query the mystery of Murphy's absence? As the recitative ended, up the stairs to the platform with white shirt, tail coat, white tie hanging loosely around his neck appeared Murphy, instrument in hand. Without the music before him he then proceeded to play in the aria with meticulous accuracy and sublime tone. The student's face which had been a mixture of white and green was suddenly flooded a rosy pink as he collapsed on to his seat. It would be interesting to know if ever at a concert the recitative had been played by one trumpeter and the aria by another. Horsfall continued to conduct as if this was the accustomed method of playing Handel. There were certainly shades of Beecham here.

There were many noteworthy concerts. Concertos were frequently given by Horsfall's friends. Maurice Aitchison, Reader in Music at Manchester University, a fine pianist with the physique of a heavyweight boxer, on March 15th, 1966, delighted the audience with a rippling, lyrical performance of Schumann's piano concerto in A minor, and followed with two further concertos, Beethoven's third in C minor on November 16th, 1968, and Tchaikowsky's first in B flat minor on November 11th, 1969. Aitchison, a graduate of Cambridge, was similar in style to John Ogdon, – exceptional technique, superb musicianship and an element of bravura particularly suitable for the big romantic works.

Another accomplished friend from the University was Peter Smith, born in Toronto, a student in New York and a lecturer in music in Manchester. The antitheses of Aitchison, small, neat, fastidious, on the 9th November 1971 he gave a highly intelligent and effective rendering of Rachmaninov's second concerto and the following year an excellent performance of the same composer's intricate 'Variations on a theme of Paganini'.

Other notable performances by Horsfall's old friends were the two violin concertos played by Clifford Knowles – former leader of the Liverpool Philharmonic Orchestra and Professor at Manchester – the Mendelssohn and the Max Bruch; and particular highlights in the orchestral pieces were the celeste and xylophone solos in Saint Saëns' 'Carnival of the Animals' suite played by Harry Massey, and the incomparable Sidney Coulston on the horn in the Nocturne from Mendelssohn's 'Midsummer Night's Dream', in Berlioz's 'Royal Hunt and Storm' interlude, and in the brilliant horn call from 'Siegfried's Journey to the Rhine' which rang like a clarion call round the Town Hall and appeared to be as effortless as if on a penny whistle. Maurice Murphy, in addition to his frequent orchestral appearances, twice played the Haydn trumpet concerto.

By this time Horsfall had been elected as a Fellow of the Royal Manchester College of Music.

Through the years he had always considered the budding professionals and thus engaged them whenever possible. Singers from the Manchester College included many who were later to make their names: tenors Robert Ferguson and Ian Caley, sopranos Barbara Walker and Caroline Crawshaw, mezzo-soprano Sandra Browne, bass-baritone Patrick McGuigan were all engaged to sing at Todmorden, as well as choirs from Burnley, Rochdale and Manchester University.

Of the amateur orchestral players, Percy Dobson three times played Mozart's clarinet concerto in A, and the leader David Lewis twice played the Beethoven Romance in F for violin and orchestra, and twice was a soloist in Bach's concerto for two violins and orchestra.

It is considered necessary to include details of the aforementioned concerts because they were inspired, directed and organised by Horsfall himself for many years. The amount of work and time he devoted to them was more than praiseworthy. He told the writer that he considered it his duty to assist the society – the musical society of the town in which he was born – for as long as he was physically capable, a duty which he performed assiduously with love and which he enjoyed. By this means he brought a considerable amount of pleasure and happiness to many people and he will always be remembered by them with great affection. It was justifiably fitting that in 1985 Todmorden Town Council elected him as an Honorary Citizen for his great contribution to music-making in the town and the surrounding districts. The sculpture of his head, by Sam Tonkiss, now stands – as it surely should – in Todmorden Town Hall.

He was a very human and a generous man. After each concert he and his wife would entertain the visitors to a buffet supper at his house.

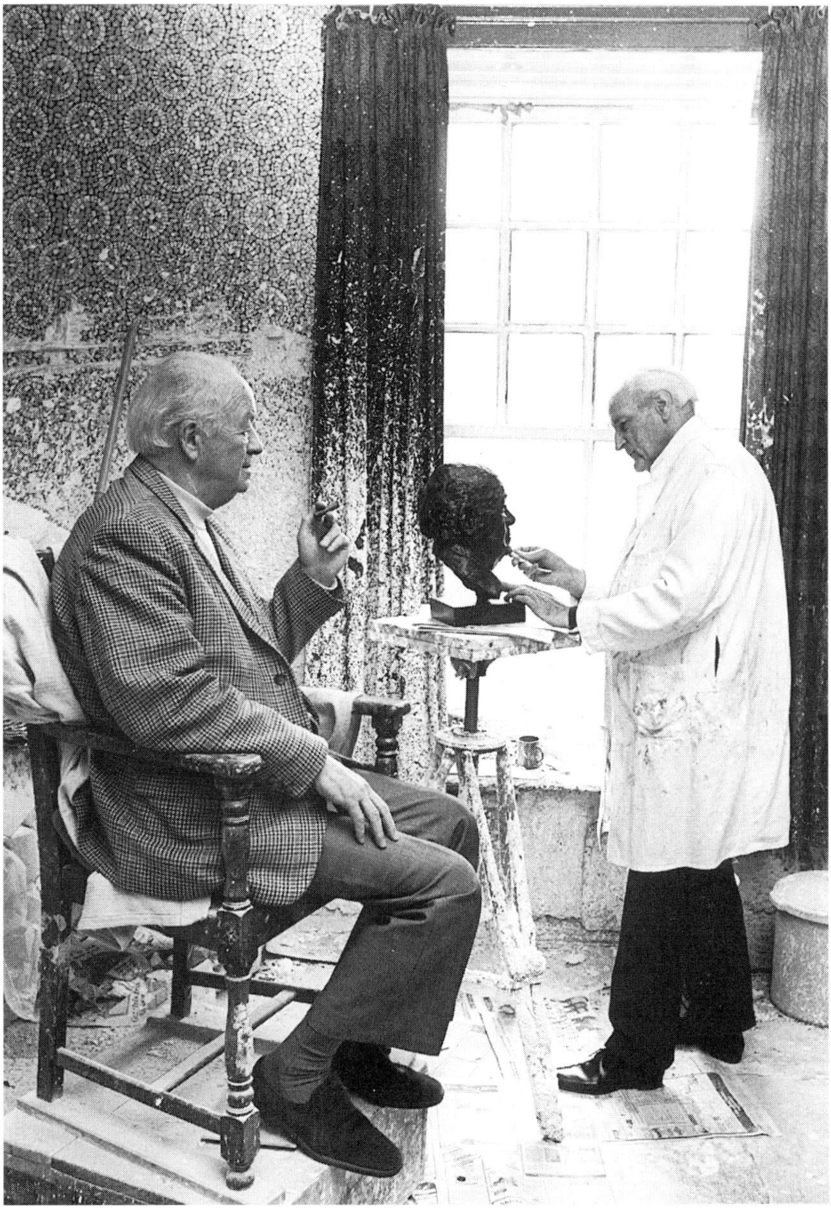

Dr Ben sitting for local sculptor Sam Tonkiss

Many of the delicacies would have been prepared by Horsfall himself as he was an excellent cook, especially as a baker. He said he had learned the art when, as a young man living in lodgings at a seaside resort, the two maiden ladies who looked after him had insisted on teaching him to cook, an acquired asset which he had never regretted. On a subsequent occasion after gaining his doctorate and staying in a private hotel he was ensnared into making a fourth at bridge – a game he loved. His partner, an elderly lady, asked politely: "Where do you practise, Doctor Horsfall?". The reply in all sincerity was: "Mostly in the back bedroom", whereupon his interrogator promptly left the table believing him to be a professional abortionist.

On an earlier occasion, in Scarborough, having a free afternoon he wandered into a nearby cinema. Leaving at the end of the film he unexpectedly met Sidney Coulston who asked him about it. In his reply he said the film was good but extremely dark to which Coulston replied he was not surprised as Horsfall had neglected to remove his sun-glasses.

He continued conducting and playing with a variety of orchestras as a freelance until the effects of his diabetic condition made it almost impossible, although he never stopped completely, and would also occasionally indulge in the rich, sweet things he loved, despite his diabetes. A heart attack with subsequent septicaemia, followed immediately by the sudden death of his wife, forced him to retire to a small flat at which, a short time afterwards, he too died suddenly on Monday, July 28th, 1986.

His funeral was held at the Todmorden Parish Church on August 1st, 1986. It was well-attended and as a tribute members of the orchestra and the choral society performed Mozart's motet 'Ave, verum corpus'.

A Memorial Concert was held at Todmorden Town Hall on Sunday, March 29th, 1987, when his old friend Clifford Knowles played the Mendelssohn violin concerto. After the concert Knowles said that he considered he had given one of his best – if not his best – performances of that particular concerto. This was followed by Beethoven's third symphony in E flat (the 'Eroica') which aptly expressed the integrity and nobility of the much-loved man.